Mass Expulsion

BRIDGING THE GAP

Series Editors
James Goldgeier,
Bruce Jentleson,
Steven Weber

The Logic of American Nuclear Strategy:
Why Strategic Superiority Matters
Matthew Kroenig

Planning to Fail:
The US Wars in Vietnam, Iraq, and Afghanistan
James H. Lebovic

War and Chance:
Assessing Uncertainty in International Politics
Jeffrey A. Friedman

Delaying Doomsday:
The Politics of Nuclear Reversal
Rupal N. Mehta

Delta Democracy:
Pathways to Incremental Civic Revolution in Egypt and Beyond
Catherine E. Herrold

Adaptation Under Fire:
How Militaries Change in Wartime
David Barno and Nora Bensahel

The Long Game:
China's Grand Strategy to Displace American Order
Rush Doshi

A Small State's Guide to Influence in World Politics
Tom Long

Cyber Persistence Theory:
Redefining National Security in Cyberspace
Michael P. Fischerkeller, Emily O. Goldman, and Richard J. Harknett

Beyond the Wire:
US Military Deployments and Host Country Public Opinion
Michael A. Allen, Michael E. Flynn, Carla Martinez Machain, and Andrew Stravers

Deploying Feminism:
The Role of Gender in NATO Military Operations
Stéfanie von Hlatky

Dangerous Instrument:
Political Polarization and U.S. Civil-Military Relations
Michael A. Robinson

Escalation Dynamics in Cyberspace
Erica D. Lonergan and Shawn W. Lonergan

Thanks for Your Service:
The Causes and Consequences of Public Confidence in the US Military
Peter D. Feaver

Military Medicine and the Hidden Costs of War
Tanisha M. Fazal

The Hand Behind Unmanned:
Origins of the US Autonomous Military Arsenal
Jacquelyn Schneider and Julia Macdonald

Coercing Syria on Chemical Weapons:
A Case Study of Deterrence and Coercive Diplomacy
Matthew Moran, Wyn Bowen, and Jeffrey W. Knopf

Mass Expulsion

The Politics of Forced Population Removal

MEGHAN M. GARRITY

OXFORD
UNIVERSITY PRESS

OXFORD
UNIVERSITY PRESS

Oxford University Press is a department of the University of Oxford.
It furthers the University's objective of excellence in research, scholarship,
and education by publishing worldwide. Oxford is a registered trade mark of
Oxford University Press in the UK and in certain other countries.

Published in the United States of America by Oxford University Press
198 Madison Avenue, New York, NY 10016, United States of America.

CIP data is on file at the Library of Congress.

ISBN 9780197829066

ISBN 9780197829059 (hbk.)

DOI: 10.1093/9780197829097.001.0001

Paperback printed by Marquis Book Printing, Canada

The manufacturer's authorized representative in the EU for product safety is
Oxford University Press España S.A. of Parque Empresarial San Fernando de Henares,
Avenida de Castilla, 2 – 28830 Madrid (www.oup.es/en or product.safety@oup.com).
OUP España S.A. also acts as importer into Spain of products made by the manufacturer.

MIX
Paper | Supporting responsible forestry
FSC
www.fsc.org
FSC® C103567

Contents

List of Figures, Tables, Maps

Figures

Tables

Maps

List of Acronyms

ACICR	Archives du Comité international de la Croix-Rouge (French name of ICRC)
AFP	Agence France-Presse
ARIF	Arakan Rohingya Islamic Front
ASEAN	Association of Southeast Asian Nations
BAC	Business allocation committee
BPP	British protected person
BSPP	Burma Socialist Programme Party
CCP	Chinese Communist Party
COW	Correlates of War (dataset)
CPB	Communist Party of Burma
CSC	Citizenship scrutiny cards
CUKC	Citizen of the United Kingdom and Colonies
CUP	Committee of Union and Progress
FBIS	Foreign Broadcast Information Service
GDP	Gross domestic product
GSME	Government-Sponsored Mass Expulsion (dataset)
ICEM	Intergovernmental Committee for European Migration
ICRC	International Committee of the Red Cross
IDMC	Internal Displacement Monitoring Centre
IO	International organization
IOM	International Organization for Migration
KANU	Kenya African National Union
KPU	Kenya People's Union
MENA	Middle East and North Africa
NLD	National League for Democracy
NRC	National registration cards
OAU	Organization of African Unity
OSV	One-Sided Violence (dataset; i.e., UCDP/OSV)
PITF	Political Instability Task Force
RIF	Rohingya Independence Front
RPF	Rohingya Patriotic Front
RSO	Rohingya Solidarity Organization
SLORC	State Law and Order Restoration Council
TMK	Targeted Mass Killing (dataset)
UCDP/PRIO	Uppsala Conflict Data Program/Peace Research Institute Oslo
UN	United Nations
UNHCR	United Nations High Commissioner for Refugees
UNSG	United Nations Secretary-General

Acknowledgments

Academic research is a series of false starts, dead ends, and rabbit holes, interspersed with periodic breakthroughs. It is never really finished—the publisher's deadline simply arrives. The process is a luxury that few are fortunate enough to pursue and crazy enough to enjoy. To persevere, and produce anything legible, requires the contributions of countless individuals who help turn what begins as an interest, an idea, or a few words on a page into a full manuscript. While I alone am accountable for the arguments and evidence presented herein, any credit is shared with the community of scholars, mentors, friends, and loved ones who have supported, guided, and encouraged me along the way.

This project began as a dissertation at the University of Pennsylvania (UPenn) with the guidance of my esteemed committee. My chair, Brendan O'Leary, was the first person I met on new students' visiting day, and our conversations about ethnic conflict, eliminationist policies, and UK and Middle East politics have continued to this day. I could not have asked for an advisor with a greater generosity of time, abundant wisdom, endless editing, and ceaseless availability. This book is a humble attempt to build on his work with John McGarry on ethnic expulsions. Beth Simmons's incisive feedback on numerous drafts, grant applications, and conference papers helped me articulate my ideas and arguments more precisely. Her Borders & Boundaries class, followed by a conference at UPenn's Perry World House, gave me my first opportunity to present my expulsion data and receive constructive feedback from an external audience—an experience that proved critical to its development. Rudy Sil's advice on theory, methods, and cross-regional comparisons was a masterclass in generating sound social science. His essay-long emails, often sent between 2 and 4 a.m., provided discerning comments and in-depth analysis on any question at hand. A course scheduling conflict fortuitously led me to Melissa Wilde's Comparative Historical Methods class, which broadened my understanding of both the method and the interdisciplinary nature of the approach. Her mentorship has been invaluable. This star-studded committee leaves all deficiencies in the book attributable to me alone.

In addition to my committee, several other scholars deserve special thanks. Guy Grossman and Alex Weisiger generously provided support, feedback, and encouragement as I presented various iterations of this project during graduate school. Devesh Kapur urged me to construct a dataset of mass expulsion events in my first summer at UPenn, and without his initial suggestion, the Government-Sponsored Mass Expulsion dataset would not have come to fruition. Harris Mylonas's response to a cold email requesting him to chair an American Political Science Association panel in 2020 sparked a multiyear collaboration exploring methodological challenges in the study of eliminationist politics. He has been an exceptional mentor and friend during this process. The PhD journey is always challenging, but a global pandemic brought an unexpected twist; throughout it all, I owe a great debt to my UPenn compatriots for their crucial feedback, inspiring discussions, spirited debates, and unwavering support. A special thanks to Sumitra Badrinathan, Christopher Blair, Archana Kaku, Joshua Schwartz, Nathaniel Shils, Troels Skadhauge, and Şule Yaylacı.

A postdoctoral fellowship at the Harvard Kennedy School's Belfer Center for Science and International Affairs was an exceptional intellectual home to spend a year transforming my dissertation into a book manuscript. A special thanks to Steven Miller and Stephen Walt, and the 2022–2023 cohort of International Security Program fellows, for their camaraderie and feedback, specifically on my theory and Uganda/Kenya chapters. The culmination of my postdoc was a book workshop where my academic inspirations read and commented on my work. This significantly improved the manuscript, and I am deeply indebted to Scott Straus, Ben Valentino, Sana Aiyar, and Harris Mylonas for their generosity of time and expertise.

During the development of this book, I benefited from the incisive feedback provided by editors and anonymous reviewers at the *Journal of Peace Research*, *Security Studies*, and *Political Science Quarterly*. Portions of articles originally published in those journals are included here.[1] I also benefited from the perceptive feedback of discussants, fellow panelists, and audience members at various conferences, including those of the International Studies Association, the American Political Science Association, the Conflict Research Society, the Western Political Science Association, and the African Studies Association. Research for this project would not have been possible without the financial support from a variety of institutions and donors,

[1] Garrity, 2022; Garrity, 2023a; Garrity, 2023b.

including UPenn's Christopher Browne Center, Perry World House, the Center for the Study of Ethnicity, Race, & Immigration, and the School of Arts & Sciences, as well as a predoctoral fellowship from the United States Institute of Peace and a generous grant from the Jewish Family Service Association.

My archival research was only possible thanks to the deeply knowledgeable archivists who helped me navigate the collections and identify pivotal documents. Heather Faulkner and Anna Haward at the United Nations High Commissioner for Refugees were extremely helpful in assisting me to identify expulsion-related documents in the online portal, and expeditiously delivered the files during my visits. At the International Committee of the Red Cross Archives, Fabrizio Bensi and Daniel Palmieri brought numerous files spanning the Red Cross's work throughout the twentieth century. Lunchtime conversations with Jean-Marie Henckaerts, International Committee of the Red Cross legal advisor and author of the definitive book on mass expulsion in international law, further enriched my research. Jacques Oberson at the League of Nations Archives helped me to locate the meeting minutes of the Lausanne Convention's Sub-Commission for the Exchange of Populations and the Records of Proceedings of the Conference at the UN Library, which were critical to my Ottoman Empire chapter. I also want to thank Lauris Olsen at the UPenn Library for his tremendous help tracking down obscure sources and making materials available during the Covid-19 pandemic. The UPenn library staff that facilitated the interlibrary loan deliveries were vital to accessing journals and book chapters while the campus was closed.

Publishing this book in the Bridging the Gap (BTG) series bridges my own background as a humanitarian aid practitioner and an academic. The BTG International Policy Summer Institute (IPSI) was my first introduction to the group. It helped hone my skills in translating research into actionable policy recommendations and widened my policy network. Fellow IPSI alumna, Rhiannon Neilsen, has been a treasured friend, reading chapter drafts, co-navigating the book publishing process, and always willing to discuss these grim topics with compassion and interest. The BTG New Voices in National Security Workshop introduced me to experts at the US Holocaust Memorial Museum, who have become dear colleagues, particularly Daniel Solomon and Lawrence Woocher. They both provided insightful comments on my policy recommendations and on other chapter drafts presented at the Peace Science Conference.

During the concluding stages of this project, I started as an assistant professor at George Mason University's Schar School of Policy and Government. I want to thank my Schar School colleagues for their advice, support, and collegiality as I put the final touches on the manuscript. A special thanks to Luis Rodriguez, Michael Hunzeker, Justin Gest, Jennifer Victor, Ahsan Butt, Mariely López-Santana, Jack Goldstone, Ellen Laipson, Christopher Berk, Philip Martin, Lucas Núñez, Ketian Zhang, and Dean Mark Rozell. In addition to the Schar faculty, the George Mason University students have shaped and refined my thinking on these topics. Their enthusiasm and energy give me optimism about future solutions and change. A massive thanks to my graduate research assistant, Sanggyu Suh. His tireless efforts analyzing numerous war and conflict datasets were instrumental in preparing the book's final revisions. I also want to express my sincere thanks to the participants at the 2024 Institute for Security and Conflict Studies Workshop at George Washington University's Elliott School of International Affairs. Their deep engagement and astute feedback on my introduction and theory chapters were crucial in refining my framing and arguments.

A final thanks to the Bridging the Gap series editors, particularly Bruce Jentleson and James Goldgeier, as well as Megan Lyons, BTG associate director, for their support of, and advocacy for, this book project. I also want to express my sincere gratitude to Oxford University Press, especially David McBride, the two external reviewers, and the Oxford editorial team. Their detailed feedback and the efficient publishing process have made this experience a pleasure.

A decade of work brings significant professional and personal growth, and I have been deeply fortunate in both areas. In the latter, a special thanks to Thomas Ginn. His enthusiasm, patience, and dedication to research on refugees and migration have been a tremendous source of support and encouragement during the final stages of this project.

This book grew out of my previous career in the humanitarian aid and development sectors, where I responded to natural and man-made disasters and to refugee movements, some very similar to those examined here. The resilience of refugees and internally displaced persons, in the face of horrific and unimaginable events, inspires my research into the root causes of eliminationist policies and the restraints that might inform prevention strategies. This is a humble attempt to contribute to those efforts. As mass atrocities continue unabated as I write this—in Sudan, Gaza, Burma, Afghanistan, and numerous other places—solutions are imperative.

I dedicate this work to my mom, Kathy Garrity. Her unending support, encouragement, advice, editing, and wisdom were essential in completing this book. Without her sacrifices along the way, none of this would have been possible.

1

Introduction

Mass expulsion is a policy of forced population removal. Since the beginning of the twentieth century, governments of more than sixty different countries have expelled an estimated 30 to 42 million people *en masse*. Expulsion is often sudden, unexpected, and chaotic. Targeted groups are caught off guard, unprepared for their abrupt uprooting, with minimal time to escape or depart. The gravity of being forced from their homes—where many have lived their entire lives—and departing to unknown and distant places, leaves expellees in shock and denial. As reality sets in, the chaos of exit ensues. Families separated, homes abandoned, livelihoods destroyed, pets deserted, graves of loved ones left behind, and in the worst cases, lives lost.

Sometimes expulsion involves physical violence. In 1991–1992, Rohingya Muslims in Burma were told, "You are not Burmese. We are torturing you so you will leave this country. We will continue until you are gone."[1] Border guards shouted at fleeing Rohingya that they would "shoot them if they returned."[2] Security officials destroyed mosques and Muslim cemeteries, evicted people from their homes, and burned their villages.[3] Seventy years earlier, in a crumbling empire, Ottoman authorities expelled 1.5 million Greek Orthodox Christians, many during a war with invading Greek forces.[4] These expulsions culminated in a horrific scene at the Smyrna (Izmir) quay. As fire engulfed the coastal city, tens of thousands of expellees congregated at the water's edge, desperately awaiting ships to transport them to safety, mostly in vain.[5]

However, unlike other atrocities, such as genocide and mass killing, most mass expulsions do not occur during war.[6] These peacetime expulsions are initiated with less physical violence but equal economic and social violence.

[1] Asia Watch, 1992, p. 18; Smith, 1994, p. 82.

[2] Amnesty International, 1992 (Sept), p. 24; Piper, 1994, p. 24.

[3] Amnesty International, 1992 (Sept), p. 24; Asia Watch, 1992, p. 1; Lambrecht, 1995, p. 4; Piper, 1994, pp. 15–16; Van Hear, 1998, p. 98; Yegar, 2002, p. 63.

[4] Morris & Ze'evi, 2019; Naimark, 2001.

[5] Clark, 2006, pp. 22–23, 255.

[6] See analysis in Chapter 2, pp. 36–38 (based on the Correlates of War and the Uppsala Conflict Data Program/Peace Research Institute Oslo datasets).

Mass Expulsion. Meghan M. Garrity, Oxford University Press. © Oxford University Press (2026).
DOI: 10.1093/9780197829097.003.0001

Leaders wield pens, not guns, to carry out the forced removals. Bureaucratic processes such as government decrees, interstate agreements, or internationally approved "population transfers" or "population exchanges" authorize the expulsions. In 1972, Ugandan President Idi Amin issued a decree that all South Asians must leave the country within ninety days, including those with Ugandan citizenship.[7] As an expellee recounted, "This came as a bolt from the blue for many. . . . 'Everybody thought, "What is this madness?" How can you suddenly leave a place where you have lived all your life?'"[8] When the expellees grasped the reality of the situation, "long lines wound out of banks, where life savings were under threat, and shelves were stripped bare as panic-buying set in—although not of the usual food staples but of suitcases."[9] A decade later, in January 1983, the Nigerian minister of internal affairs pronounced the expulsion of 2 million "illegal migrants" at a press briefing, giving them two weeks to depart.[10] People scrambled to leave by land, sea, and air. A local journalist described the scene: "The borders were a disaster, crammed with desperate people carrying chairs on their heads, dragging their checked bags and selling off whatever they couldn't lift to make money to pay for fares that had doubled. Millions streamed out through any possible exit they could find."[11] Many suffered from hunger, dehydration, exhaustion, and exposure as they waited at closed border points in the sweltering heat with minimal provisions.[12]

Regardless of the form of coercive force governments use to expel, in all instances people are targeted on the basis of their membership in a particular group. The individual conduct of expellees, or their individual legal status, is immaterial. Mass expulsion allows no room for individual appeal. It is a permanent group sentence to depart and never return.

Despite the frenzied and brutal nature of mass expulsion, the phrase "orderly and humane" frequently encapsulates the rhetoric of this phenomenon. After World War II, the Allied Powers authorized the expulsion of over 9 million ethnic Germans from Poland, Czechoslovakia, and Hungary

[7] Statement by H. E. The President of Uganda Concerning the Status of the Asian Community in Uganda, 09 August 1972; 11/2/64-641.UGA[c] Expulsion and Deportation—Uganda [1972–1984] Volume 3; Series 2, Box 1281; Fonds 11, Records of the Central Registry; Archives of the United Nations High Commissioner for Refugees (hereafter Series 2, Box 1281; Fonds 11; UNHCR).

[8] Fulford, 2023, p. 84.

[9] Fulford, 2023, p. 91.

[10] Nigerian External Publicity Division, 1983.

[11] Lawal, 2019.

[12] Bentsi-Enchill, 1983a; Bentsi-Enchill, 1983b; Verdon, 1983.

in the Potsdam Agreement.[13] Article XIII of the communiqué stated: "The Three Governments, having considered the question in all its aspects, recognize that the transfer to Germany of German populations . . . will have to be undertaken. They agree that any transfers that take place should be effected in an *orderly and humane* manner."[14] Three decades later, United Nations High Commissioner for Refugees (UNHCR) Deputy High Commissioner Charles Mace used the same language in a cable sent to the organization's headquarters in Geneva after Amin's expulsion of South Asians from Uganda. Mace wrote, "We and international public opinion generally would wish departure (if it has to take place) to be conducted in [an] *orderly and humane* way."[15]

Expelling governments have employed the same rhetoric. Nigerian government officials referred to the "*orderly departure* of aliens"[16] and explained the government's extension of the expulsion timeline from two to six weeks "in order to allow for *smooth and orderly* exist [sic] of the affected people."[17] In 1978, after almost a year of expulsions, the Vietnamese government in Hanoi announced a "seven-point programme" for the "*orderly departure*" of hundreds of thousands of ethnic Chinese expelled from Vietnam.[18] No other atrocity—genocide, ethnic cleansing, mass killing—is described in this way.

Democratic liberal leaders, alongside their authoritarian brethren, have championed and deployed expulsion policies throughout the modern era. Influential political figures such as Greek Prime Minister Eleftherios Venizelos, British Prime Minister Winston Churchill, and United States President Herbert Hoover, have advocated for expulsion policies to bring about peace and end deadly wars.[19] At least nine Nobel Prize laureates have endorsed and supported expulsion,[20] with Burma's Aung San Suu Kyi the latest addition.[21]

[13] Douglas, 2012; Garrity, 2022; Mazower, 2009.
[14] U.S. Department of State—Office of the Historian, 1945.
[15] Outgoing Cable from UNHCR Deputy High Commissioner, Mace, to Dadzie, UNHCR Director Protection Division, 05.09.1972; 11/2/10-100.UGA.ASI[b]—Refugees from Asia in Uganda [Volume 2-1.UGA.ASI]; Series 2, Box 204; Fonds 11; UNHCR.
[16] Nigerian External Publicity Division, 1983, p. 11.
[17] Nigerian External Publicity Division, 1983, p. 4.
[18] Chang, 1982, p. 220.
[19] Frank, 2017; Mazower, 2009.
[20] Frank, 2017, p. 17, footnote 13.
[21] In 1991, Aung San Suu Kyi was awarded the Nobel Peace Prize for her nonviolent struggle for democracy and human rights. However, under her leadership as state counsellor of Myanmar (the de facto head of government), the Myanmar military expelled over 800,000 Rohingya from Arakan (Rakhine) State (UN Human Rights Council, 2018).

While its perpetrators use the rhetoric of "orderly and humane," this book is about the politics of the *disorderly and inhumane* policy of mass expulsion. Examining cases of cross-border expulsion from the twentieth and twenty-first centuries, it explicates the who, what, when, where, why, and how of these events. What is mass expulsion? Who implements these atrocities, and who are the targets? When does it happen? Where does it occur? Why do governments choose this policy? And how do they carry it out? Mass expulsion is defined as a systematic government-sponsored policy to remove an ethnic, racial, religious, or national group as such, with no individual legal review and no recognition of the right to return.[22] With new, original data and detailed case studies of critical events, this work provides the first comprehensive, systematic analysis of mass expulsion over the *longue durée*.

Like other atrocities, mass expulsion is an extreme choice. It is not the first option governments turn to when deciding how to deal with "unwanted" populations. Governments of plural societies must determine how to manage the diverse populations that live within their borders. Most choose policies of coexistence, including control, arbitration, autonomy, federation, or consociation.[23] Less frequently, governments choose to eliminate diversity by targeting specific groups with extreme strategies of genocide, mass expulsion, coercive assimilation, or territorial elimination (i.e., secession or partition).[24] There is excellent research on many of these eliminationist policies;[25] however, in the study of ethnic conflict, political violence, and forced migration, one atrocity has been conspicuously neglected: mass expulsion.

While mass expulsion is a historical phenomenon—Assyrians expelled the Israelites in the eighth century BCE[26]—it continues to the present day. Between 2015 and 2020, over 2 million people were expelled around the world. Governments repeatedly choose this policy of forced population removal, with an average of 1.56 expulsions per year over the last 50 years. These are not small events. Of the 139 cross-border expulsions initiated between 1900 and 2020, an average of 200,000 to 300,000 people were forcibly expelled in each episode.

22 Garrity, 2022.

23 McGarry & O'Leary, 1993, p. 4; O'Leary, 2001, p. 29.

24 O'Leary, 2001, p. 28.

25 See Bulutgil, 2016; Butt, 2017; Garrity & Mylonas, 2025; Mann, 2005; Midlarsky, 2005; Mylonas, 2012; Semelin, 2007; Stanton, 2016; Straus, 2015; Ther, 2014; Valentino, 2004.

26 Bell-Fialkoff, 1999, p. 8; Tägil, 1990, p. 64.

Yet despite its significant human costs, and serious economic and security implications, we know surprisingly little about mass expulsion. Much more ink has been spilled, deservedly, explaining the most heinous atrocities, such as genocide and mass killing.[27] Existing research has examined the causes of these extreme eliminationist policies as well as variation in their use during periods of war and armed conflict.[28] Others have studied variation across strategies of eliminating and managing ethnic differences, such as when governments implement nation-building policies of exclusion, assimilation, or accommodation.[29] One key unanswered question relates to variation within the overarching category of eliminationist policies—how do governments decide between genocide, mass expulsion, coercive assimilation, or territorial elimination? However, to answer that question, we need a detailed understanding of each of the policy options in a government's repertoire of elimination. We lack this for mass expulsion. To assess how existing explanations of other eliminationist policies may, or may not, apply to mass expulsion, we must first empirically isolate and document this phenomenon.

Some scholars have included mass expulsion under the broader concept of "ethnic cleansing," examining instances of genocide, expulsion, and coercive assimilation together.[30] While this research sheds important light on the causes of this macro strategy, it obscures the distinct drivers of the specific policy of expulsion. Expulsion aims *to remove* a target population from the territory of a state, while genocide aims to annihilate or destroy the target group,[31] and coercive assimilation intends to eliminate a group's unique cultural identity.[32] Additionally, the most prominent cross-national studies of ethnic cleansing are exclusively focused on Europe.[33] The research presented here geographically extends our empirical understanding of mass expulsion to assess how existing explanations of European ethnic cleansing may travel to other world regions. Furthermore, existing research on mass atrocities has

[27] Midlarsky, 2005; Semelin, 2007; Straus, 2015; Valentino, 2004.

[28] Chirot & McCauley, 2006; Downes, 2011; Lichtenheld, 2020; Stanton, 2016; Straus, 2015.

[29] Mylonas, 2015.

[30] Much of the existing data on mass atrocities (Bellamy, 2011), state-sponsored mass killing (Ulfelder & Valentino, 2008), and targeted mass killing (Butcher et al., 2020) aggregates incidents of genocide, mass expulsion, and coercive assimilation. Not all scholars of ethnic cleansing include coercive assimilation within their concept (Bulutgil, 2016; Müller-Crepon et al., 2024; Mylonas, 2012), but others do (Mann, 2005; Mirković, 1996).

[31] Lingaas, 2020, pp. 73–75; Naimark, 2001; Schabas, 2000; Straus, 2016.

[32] Garrity, 2023b, pp. 475, 483–487; Schabas, 2000, p. 200.

[33] Bulutgil, 2016; Müller-Crepon et al., 2024.

primarily focused on the targeting of citizens, excluding noncitizens, while the few studies on mass expulsion have largely concentrated on immigrant expulsions in sub-Saharan Africa.[34] We lack a comprehensive theory of mass expulsion regardless of the target population's citizenship status. To fill these gaps, this study examines mass expulsion across regions, over the *longue durée*, and includes the targeting of citizens (i.e., nationals) and noncitizens (i.e., foreign nationals, resident aliens, and refugees).

Two central research questions organize the following investigation of mass expulsion. First, why do governments expel? What motivates them to use this extreme eliminationist policy to remove populations *en masse*? Second, how do governments expel? What is the process of mass expulsion? What conditions and factors give rise to this policy, and what may restrain motivated governments from implementing expulsion? To answer these questions, I document cross-border mass expulsion events around the world from 1900 to 2020 in my Government-Sponsored Mass Expulsion (GSME) dataset (see Map 1.1).[35] Using this data, I provide the first comprehensive account of mass expulsion—when and where it occurs, who is targeted, and what regimes are most likely to carry it out.

Patterns in the data inform my theory of mass expulsion, explicated in two parts. First, I present a typology of mass expulsion. The typology identifies two general categories of expulsion—security and economic—and four corresponding, distinct types: counter-irredentist, counter-subversive, reprisal, and nativist. Governments implement mass expulsion to remove target groups they believe pose a security or economic threat to the state. The first three types are variants of the security category, the fourth a variant of the economic category. Counter-irredentist expulsions are driven by the desire for territorial control. They target groups with real or alleged ties to an external state in order to resist that state's irredentist claims. These expulsions aim to remove populations in order to eliminate security threats to the state's territorial integrity and to secure its land for the dominant group. Counter-subversive expulsions, in contrast, are not about territory, but instead are driven by securing the regime's internal political control and stability. They target groups that support, or are perceived to support, efforts to subvert the existing government. Reprisal expulsions, the third type under the security category, are driven by a government's desire for retaliation or revenge against an external state. These expulsions respond to

[34] Adepoju, 1984; Adida, 2014; Honig, 2016.
[35] Garrity, 2022.

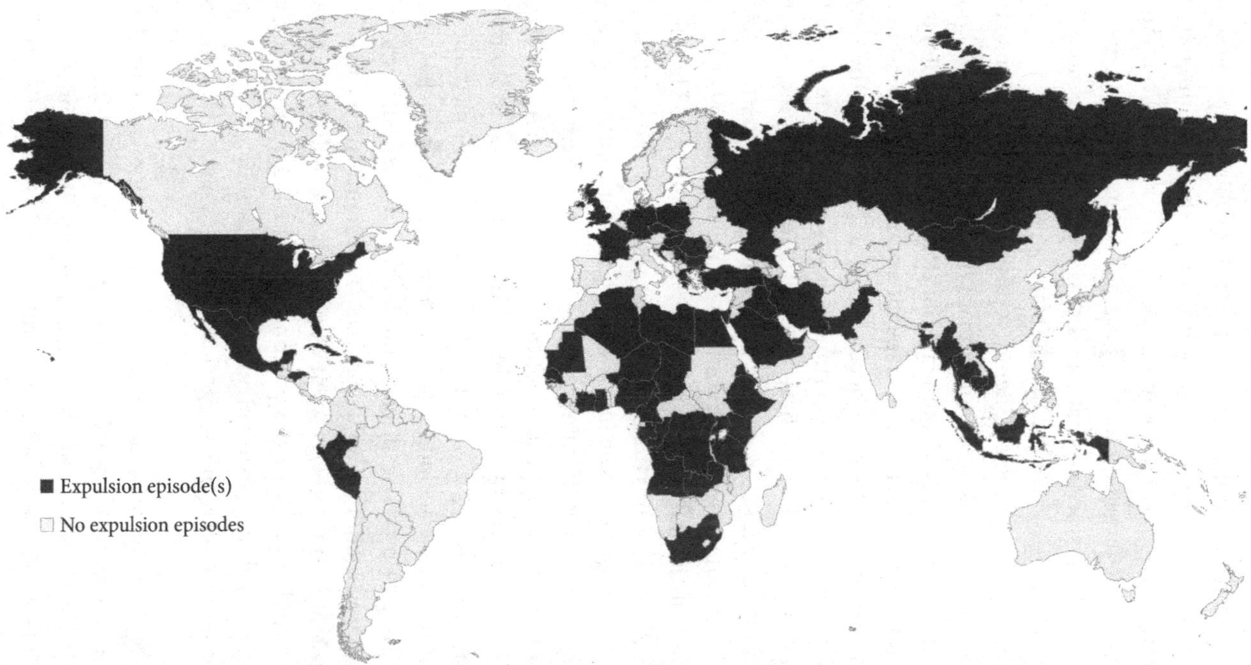

Map 1.1 Mass expulsion episodes around the world (1900–2020)[36]

[36] This map was created using MapChart.

an external government's unfavorable foreign policy position, or decision, by expelling a group with ties to that state. While many mass expulsions are driven by security concerns, over one-third of expulsion episodes are motivated by economic concerns. In juxtaposition to the other three types of expulsion, nativist expulsions aim to remove a real or alleged economic threat to the state. The targeted group is resented because of its perceived encroachment on the economic rights and privileges of "indigenous" or "native" inhabitants, however defined by the state.

Armed with an understanding of different types of expulsion, I turn to the question of how governments expel and explain the process of mass expulsion. My theoretical framework documents the structural, proximate, precipitating, and intervening factors that shape the context and circumstances in which expulsion does or does not occur. Structural shocks to the status quo change relations between the government and a target group, increasing the likelihood of expulsion. These external shocks may include the dissolution of multinational empires and the creation of new nation-states, the outbreak of interstate or intrastate conflicts, or major financial crises, all of which rearrange structural hierarchies and alter the status quo. The effects of these shocks give rise to proximate factors—specifically, the motivations outlined in the typology for expelling a target group in order to counter irredentism, to counter internal subversion, to retaliate against an external government, or to reclaim indigenous control of the economy. At this stage, the government must assess the suitability of this eliminationist policy to address the identified threat. Thus, the theory details four key preconditions for mass expulsion. These include a governing elite with an exclusionary ideology, a target group whose threat would be neutralized if removed, the presence or construction of an alternative "homeland" state where the target group "belongs," and a government with adequate capabilities to push out the target population. With the preconditions satisfied, precipitating factors—political instability, external attacks, post-conflict negotiations, critical elections—stimulate the trigger event that sparks the decision to expel.

In cases where the motivation and necessary preconditions are in place, there is still the question of feasibility. Existing research on other eliminationist strategies has focused on the causes and conditions under which governments implement these policies. While many of these theoretical expectations hold when examining positive cases of expulsion, they fall short when applied to negative cases—cases with similar probabilities of expulsion but where governments did not expel.[37] Many of the same factors the existing literature suggests should lead to expulsion—war, territorial disputes, ethnonationalism, exclusionary ideologies, regime type, history of previous expulsions, economic decline—are present in cases where expulsion policies are not enacted. Theories accounting for variation among these cases with similar conditions are underdeveloped.[38]

Therefore, the theoretical framework introduced here identifies key intervening factors that enable or restrain/constrain[39] expulsion: the ruling elites' alliances, the "homeland" state of the target group, and pertinent international organizations (IOs). When motivations and preconditions are held constant, these three factors are central in differentiating governments that expel from those that do not expel. Critical to a government's expulsion calculus are the potential political and economic benefits or harms to its domestic and transnational alliances, and whether those allies support, ignore, or actively discourage expulsion. The "homeland" state, where expellees are alleged to "belong," also plays an important role in enabling or constraining expulsion. Vital here is the strength of ties between the government and the "homeland" state and the decision, or anticipated decision, of the "homeland" to deny entry to expellees or to acquiesce and resettle them. The third intervening factor, pertinent IOs, points to the significance of the relationship between IOs and a government considering expulsion, as well as the IOs' response, or anticipated response, to an expulsion decision. Individually, each of these factors can influence expulsion decisions; however, they are most effective when they operate in combination.

The research design for this study is a mix of quantitative cross-national data analysis and qualitative in-depth case studies. To establish the universe of cases, I developed the GSME dataset, documenting cross-border expulsion events around the world from 1900 to 2020.[40] This comprehensive and systematic survey of mass expulsion introduces a significant amount of new data to the field with its distinct concept, extended duration, cross-national nature, and inclusion of citizens and noncitizens. To determine the enabling conditions that facilitate expulsion in some cases,

[37] Mahoney & Goertz, 2004.

[38] Straus, 2012.

[39] The term "restraints" connotes measures or conditions of self-control, indicating internal moderation of behavior. The term "constraints" refers to limitations or restrictions placed on something to inhibit actions or behavior, which are more aligned with external factors. Both restraints and constraints are relevant to mass expulsion.

[40] Garrity, 2022.

and the restraining/constraining conditions that deter it in others, I used a paired-comparison case study design. The three case studies include:

- Greek Orthodox Christians in the Ottoman Empire/Turkish Republic (1913–1923): expelled from the Aegean and Pontic littorals, but not from the imperial capital, Istanbul
- South Asians in postcolonial East Africa: expelled from Uganda (1972) but not from Kenya (1967–1969)
- Rohingya in Burma in the early 1990s: expelled from Arakan (Rakhine) State (1991–mid-1992), but then swiftly repatriated under a new regime (mid-1992–1995)

The three expulsion cases—Ottoman Empire, Uganda, and Burma—are crucial cases, albeit each for different reasons.

The Ottoman/Turkish expulsion of Greek Orthodox Christians included the first internationally sanctioned, compulsory "population exchange"[41] agreement. Although the Ottomans had enacted a "population exchange" with Bulgaria in 1913, that agreement was in theory voluntary, despite force being used by each side to remove the opposing population from the border regions. The Lausanne Convention of 1923, in contrast, was part of an internationally negotiated postwar treaty in which both the Turkish and Greek governments agreed to forcibly expel their Greek Orthodox Christian and Muslim populations, respectively. This agreement set an international precedent and was used as a model for future expulsions. Uganda's expulsion of South Asians in 1972 is a classic case of what some refer to as "middleman minority" expulsions.[42] It garnered international attention, given the removal of tens of thousands of British nationals of South Asian descent alongside South Asians with Ugandan citizenship. The citizenship dynamic is especially important in this case, drawing attention to "hybrid" expulsion episodes where citizens and noncitizens are expelled simultaneously. Burma's expulsion of the Rohingya is significant both for its contemporary relevance, with over 800,000 Rohingya expelled to Bangladesh in 2016–2018, and its persistent nature, with expulsion episodes initiated in

[41] "Population exchange" is placed in quotation marks throughout the text to indicate the contested nature of the phrase, which is often used as a euphemism for mass expulsion. While the idea of an "exchange of peoples" connotes a neutral, organized, peaceful, voluntary process, in practice these "exchanges" were forced, disorganized, and chaotic, masking the harsh realities of those directly affected by their implementation.

[42] Blalock, 1967; Bonacich, 1973.

1978, 1991, 2012, and 2016. This case is also distinct because of the precarious citizenship status of the target group, many of whom were stateless at the time of the expulsion.

In addition to the crucial nature of each case and the distinct government motivations, the three expulsion cases vary in terms of period, region, target group, target group citizenship status, and regime type.[43] Temporally, the expulsion cases occurred throughout the twentieth century—one before 1950 and two after. Regionally, the cases are drawn from Europe, sub-Saharan Africa, and Southeast Asia. In each expulsion, the government targeted a different category of persons. According to the 1923 Lausanne "population exchange," Greeks were expelled because of their Greek Orthodox Christian religion, but their Greek ethnic roots were also a key factor, making them an ethno-religious target. The South Asians in Uganda were both ethnically and racially distinct from the Black African majority and thus targeted as an ethno-racial group. And in Burma, the Rohingya were targeted based on their Islamic religion (in opposition to the Buddhist majority) as well as their ethnicity and race, being excluded from the government's list of "national ethnic races."[44] The citizenship status of the target group also varied across the cases, with citizens (nationals) and noncitizens (resident aliens) expelled as well as a large stateless population. Last, the regime type varied among expelling governments, which included autocracies and anocracies.

To ensure variation on the key dependent variable—mass expulsion—I identified three negative cases in which conditions and contexts were similar, where governments seemed likely to expel, but expulsion did not occur. Negative cases are apposite to analyses of eliminationist policies, where identifying key factors that constrain their occurrence is paramount.[45] Focusing on the absence of rare phenomena has led to important insights into genocide and large-scale killing of civilians, sexual violence during conflict, and revolutions.[46] However, among qualitative research of eliminationist policies, there is a dearth of negative case studies.[47] Some scholars include shadow or counterfactual cases in their analyses to test and validate arguments, but these are distinct from negative cases. Shadow cases are ancillary

[43] Regime types are drawn from the Polity V data (Marshall, 2021).
[44] Center for Diversity & National Harmony, 2018, p. 202; Cheesman, 2017, p. 468; MacLean, 2019, p. 88.
[45] Garrity, 2023a; Straus, 2012.
[46] Skocpol, 1979; Straus, 2015; Wood, 2006.
[47] Straus, 2015.

case studies, typically at the end of a scholarly work, that further explore the emergent hypotheses. They can be positive or negative and are explored just enough to suggest that the argument from the central (positive) case studies is generalizable.[48] Negative cases, by contrast, are central to the main argument. Rather than playing a complementary role, they are examined at length alongside the positive cases, and are deployed at the start of the research design to build theory and generate new hypotheses.[49] Utilizing the "possibility principle," negative cases are not simply zeros in a binary coding schema but cases in which the outcome of interest had a real possibility of occurring, but did not.[50] The negative cases examined here are contexts in which existing theory would predict mass expulsion was likely, where it was poised to occur, but in which governments did not implement the policy.[51]

Employing a most-similar systems design, the selected negative cases match the positive cases of expulsion along a series of key attributes that existing theories suggest should explain the variation: the security environment, economy (gross domestic product (GDP), GDP per capita, dominant sectors), region, geography, regime type, population size, target group (size, percentage of total population), colonizer, and public sentiment toward the target group. Holding these attributes constant, I deduced the key contributing factors that explain government decisions to expel versus decisions to refrain. The three negative cases are Istanbul (1913–1923), Kenya (1967–1969), and Burma (mid-1992–1995). Istanbul and Burma are within-case comparisons, and Kenya is a cross-case comparison. The within-case comparisons examine geographic and temporal variation. The Ottoman Empire case investigates variation in the decision to expel Greek Orthodox Christians from the Aegean and Pontic littorals and from Anatolia, but not from Istanbul. The Burma case examines variation in the Tatmadaw's expulsion of the Rohingya between March 1991 and July 1992, and the abrupt policy reversal and repatriation under new leadership from mid-1992 through 1995. Cross-case comparisons are more challenging in holding key variables constant. Nevertheless, postcolonial Kenya and Uganda were East African neighbors with similar histories and structural conditions in the late 1960s/early 1970s, making Kenya a strong negative case.[52]

[48] Goertz, 2017; Soifer, 2020.
[49] Straus, 2015.
[50] Mahoney & Goertz, 2004; Ragin, 2000; Straus, 2012, 2015.
[51] Garrity, 2023a.
[52] Garrity, 2023a.

To find evidence for the case studies, I conducted archival research at the United Nations High Commissioner for Refugees (UNHCR), the International Committee of the Red Cross (ICRC), and the League of Nations Archives in Geneva, Switzerland. These sources were necessary because most expulsionist governments are not transparent in their decision-making processes, nor do they have open-access records on this topic. Telegrams, cables, confidential memos, meeting minutes, reports, and documented conversations with expelling government officials helped to discern government motivations, identify new cases, and uncover the responses of IOs. By triangulating this data with government public statements, I was able to capture the discourse of mass expulsion. The archival evidence was complemented with other primary sources, including government documents and speeches, memoirs of key government officials, Foreign Broadcast Information Service (FBIS) daily reports, and various news articles from a wide array of international media outlets.

Additional evidence was gathered from reports and briefs published by the United Nations and relevant agency affiliates, human rights organizations—particularly Human Rights Watch (including the regional watch organizations before 1988) and Amnesty International—humanitarian organizations, and think tanks. These sources proved invaluable for understanding how governments used different tactics on the ground and the systematic nature of the expulsion episodes. Secondary historical sources, including historical records of events, such as *Keesing's Contemporary Archives* and *African Contemporary Record*, were useful in understanding decision-making processes and external events unfolding at the time.

The starting point for this research was to understand the phenomenon of mass expulsion—a prominent, recurring policy affecting millions of people that had largely escaped careful examination. It was also to investigate an atrocity described by perpetrators, international actors, observers, and scholars as "orderly and humane," while all the evidence of expellees' experiences pointed to the contrary. The analysis that follows reveals that mass expulsion is most emphatically *disorderly* and *inhumane*. Yet, the analytical focus on the state, in line with much of the existing research on eliminationist policies, risks overlooking the victims and survivors of mass expulsion.[53]

[53] There are many outstanding books of nonfiction and fiction that focus on the lives of expellees and offer perspectives of the lived experience of expulsion, such as *Twice a Stranger:*

Acknowledging that limitation, the conclusion offers a discussion of policy implications and recommendations that aim to reduce the number of future expellees. Three main prevention strategies emerge from the research findings: (1) target and monitor domestic and transnational allies of high-risk countries as key levers of influence; (2) engage "homeland" states of target groups as key partners in prevention efforts; and (3) increase international and regional organizations' involvement to deter expulsion by integrating and lobbying high-risk countries to join, and engage with, these institutions and ensure accountability for mass expulsion when prevention fails.

The book proceeds as follows. Part I outlines the concept and theory of mass expulsion. Chapter 2 presents a conceptual analysis of mass expulsion and a comprehensive overview of the phenomenon over the *longue durée* using the GSME data. Chapter 3 introduces a typology of mass expulsion explaining four distinct types of the phenomenon: counter-irredentist, counter-subversive, reprisal, and nativist expulsions. Chapter 4 details the process of mass expulsion and develops a theoretical framework that explains both why some governments decide to adopt this specific eliminationist policy and why others, despite similar motives and conditions, do not follow through with its implementation.

Part II provides the empirical evidence for the theoretical framework. Chapters 5–7 are each dedicated to a different type of expulsion: nativist, counter-irredentist, and counter-subversive. Each case study includes a negative case, where expulsion seemed likely but did not occur, to illustrate the key intervening factors that facilitate or deter expulsion. Chapter 5 investigates South Asian minorities in postcolonial Uganda and Kenya, who were expelled from the former but not from the latter, despite widespread anti-Asian sentiment throughout both countries. Chapter 6 examines Greek Orthodox Christians in the Ottoman Empire expelled, between 1913 and 1923, from the Aegean and Pontic littorals but not from Istanbul, despite the wealthiest, most politically active, irredentist Greeks living in the imperial capital. Chapter 7 then turns to Southeast Asia and examines the Rohingya

The Mass Expulsions That Forged Modern Greece and Turkey (Clark, 2006), *Birds Without Wings* (De Bernières, 2004), *Orderly and Humane: The Expulsion of the Germans After the Second World War* (Douglas, 2012), *From Citizen to Refugee: Uganda Asians Come to Britain* (Mamdani, 2022), and *First, They Erased Our Name: A Rohingya Speaks* (Habiburahman & Ansel, 2019), among many others.

in Burma from 1991 to 1995, a period in which they were expelled *en masse* and then in an abrupt volte-face the expulsions were halted and the refugees repatriated under a new regime. Last, Chapter 8 summarizes the contributions to the fields of international security, ethnic violence, and forced migration and discusses key policy implications and recommendations for deterring the use of mass expulsion. Given the understudied nature of this phenomenon, the conclusion also outlines some of the many remaining questions that require further investigation.

Let us begin with the foundational question: What is mass expulsion?

PART I

CONCEPTS & THEORY

2

Concepts and Data

2.1 What Is Mass Expulsion?

Mass expulsion is not a new concept.[1] Although it lacks an official international legal definition, it is codified in international law in various human rights conventions with many well-documented cases.[2] I am introducing mass expulsion as a neovalent—an existing term given new meaning through an expansion of its defining attributes.[3] Therefore, I define the concept as a systematic government-sponsored policy to remove an ethnic, racial, religious, or national group as such, with no individual legal review and no recognition of the right to return.[4] Stemming from the definition are six specific attributes of the concept, each of which is expounded upon below.

2.1.1 Government Sponsored

The first attribute of mass expulsion is that governments are the perpetrators. This encompasses both state-ordered and state-directed expulsion policies. State-ordered expulsions involve explicit government-issued expulsion decrees or treaties as well as the physical removal of the target group by state military, police, or intelligence forces. State-directed expulsions are executed by various agents of the state, including paramilitary non-state actors

[1] In the few texts explicitly devoted to mass expulsion, the concept has been defined as "an act, or failure to act, by an authority of a State with the intention and with the effect of securing the removal of a person or persons from the territory of that State" (Coles, 1983, p. 3); "that exercise of State power which secures the removal, either 'voluntarily', under threat of forcible removal, or forcibly, of an alien from the territory of a State" (Goodwin-Gill, 1978, p. 201); and "an expulsion of a group of people on the very ground of belonging to that specific group . . . [with] no individual review of each expulsion" (Henckaerts, 1995, p. 21). My concept and definition build on Henckaerts's magisterial legal analysis in his 1995 book *Mass Expulsion in Modern International Law and Practice.*

[2] Expulsion—of nationals and "aliens" or non-nationals (including migrant workers and refugees)—is explicitly prohibited in various human rights conventions (see Appendix A).

[3] Sartori, 1984, p. 40.

[4] Garrity, 2022.

Mass Expulsion. Meghan M. Garrity, Oxford University Press. © Oxford University Press (2026).
DOI: 10.1093/9780197829097.003.0002

that are supported by government officials. The focus on the state as the main actor, or perpetrator, of mass expulsion is in line with existing research and data on other eliminationist policies.[5] The exclusion of non-state actors as perpetrators minimally impacts the overall sample. As Scott Straus notes regarding his data on large-scale violence against civilians in Africa—which includes state and non-state actors as perpetrators—"state actors are the lead perpetrators in nearly every case."[6]

2.1.2 Intent to Systematically Remove

The second attribute of mass expulsion is the intent to systematically remove the target group from the territory of the state.[7] "Systematic" refers to organized, coordinated, intentional actions that aim to remove the target population from the country.[8] This is the core aspect of mass expulsion and distinguishes it from other eliminationist policies. Expulsion intends *to remove* the target population from the territory, whereas genocide intends *to annihilate or destroy* the target group,[9] and coercive assimilation intends *to eliminate the group's unique cultural identity*.[10] Some scholars include mass expulsion under the umbrella concept "ethnic cleansing," examining instances of genocide, mass expulsion, and coercive assimilation together.[11] However, this blurs the distinct intent of the three policies. Extracting mass expulsion from this umbrella allows us to more clearly identify the drivers of this specific eliminationist strategy.[12]

[5] See datasets by Bulutgil (2016); Harff (2003); Lichtenheld (2020); Müller-Crepon et al. (2024); Ulfelder & Valentino (2008).

[6] Straus, 2015, p. 90.

[7] There is an important distinction between the intent of the perpetrator and their motive. Intent refers to the purpose or aim in committing a specific act (in this case, removing a target group from the territory of a state), whereas motive is the underlying reason or cause for the action. A four-tiered typology of expulsion motivations is explained in Chapter 3.

[8] Garrity, 2023b, p. 475; Schabas, 2000, p. 200.

[9] Lingaas, 2020, pp. 73–75; Naimark, 2001; Schabas, 2000; Straus, 2016. These scholars note a distinction between genocide and ethnic cleansing, the latter which they suggest connotes the goal of removal. I argue that mass expulsion is a more precise concept than ethnic cleansing (Garrity, 2023b, p. 478).

[10] Garrity, 2023b, pp. 475, 483–487; Schabas, 2000, p. 200.

[11] Not all scholars of ethnic cleansing include coercive assimilation within their concept (Bulutgil, 2016; Müller-Crepon et al., 2024; Mylonas, 2012), but others do (Mann, 2005; Mirković, 1996). And much of the existing data on mass atrocities (Bellamy, 2011), state-sponsored mass killing (Ulfelder & Valentino, 2008), and targeted mass killing (Butcher et al., 2020) aggregates incidents of genocide, mass expulsion, and coercive assimilation.

[12] Garrity, 2023b.

Rather than focusing on government intent, much of the existing research in this field has defined its concepts based on government practices or tactics (e.g., murder, deportation, displacement).[13] This conceptually muddies the boundaries between related concepts within this semantic field. The methods used to expel a group may in some cases be the same as those used by governments implementing other atrocities. Killing is a tactic used by governments with varied intentions—sometimes to destroy a group (genocide), sometimes to remove them (mass expulsion), and other times to force their subjugation (control).[14] While most genocides involve large-scale killing, not all mass killings are genocidal. Similarly, while some mass expulsion episodes involve killing to coerce a population to flee an area, not all mass killing events are episodes of mass expulsion. Defining mass expulsion based on its intention to remove is more definitionally precise and allows for improved theorizing of the causes and consequences of this abhorrent phenomenon.

Given the centrality of intention to this definition, identifying an episode of mass expulsion requires an empirical determination of a government's *mens rea,* or mental element, as it is known in legal parlance. Government intent may be explicit or implicit; the former is much easier to identify and document than the latter. In some expulsion cases, the government's intention is unequivocal. State authorities officially announce an expulsion order or decree (e.g., Mexico, 1931; Uganda, 1972; Nigeria, 1983) or consent to a bilateral or multilateral "population transfer" or "population exchange" agreement (e.g., Lausanne Convention, 1923; Potsdam Agreement, 1945; Czechoslovakia–Hungary Agreement, 1946). In other cases, historical evidence of intent is found in archival records.

However, given the severe nature of this policy, most governments do not have open-access archives that can be analyzed to determine intent. Nor do they have written documentation to evaluate because expulsion orders and decisions were communicated verbally without a paper trail. Thus, in many instances, government intent is "a logical deduction that flows from evidence of the material acts."[15] In other words, the intent to remove is

[13] Bellamy, 2011; Bulutgil, 2016; Butcher et al., 2020; Harff, 2003; Lichtenheld, 2020; Orchard, 2010; Ulfelder & Valentino, 2008.

[14] Garrity, 2023b, pp. 485–487; Schabas, 2000, p. 200.

[15] Schabas, 2000, p. 222.

inferred from official state actions. These actions may include announced and unannounced police or military "clearance operations" (e.g., Uganda, 1982; Greece, 1993; Burma, 2016), organized raids that corral target populations and force them across borders, sometimes transporting them directly (e.g., United States, 1929; Russia, 2006; Algeria, 2016), and instances where governments destroy or confiscate legal documents accompanied by orders for the population to leave (e.g., Dominican Republic, 1991; Tanzania, 2006; Angola, 2008). In all these cases, physical force is used but deadly violence is limited.

In a small number of episodes, government intentions are more difficult to discern. During wars or armed conflicts, killing may be used to induce flight (e.g., Greece, 1912; Cyprus, 1974; Burma, 2016). However, large-scale killing is also a tactic of other eliminationist policies, such as genocide. In these cases, further contextual evidence must be evaluated to assess a government's intention. Evidence of expulsion may include the use of tactical, as opposed to wholesale, state killing to provoke flight, or reports of state or state-sponsored actors threatening the target group to leave "voluntarily" or face violence. Other evidence of expulsion includes perpetrators opening exit routes to encourage forcible departure, in contrast to perpetrators blocking or closing borders, which may be preliminary evidence of plans for mass killing or genocide. Acts of intentional omission are also important signals for expulsion—for example, when governments fail to restrain militias that are forcibly removing populations.

In implementing the intentional removal of a target group, the necessary level of government coercion depends on the specific country context. In the case of bilateral or multilateral "population exchange" agreements, target populations may leave the state upon learning that an agreement has been signed, with minimal government coercion required. In other instances, fear of violence, threats of violence, or knowledge of previous episodes of violence may induce populations to depart following a government's expulsion announcement in the absence of direct force. Sometimes large-scale violence in an area—arrests and killings of members of the target group, burning homes, confiscating assets—precipitates the forcible departure of other members of the group. Regardless of the level of coercion used, mass expulsion is defined based on the government's aim of intentionally removing a specific target group. The level of force used to execute the removal will vary depending on the context.

2.1.3 Group-Based Phenomenon

The third attribute of mass expulsion is the targeting of specific ethnic, racial, religious, or national groups. These four categories are in line with a broad conceptualization of ethnicity as groups with descent-based attributes.[16] They each conform to the key properties of constrained change and visibility.[17] They are "sticky" and hard to change in the short term, making it difficult to escape group-based government targeting. They also match those in existing international human rights treaties like the 1948 Genocide Convention[18] as well as the African Charter on Human and Peoples' Rights. The latter states in Article 12(5), "Mass expulsion shall be that which is aimed at national, racial, ethnic or religious groups."[19]

It is essential to emphasize that these categories of group identity are socially constructed and sometimes overlapping.[20] They are projected by the perpetrator onto others to distinguish the non-core "out group" from the dominant core "in group."[21] It is well documented that the four groups included in the Genocide Convention, and those that were excluded (namely political and class groups), were heavily disputed and influenced by post-WWII geopolitics.[22] Nevertheless, political and economic groups are more fluid than the ones included in the mass expulsion definition. One can easily and quickly change political parties, affiliations, or beliefs. One can also, depending on the context, raise one's socioeconomic status. But one cannot easily change ascriptive characteristics such as ethnicity and race. While one can convert to a different religion, governments eager to expel religious groups often ignore conversions, as was the case in Nazi Germany with Christian Jews.[23] Religious identity, in some cases, is also visible with physically identifiable amulets or clothing (e.g. Sikh turbans, Jewish yarmulkes, Catholic crucifixes, or Muslim hijabs). Nationality is also not easily changed in the short term. While in some countries one can obtain dual nationality, in many cases nationality is inextricably linked to other ascriptive characteristics, including race, ethnicity, and religion. Many states also

[16] Chandra, 2006; Horowitz, 1985.
[17] Chandra, 2006.
[18] United Nations, 1948 (see Article II).
[19] African (Banjul) Charter on Human and Peoples' Rights, 1981.
[20] Lingaas, 2020, p. 70.
[21] Lingaas, 2020, pp. 41, 73; Mylonas, 2012, pp. 23–29.
[22] Lingaas, 2020, pp. 59–63.
[23] Evans, 2005, pp. 545–546; Harff, 2003; Lingaas, 2020, p. 105.

prohibit dual nationality. Although there are tradeoffs to excluding political and class groups, the four categories included in the mass expulsion definition—ethnicity, race, religion, and nationality—reflect descent-based characteristics that are difficult to change in the short term.

2.1.4 "As Such" (Instrumentally, Not Incidentally, Targeted)

In addition to mass expulsion being a group-based phenomenon, the fourth definitional attribute is that the group must be targeted on the basis of its shared group characteristics, not as a result of larger indiscriminate violence that causes displacement. The relevant group must be instrumentally, not incidentally, removed. While all mass expulsion episodes forcibly displace populations, not all forced migration events are mass expulsions. The indiscriminate targeting of civilian populations causing all people in an area to flee is not mass expulsion, nor is general political instability that leads to large-scale emigration. For example, Syrian refugee flows resulting from the 2011 civil war, or the large-scale exodus of Libyans from Libya during the First and Second Libyan Civil Wars (2011; 2014–2020), are cases of forced displacement but not mass expulsion. In those cases, groups were not specifically targeted on the basis of shared ascriptive characteristics. Additionally, while mass expulsion creates refugees when citizens are expelled from their country of origin, not all expulsion events target citizens, and thus not all expellees are refugees. Expelled noncitizens (e.g., foreign nationals or resident aliens) can return to their state of citizenship; therefore, they are not refugees. In other situations, governments explicitly expel refugees, sending them back to their home country or a neighboring third country where they still face a fear of persecution, a clear case of *refoulement*.[24]

The "as such" clause is critical to the definition of mass expulsion because it differentiates general population removal (i.e., forced migration or displacement) from forced population removal of a specific identity group (mass expulsion). Governments deploy mass expulsion policies to remove a target group as a separate and distinct entity. Individual expellees are targeted on account of their membership, or alleged membership, in a particular group. It is the group itself that is the ultimate target of expulsion.[25] Empirically, this can be deduced by assessing if locations with high

[24] Article 33 of the UN Refugee Convention prohibits the expulsion of refugees (UNHCR, 1951).
[25] Lingaas, 2020, p. 67.

percentages of the target group are affected, or if the perpetrator excludes members of other groups in the same area.

2.1.5 Absence of Individual Legal Review

The fifth attribute of mass expulsion—the absence of individual legal review—complements the fourth attribute, with further specification to indicate the broad targeting of a group. In mass expulsion episodes, persons are expelled irrespective of their individual actions or legal status. This distinguishes mass expulsion from individual expulsion. Governments have authority over their territorial sovereignty, including immigration decisions, and may legally expel noncitizens (citizens may not be legally expelled[26]). However, international law demands due process, including individual evaluation of each person's case and the prospect of appeal. If individuals are expelled from the territory after their documentation (or lack thereof) has been legitimately reviewed by the respective governing authorities and deemed to be in violation of domestic law, this is an individual—not a mass or group—expulsion. Governments that use legal means to remove noncitizens (e.g., requiring new forms of documentation, adding additional regulations for noncitizen residence, changing business licensing requirements) are not instances of mass expulsion. Mass expulsion is predicated on the absence of legitimate individual assessment.

2.1.6 No Recognition of the Right to Return

The sixth and final attribute of mass expulsion is that it is a rapid onset event with the aim of immediate, permanent, forced removal not recognizing expellees' right to return. Expelling governments may force expellees to sign declarations admitting to criminal offenses, attesting to voluntary departure, or relinquishing their property rights. They may confiscate their assets upon exit, destroy their legal documentation, or revoke their

[26] In some cases, countries remove citizenship from groups (through legal or illegal means) and then expel the noncitizens. For example, while a U.S. citizen cannot legally be expelled, the citizenship of a naturalized citizen may be revoked for reasons of naturalization fraud—illegal procurement of naturalization, concealment or willful misrepresentation on the naturalization application and/or examination, or membership/affiliation with certain organizations (i.e., terrorist groups). A natural-born citizen may also relinquish US citizenship through voluntary conduct (see Immigration and Nationality Act, § 349, 8 U.S.C. 1451, 2025a; § 349, 8 U.S.C. § 1481, 2025b). If naturalized citizenship is revoked, the legal process for expelling an individual noncitizen would apply.

citizenship. Governments may also resettle dominant populations into residences vacated by expellees to further solidify their permanent removal. The irreversibility aspect of mass expulsion distinguishes the phenomenon from the policy (not to be confused with the tactic) of deportation. While deportation regulations vary across states, most countries require a "cooling-off period" in which a deported person must wait before attempting to reenter the country.[27] After several years, a person may reapply to legally return to the country; whether entry is granted is at the discretion of the country's immigration authorities. The distinction with mass expulsion is that, at the time of removal, there is no hope of return, indicating a permanence, or intended permanence, albeit not always permanent in practice. There have been cases where governments have claimed that expellees have no right to return but where the population has come back to the country (e.g., Dominican Republic: 1991, 1996, 1999; Angola: 2003, 2008, 2011). Nevertheless, expelling governments do not recognize expellees' right to return at the time of the expulsion decision.

*

The six attributes of mass expulsion—government sponsored, intent to systematically remove, group based, instrumental targeting, absence of individual legal review, and no recognition of the right to return—define and delimit the boundaries of the concept and distinguish mass expulsion from other related but distinct concepts. There are tradeoffs to employing a narrow concept focused on a single eliminationist policy with a distinct intent as opposed to a broader concept like ethnic cleansing that includes multiple eliminationist policies (i.e., genocide, expulsion, and coercive assimilation).[28] A broader concept provides insight into the macro causes of group elimination.[29] However, this assumes that all eliminationist policies are driven by the same factors and by the same aims. Yet governments have explicitly stated that they strategically use different eliminationist policies toward different groups at different times.

In the early twentieth century, the Ottoman Empire targeted various minority groups within its territory with annihilation (Armenians), mass expulsion (Greek Orthodox Christians), and coercive assimilation (Kurds).[30] As historian and sociologist Taner Akçam writes:

[27] Immigration and Nationality Act, § 212(a)(9)(A), 8 U.S.C. § 1182(a)(9)(A), 2025c.
[28] Bulutgil, 2016; Mann, 2005; Mirković, 1996.
[29] Bulutgil, 2016; Mylonas, 2012.
[30] Garrity, 2023b, p. 483.

> Extant Ottoman documents reveal that the Unionist government made clear distinctions in its wartime policies between the Armenians and the empire's other Christian communities. The Greeks . . . were *deported and expelled* with brutality, but the Armenians were targeted for outright *annihilation* [emphasis added].[31]

Archival evidence from the Prime Ministerial Ottoman Archive documents conversations between senior Ottoman authorities and local officials indicating different intentions for different groups. In a telegram sent by Talat Pasha, Ottoman minister of interior affairs, to the governor of Diyarbakır province, Pasha rebuked the governor for using violence equally against all Christians: "The policy of annihilation was to be limited to the Armenians and not to include other Christian groups [e.g., Greek Orthodox]."[32] The eliminationist policies were not only limited to the Ottoman Empire's Christian population. While Armenians and Greeks were eliminated from the empire through genocide and expulsion policies, respectively, the Kurds were violently forced to assimilate into the dominant Turkish culture.[33] The Ottomans, and later the Turkish regime, prohibited their language, closed their religious and cultural institutions, and forcibly settled Turks in Kurdish areas.[34]

Similar patterns can be seen across space and time. In the 1970s, Ugandan President Idi Amin expelled South Asians *en masse* while simultaneously massacring rival Acholi and Langi ethnic groups. Over the course of four decades, the Burmese Tatmadaw repeatedly expelled the Rohingya minority while using a combination of control and coercive assimilationist strategies against the Karen, Kachin, and Chin minorities. While it is not necessary to debate the horrors of various atrocities, it is analytically important to acknowledge that governments use different eliminationist policies to achieve different aims.

This study does not examine why governments may choose to implement different types of eliminationist policies; that is a subject for another volume. Rather, it provides the first comprehensive analysis of why governments choose, or refrain from choosing, the specific policy of mass expulsion. Focusing on a single eliminationist policy defined by its intention, rather than by the perpetrator's practices or tactics that cut across policies,

[31] Akçam, 2012, p. 125.
[32] Akçam, 2012, p. 210.
[33] Garrity, 2023b, p. 483.
[34] McDowall, 2000; Yegen, 2009.

enables a clearer understanding of government motivations and, in turn, the causes of, and constraints on, mass expulsion.

2.1.7 Scope Conditions

In addition to meeting the definitional attributes of mass expulsion outlined above, two important scope conditions limit the cases examined. The first is that the target population must be expelled across an international border or from newly annexed or ceded territory. Thus, incidents of internal expulsion are excluded. Cross-border expulsion is distinct from internal expulsion. In the former, the state abdicates all responsibility for individuals of the target population. In these cases, governments define the expelled target group as belonging someplace else—possessing an alternative "homeland"—and consequently assign responsibility for them to another state. This is distinct from governments seeking to marginalize or disenfranchise a target group within their state by internally relocating them. In these instances, the target population is still the government's responsibility, although they may not be treated equally to the dominant core group.

There are also operational considerations for this scope condition. There are severe barriers to systematic data collection of internal expulsion cases since 1900. Internal displacement was not a significant focus of the international community until more recently. While some studies on European ethnic cleansing include internally displaced populations,[35] data like this outside of the European context from the first half of the twentieth century is not available in extant datasets or from international organizations. The Internal Displacement Monitoring Centre, "the world's definitive source of data and analysis on internal displacement,"[36] does not begin its data collection until 1998. Coding internal expulsions would also require a much larger number of, rather subjective, determinations for inclusion. In cases of development-induced internal displacement, it is often difficult to assess whether a government is removing a group because they are "in the way" of a development project or specifically because of their group characteristics. In cases of internal displacement resulting from natural disasters, a government's neglect in preventing or mitigating the disaster may

[35] See Bulutgil, 2016; Pohl, 1999.
[36] Internal Displacement Monitoring Centre, 2024.

disproportionately affect a specific ethnic group, but this may not be a deliberate policy of expulsion. Internal expulsions also open the question of segregation. Government "red-line" policies that limit access to financing may disproportionately affect one group and force them to relocate; however, the coordinated and systematic nature of these efforts may be opaque. For all these reasons, this study focuses exclusively on cross-border mass expulsion.

The second scope condition is a minimum threshold of at least 1,000 persons expelled during a one-year period. Quantifying the "mass" in mass expulsion is an inherently contentious exercise. In one of the foremost legal analyses of mass expulsion, Jean-Marie Henckaerts writes, "There is no absolute answer as to what size group constitutes a mass and what does not. In international law this dead end has been avoided by providing qualitative, not quantitative, standards."[37] Yet, for the purpose of empirical analysis, a quantifiable benchmark is needed. Most works on eliminationist policies use an absolute number of persons killed or displaced,[38] although the thresholds vary widely from 25 to 100,000 persons affected.[39] One issue in using absolute thresholds is the unreliability of reporting and incomplete or missing data. A relative proportion of the group affected would be a better measure, and some scholars take this approach.[40] Relative measures may better capture the impact of the expulsion, as 1,000 persons expelled in a country of 2 million is proportionally the same as 10,000 out of 20 million or 100,000 out of 200 million. However, using a relative threshold introduces a second unreliable quantitative measure: census figures of the target group size. Census data is highly uncertain, particularly in many of the contexts examined here where regular censuses are not conducted or are imprecise. Manipulation and deliberate under-counting of ethnic minorities is also a chronic deficiency with country-level population data.[41] Further, many countries do not have accurate estimates, or any estimates, of the total number of noncitizens in the country, a critical component of this analysis. Therefore, a minimum absolute threshold of 1,000 persons expelled over the course of an annual period is used. One could raise the

[37] Henckaerts, 1995, p. 1.
[38] E.g., Adida, 2014; Butcher et al., 2020; Orchard, 2010; Straus, 2015; Ulfelder & Valentino, 2008.
[39] Garrity & Mylonas, 2025.
[40] E.g., Bulutgil, 2016; Mylonas, 2012.
[41] Mylonas, 2015; Ulfelder & Valentino, 2008.

threshold of persons expelled above 1,000, but mass expulsion still remains a significant phenomenon regardless.[42]

2.1.8 Coding Cases

Having explained the core attributes of the mass expulsion definition, and corresponding scope conditions, we turn to its operationalization. For an event to be coded as a mass expulsion episode in the Government-Sponsored Mass Expulsion (GSME) dataset, five questions depicted in the coding criteria decision tree must be answered in the affirmative (see Figure 2.1).[43] First, was the event ordered or directed by the government? Second, was the intent to systematically remove the target group? Third, was the target an ethnic, racial, religious, or national group? Fourth, was the group targeted on the basis of its shared characteristics? And fifth, was there no recognition of the group's right to return? If the answer to any of these questions is no, then the case is not coded as an episode of mass expulsion. While the questions may seem straightforward, some cases are more ambiguous than others. The coding criteria are particularly instructive in assessing gray area cases where it is difficult to determine whether the episode is a mass expulsion. A brief case illustration of postcolonial Uganda and Kenya demonstrates how applying the coding criteria helps to clarify the difference between two seemingly similar cases—the former a mass expulsion episode, the latter not.[44]

First, *was the event ordered or directed by the government?* In August 1972, Ugandan President Idi Amin announced the expulsion of South Asians from Uganda and issued an official decree documenting the government's decision, clearly meeting the first criterion. In 1967, the Kenyan government passed two pieces of legislation—an immigration bill and a trade licensing bill—that had the effect of reducing the *noncitizen* South Asian population in Kenya. The legislation passed by the parliament was clearly a government initiative, also meeting the first criterion.

Second, *was the intent of the government to systematically remove the target group?* In the case of Uganda, Amin's aim to remove South Asians from Uganda was officially documented in Decree 17 and was further indicated

[42] The 1,000-person expelled minimum threshold results in 139 expulsion cases between 1900 and 2020. If that threshold were raised to 5,000, the total cases would be 119; if raised to 20,000, 99 cases; if raised to 50,000, 73 cases.

[43] The five questions encompass the six definitional attributes. The "as such" and "absence of individual legal review" attributes are combined into question number four.

[44] See Chapter 5 for a detailed account of these two cases.

Question	No / Yes	Relevant evidence includes but is not limited to:
1) Was the event ordered or directed by the government?	No. Expulsion driven by non-state actors Yes	• *Explicit government-issued expulsion decree or policy* • *Involvement of state military, police, intelligence, and/or paramilitary forces (supported by the state) in the physical removal of the target group* • *No government intervention to prevent target group removal*
2) Was the intent to systematically remove the target group?	No. Government had alternative intention (*e.g., to destroy, to coercively assimilate, to control, etc.*) Yes	• *Government-announced expulsion policy* • *Multilateral or bilateral "population transfer/exchange" agreement* • *Reports of organized and coordinated state or state-sponsored actions (e.g., evicting/corralling expellees toward borders and coastlines; encouraging exit rather than restricting departure; providing transport to border crossings; destroying/confiscating legal documents)* • *Tactical state or state-sponsored violence to provoke and accelerate flight; threatening the target group to leave "voluntarily" or face violence*
3) Was the target an ethnic, racial, religious, or national group?	No. Population targeted based on other attributes (*i.e., political opposition, socio-economic status, sexual orientation*) Yes	• *Government expulsion decree explicitly mentions or describes one of the four groups* • *Host governments and/or response organizations document expellees as belonging to one of the four groups*
4) Was the group targeted on the basis of its shared characteristics?	No. Population indiscriminately targeted, or individual status evaluated Yes	• *Target group is instrumentally, not incidentally, removed* • *Expellees originate from locations with large populations of the target group* • *In mixed areas the target group is removed but other residents are excluded* • *Absence of individual legal review of expellees*
5) Was there no recognition of the right to return?	No. Government intends to temporarily remove target group Yes	• *Government authorities prevent expellees from returning home; burn target group residences* • *Expellees forced to sign documents declaring "voluntary" departure, admitting to offenses, and/or relinquishing property rights* • *Confiscation of expellees' property, assets, and/or documentation; revocation of citizenship* • *Resettling dominant populations into expellees' vacated residences/areas* • *No mention of timeframe for which expellees may apply to re-enter the country*

Figure 2.1 Mass expulsion coding criteria decision tree

in his regular public announcements in which he expanded his intent to remove both South Asian citizens of Uganda as well as South Asian noncitizens. His coordination with the United Nations to physically remove the South Asians further indicated his intent to remove, rather than to destroy, coercively assimilate, or control them within the territory.[45] In Kenya, rather than systematically removing South Asians from the country, the legislation passed was intended to *selectively remove* individual noncitizens working in specific sectors and locations and those not employing and training Africans in their businesses. These legislative maneuvers did not affect South Asians with Kenyan citizenship, nor noncitizen South Asian manufacturers who were crucial for the continued growth of the Kenyan economy. The Kenyan government's intent was not the systematic removal of the South Asian population from Kenya, but rather the implementation of a more restrictive immigration policy with exemptions for select noncitizens.

Third, *was the target an ethnic, racial, religious, or national group?* In Uganda, the expulsion order outlined specific ethnic and national targeting: "any person who is of Asian origin, extraction or descent and who is subject or citizen of [the United Kingdom, India, Pakistan, or Bangladesh]."[46] While at first it may have seemed like Amin was only targeting South Asian noncitizens, he later announced that all South Asians, regardless of citizenship status (including South Asians with Ugandan citizenship), would be expelled, further cementing the ethno-racial nature of the expulsion. In Kenya, the immigration and trade licensing legislation did not explicitly have an ethnic, racial, religious, or national component. The new laws applied equally to all permanent residents and businesses engaged in trade. However, most of the traders affected were South Asians, who dominated the commercial sector in Kenya. As a result, South Asians were not the de jure target of the policies, but they were the de facto target. Thus, the Kenya case would meet the third criterion.

Fourth, *was the group targeted on the basis of its shared characteristics?* In Uganda, South Asians were expelled on the basis of their shared South Asian descent. While the Ugandan government's "verification exercise" had the façade of individual legal evaluation, thousands of South Asians had their

[45] Confidential Cable from Komorsky (UNHCR Representative Kampala) to UNHCR High Commissioner, 20.10.1972; 13/1/4-18, Uganda Asians [Volume 1]; Series 4, Box 43; Fonds 13, Sub-Fonds 1; UNHCR.

[46] Confidential Memorandum from The Representative, UNHCR Branch Office for Uganda—photostat copies of Decree No. 17 and Statutory Instrument No. 124/72, 14 September 1972; 11/2/64-641.UGA[a] Expulsion and Deportation - Uganda [1972] Volume 1; Series 2, Box 1281; Fonds 11; UNHCR.

legitimate citizenship claims revoked on discriminatory grounds in a blanket ethnic expulsion. In Kenya, the new immigration and trade licensing legislation targeted certain categories of persons (permanent residents) and certain sectors (commerce). Permanent residency certificates were canceled and replaced with work permits that were costly to obtain and restrictive. Work permits were only issued to businesses that employed and trained Kenyan citizens, and the new law restricted the types of goods that could be sold and the location of business operations. While South Asians were disproportionately affected by the new legislation because they were largely foreign nationals and were dominant in trade, their cases were individually evaluated. If they met the new requirements (e.g., they paid for the work permits and employed Kenyan workers in their businesses), they were allowed to remain in Kenya. Consequently, in Kenya, the policy was not targeted at South Asians based on their shared group characteristics.

Fifth, *was there no recognition of the right to return?* To prevent the South Asian's return to Uganda, the government confiscated their assets and property and rescinded the Ugandan citizenship of those with Ugandan passports. Despite Amin's assurances that the expelled South Asians would be fully compensated, this did not happen during his rule.[47] In Kenya, by contrast, the noncitizen South Asians who decided to leave were not denied the right to return. Under the new legislation, those who did not obtain work permits had to leave the country for their place of citizenship (largely the United Kingdom), but they were not excluded from reapplying to return to Kenya in the future. In sum, the Uganda case answered all five questions affirmatively and was coded as a mass expulsion, whereas the Kenya case answered only two questions affirmatively and was therefore not coded as an expulsion.

2.2 Data: The When, Where, Who, and What of Mass Expulsion

To fully understand mass expulsion, we need to know when and where it occurs, who it targets, and what types of governments carry it out. The GSME dataset is the first comprehensive aggregation of cross-border mass

[47] Confidential Memorandum from the Representative, UNHCR Branch Office for Kampala, 18 December 1972; 11/2/64-641.UGA[c] Expulsion and Deportation—Uganda [1972–1984] Volume 3; Series 2, Box 1281; Fonds 11; UNHCR.

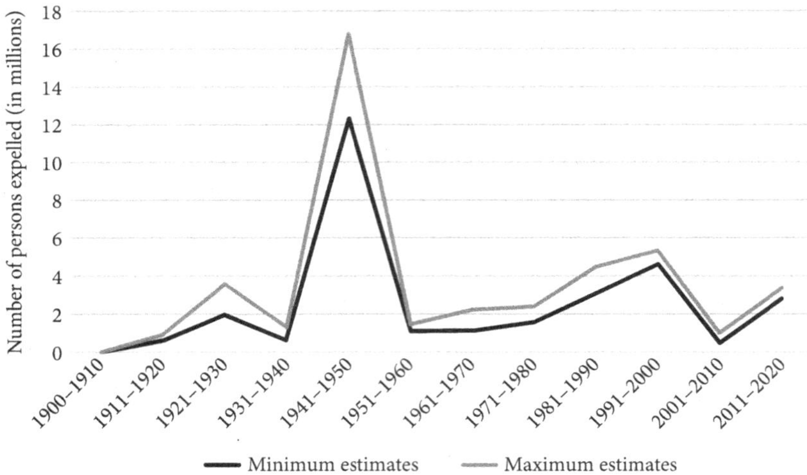

Figure 2.2 Total number of persons expelled (1900–2020)

expulsion events around the world between 1900 and 2020.[48] This section presents an expository analysis of the phenomenon.

It is first important to understand the magnitude of this grim policy. Between 1900 and 2020, over 30.3 million people were expelled from their homes and forced to leave the country. Given the chaos of mass expulsion, data on the number of persons expelled is imprecise. More than 30 million is a minimum estimate. The total number of expellees may reach as high as 42.9 million (see Figure 2.2).

During the period examined, the magnitude of the 139 expulsion episodes has varied widely, from fewer than 5,000 people expelled to more than 1 million (see Figure 2.3). The modal expulsion size is between 100,001 and 250,000 persons in thirty distinct episodes, a significant assault on civilians. The scale of this phenomenon remains consistent over time. Examining the three most recent decades in the dataset (1990–2020), the modal expulsion size is the same as the total sample, with thirteen episodes affecting between 100,001 and 250,000 persons. The data show that hundreds of thousands of individuals and families have been expelled throughout the twentieth and early twenty-first centuries, and they continue to be expelled in significant numbers today.

[48] Garrity, 2022.

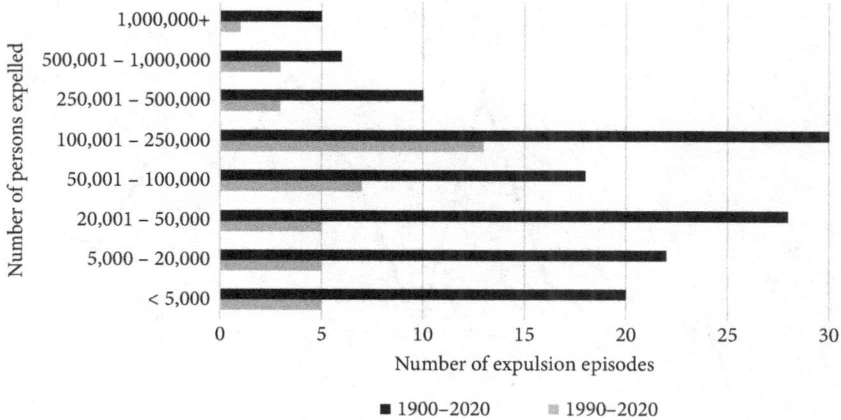

Figure 2.3 Magnitude of expulsion episodes

2.2.1 When Has Expulsion Occurred?

In the 120 years examined, governments have initiated 139 expulsion episodes around the world. Beginning in 1900, governments initiated ten or more mass expulsions in eight of the twelve decades (see Figure 2.4). The early twentieth century saw the culmination of the age of global empires followed by their progressive dissolution into nation-states. As this transition unfolded, mass expulsion was a favored policy to "unmix" multiethnic populations. The earliest expulsion cases between 1900 and 1923 took place amid the collapse of the Ottoman Empire—during the Balkan Wars (1912–1913) and in the immediate aftermath of World War I. Far from a Eurocentric phenomenon, other countries in the 1930s also expelled ethnic groups, including the US, Mexico, Cuba, and the Dominican Republic. During World War II, and the subsequent postwar peace agreements (1938–1948), there was a surge in mass expulsions, with over twenty European cases.

Decolonization across Africa and Asia (1960–1980) brought additional waves of expulsion as new states emerged following the collapse of colonial empires and as new governments vied to maintain and control power. Similar political upheavals in the 1990s, including the Gulf War, the collapse of Yugoslavia, and the aftereffects of the Rwandan genocide sparked further expulsion episodes in Saudi Arabia, Kuwait, Croatia, Serbia, and Tanzania. More recently, twenty-two expulsion episodes were initiated between 2000

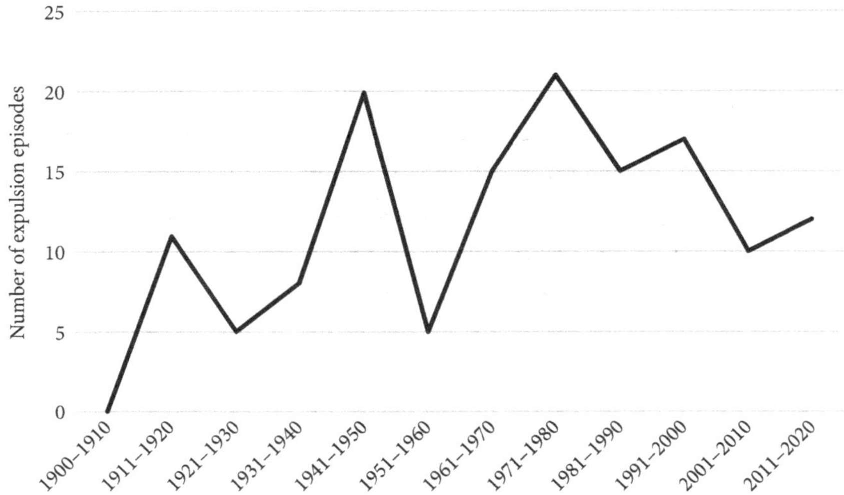

Figure 2.4 Mass expulsion episodes initiated (1900–2020)

and 2020. Far from a historical phenomenon, in 92 of the 120 years catalogued, there was at least one ongoing mass expulsion event somewhere in the world. Over the last fifty years (1970–2020), governments implemented approximately three expulsions every two years, affecting between 300,000 and 400,000 persons.

A frequently asked question related to the "when" of mass expulsion is: Does expulsion typically occur during war? Most genocides and mass killings occur during war and armed conflict; thus, we might expect a similar pattern for a related eliminationist policy.[49] Comparing the GSME dataset and the Correlates of War (COW) dataset, between 1900 and 2020, only one-third of mass expulsions were initiated during wars. Of these forty-four expulsion events, 68 percent were initiated during interstate wars, 25 percent during intrastate or civil wars, and 7 percent during simultaneous

[49] An analysis of existing genocide/politicide datasets shows that 89–93 percent of genocides/politicides have occurred during wars or armed conflicts. [Of the Political Instability Task Force (PITF) dataset's unique genocide/politicide observations (i.e., DESC 2 = 1), 93 percent occurred during a COW-coded interstate or intrastate war and 89 percent during a Uppsala Conflict Data Program/Peace Research Institute Oslo (UCDP/PRIO) interstate, intrastate, or internationalized–intrastate armed conflict. Relatedly, a high number of Targeted Mass Killing (TMK) events during an ongoing genocide/politicide occurred during a COW-coded interstate or intrastate war (66 percent) or during a UCDP/PRIO interstate, intrastate, or internationalized–intrastate armed conflict (70 percent) (Data from Butcher et al., 2024; Center for Systemic Peace, n.d.; Gleditsch et al., 2002; Sarkees, 2021; Sarkees & Wayman, 2010)].

interstate and intrastate wars.[50] These patterns are similar across other datasets such as the Uppsala Conflict Data Program/Peace Research Institute Oslo (UCDP/PRIO) data,[51] which measure interstate and intrastate armed conflicts.[52] Regardless of the war or conflict dataset used, most expulsion events over the past 120 years were initiated during peacetime.[53]

Another question pertaining to when expulsion occurs is: Does mass expulsion coincide with other atrocities, such as genocide and mass killing? Comparing the GSME dataset and the Targeted Mass Killing (TMK) dataset, between 1946 and 2020, 15 expulsion episodes (out of a total of 102 during this period) were initiated during TMK events.[54] Of those fifteen episodes, nine were initiated during ongoing genocides or politicides.[55] This pattern is similar using the Political Instability Task Force (PITF) data, with eight mass expulsion events initiated during PITF-coded genocides or politicides (1955–2018).[56] Thus, there is relatively limited overlap between the onset of mass expulsion and the onset of targeted mass killings (15 percent) or genocides/politicides (9 percent). These findings also hold when examining the relationship between the onset of mass expulsion and the onset of one-sided government violence (OSV). Using the UCDP/OSV dataset,[57] between 1989 and 2018, only six mass expulsions (of the forty-six during this period) were initiated during major OSV events, a similarly low level of overlap.[58]

In total, 40 percent of mass expulsions in the GSME dataset were initiated during periods of significant violence—war, armed conflict, mass killing,

[50] This analysis is based on COW interstate (1900–2007) and intrastate war (1900–2014) data. The start year of the analysis is 1900 because that is the first year of the GSME dataset, it ends in the last year of COW data collection (Sarkees, 2021; Sarkees & Wayman, 2010).

[51] Gleditsch et al., 2002.

[52] Between 1946 and 2020, one-fifth of mass expulsions were initiated during major armed conflicts, as defined by UCDP/PRIO. Of the twenty-one expulsion episodes, 43 percent were initiated during interstate armed conflicts, and 57 percent during intrastate armed conflicts. UCDP/PRIO captures armed conflicts with varying intensity levels: (1) minor (25–999 battle-related deaths) and (2) war (at least 1,000 battle-related deaths). To better compare to the COW data (which uses a minimum threshold of 1,000 battle-related deaths), these figures reflect UCDP/PRIO (Types 2, 3, and 4) with intensity level 2 (i.e., war). Note that the UCDP/PRIO and COW data have different start and end dates. Holding these constant, in the COW (1946–2014) and UCDP/PRIO (1946–2014) data, the percentage of mass expulsions during war/armed conflict (intensity level 2) remain similar across the two datasets: 24 percent for COW and 21 percent for UCDP/PRIO.

[53] Sixty-seven percent using COW data, or 79 percent using UCDP/PRIO data.

[54] Butcher et al., 2024.

[55] Butcher et al., 2024.

[56] Center for Systemic Peace, n.d.

[57] Eck & Hultman, 2007.

[58] Only OSV events with at least 1,000 fatalities are included here in order to better compare to the COW and UCDP/PRIO (intensity level 2) data.

genocide/politicide, or one-sided violence.[59] While wars and armed conflicts are an important aspect of the context in which expulsion may occur, most expulsion events occur during peacetime, a distinct feature of mass expulsion in comparison to other eliminationist policies.

2.2.2 Where Does Expulsion Happen?

Mass expulsion occurs all over the world; no region has been spared (see Figure 2.5). Since 1900, most expulsions have occurred in Europe, with fifty-one cases, or 37 percent of the total sample. Interestingly, 73 percent of European expulsion events occurred in the first half of the twentieth century, with just fifteen cases occurring after 1949. Sub-Saharan African governments have implemented nearly a third of mass expulsions (forty-three episodes, or 31 percent), all concentrated in the latter half of the twentieth and beginning of the twenty-first century, which correlates with the onset of decolonization on the continent. The Middle East and North

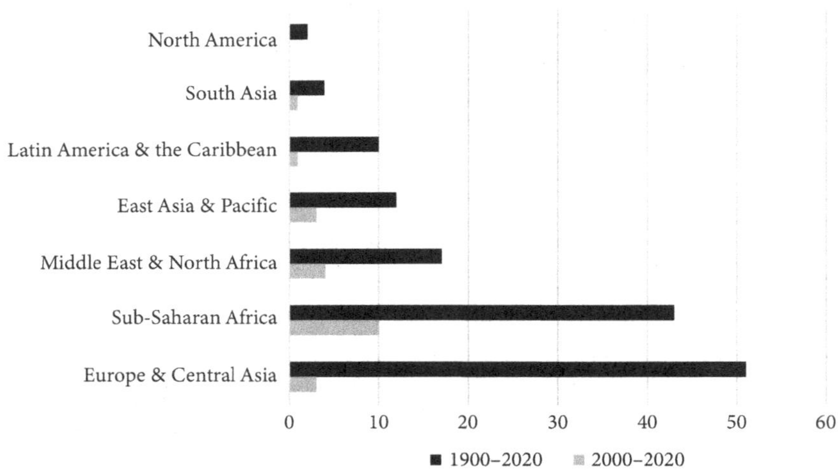

Figure 2.5 Number of mass expulsion episodes, by world region[a]

[a]These regions correspond to the World Bank's classification (World Bank, 2025a).

[59] Forty percent is calculated by aggregating the total number of expulsions that were initiated during COW interstate or intrastate wars, UCDP/PRIO intensity level 2 interstate/intrastate/internationalized–intrastate wars, TMK episodes, PITF genocide/politicide episodes, or OSV events with at least 1,000 fatalities, while excluding all duplicates: 56 out of 139 total expulsion episodes.

Africa (MENA), East Asia and Pacific, and Latin America and the Caribbean regions together comprise another third of worldwide expulsions, with approximately 10 percent each of the total cases (seventeen, twelve, and ten expulsion events, respectively). South Asia and North America were the least likely regions to expel, with 3 percent and 1 percent (or four and two episodes), respectively, of the total caseload.

To see how the regional distribution of expulsion has changed over time, the gray bars in Figure 2.5 show the geographic breakdown of mass expulsion events between 2000 and 2020. While the top-three expulsionist regions remain the same, the order changes. Sub-Saharan Africa is the leading expelling region (ten episodes, 45 percent), followed by MENA (four episodes, 18 percent), and then Europe (three episodes, 14 percent). The other regions remain in similar positions compared to the full period, although East Asia and Pacific's share rises (tied with Europe at 14 percent), while North America drops out of the sample, with zero expulsion events during the last twenty years (2000–2020).

Figure 2.6 shows the regional distribution of the sixty-one countries that account for all the expulsion events examined. There is a relatively high

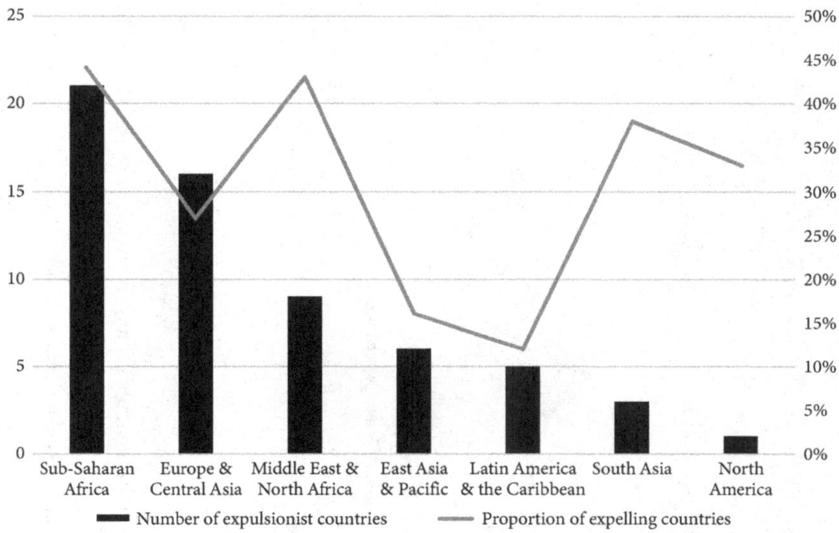

Figure 2.6 Number of unique expulsionist countries and proportion of expelling countries, by world region[a]

[a]World Bank, 2025a.

Map 2.1 Frequency of mass expulsion around the world (1900–2020)[60]

[60] This map was created using MapChart.

proportion of expelling countries in five of the seven regions indicated by the gray line. In four regions—sub-Saharan Africa, MENA, South Asia, and North America—over 30 percent of countries have expelled, closely followed by 27 percent in Europe.[61] Map 2.1 geographically shows the sixty-one expelling countries and the number of times they have implemented an expulsion policy.[62]

Over half of expulsionist countries (56 percent) are repeat offenders, having implemented an expulsion policy more than once: 21 percent have expelled twice, 18 percent three times, 7 percent four times, and 10 percent five times or more. The remaining 44 percent of countries have implemented a policy of mass expulsion only one time.

2.2.3 Who Is Targeted for Expulsion?

Governments that implement mass expulsion target ethnic, racial, religious, or national groups; yet, within these groups, individuals have a range of legal statuses. The GSME dataset captures four categories of persons who may be expelled: nationals, foreign nationals, resident aliens, and refugees. The term *nationals*, used interchangeably with *citizens*, refers to persons legally recognized by a state, either native or naturalized, entitled to full rights and protections. *Foreign nationals* refer to persons temporarily in a country of which they are not citizens. *Resident aliens* are also foreign nationals, but they are lawful permanent residents of the country in which they reside. *Refugees* refer to persons outside their country of origin who are seeking the protection of another state because of fear of persecution in their home country. In a few rare instances, some of the population

[61] Note that not all World Bank regions include the same number of countries (World Bank, 2025a). North America only includes three countries (US, Canada, Bermuda), and South Asia includes eight. The other regions are much larger: Europe and Central Asia (fifty-eight countries), sub-Saharan Africa (forty-eight countries), Latin American and the Caribbean (forty-two countries), East Asia and Pacific (thirty-eight countries), and MENA (twenty-one countries). With the end of colonization, the number of countries in a region has changed dramatically over the period examined. Nevertheless, it is useful to see the absolute and relative numbers of expelling states per region.

[62] Reproduced with permission from SAGE Journals, Garrity, M. (2022). Introducing the government-sponsored mass expulsion dataset. *Journal of Peace Research*, *59*(5), 767–776. https://doi.org/10.1177/00223433211068633.

expelled included stateless persons.[63] In these cases, which involved Palestinians and Rohingya (e.g., Israel, 1967; Kuwait, 1991; Bangladesh, 1992; Burma, 1991, 2012, 2016), stateless members of the group were expelled alongside national, resident alien, or refugee co-ethnics. While the four main categories of persons expelled indicate different legal statuses within a target population, governments often remove multiple categories of people simultaneously.

Over half of the 139 expulsion events targeted nationals, or citizens, of the expelling state (seventy-eight episodes, or 56 percent). Of the 78 episodes, however, only 47 incidents (out of 139) *exclusively* targeted citizens—34 percent of the total caseload (see Figure 2.7). Almost all of the forty-seven cases that only targeted citizens occurred in Europe (89 percent), and 74 percent of those incidents took place in the first half of the twentieth century. The existing literature's heavy focus on European ethnic cleansing offers insight into why noncitizen expulsions have been largely overlooked.

The fact that only twelve cases of citizen-only expulsion occurred after 1950 may at first seem to suggest that the customary international law against expelling citizens has diffused around the world. On the contrary, the evidence indicates that expelling states have simply modified their strategy by removing citizens simultaneously with noncitizens. There are thirty-one documented cases (22 percent) of hybrid—citizen

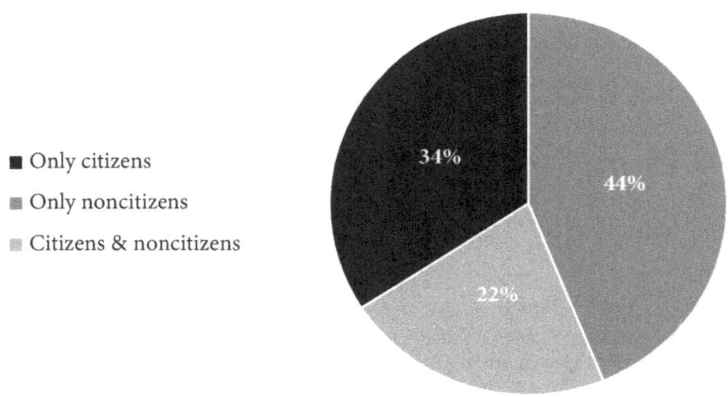

Figure 2.7 Percentage of total expulsion episodes by category of persons expelled

[63] Article 1 of the 1954 Convention Relating to the Status of Stateless Persons defines a stateless person as "a person not considered a national by any State under the operation of its law" (United Nations, 1954).

Table 2.1 Noncitizen-Only Expulsions

Category of Persons Expelled	*Total Cases (percentage)*
Expulsion of only foreign nationals and/or resident aliens	41 (67%)
Expulsion of foreign nationals and/or resident aliens, and refugees	11 (18%)
Expulsion of only refugees	9 (15%)

and noncitizen—expulsions, of which twenty-six cases (84 percent) have occurred after 1950. These hybrid expulsions include the removal of citizens along with a variety of combinations of foreign nationals, resident aliens, and refugees.

Perhaps surprisingly, the plurality of expulsion cases between 1900 and 2020 targeted only noncitizens (44 percent). As illustrated in Table 2.1, most of these noncitizen-only expulsions exclusively targeted foreign nationals and/or resident aliens (67 percent). The remaining 33 percent expelled foreign nationals and/or resident aliens along with refugees (18 percent) or only targeted refugees (15 percent). Refugees are often swept up in the expulsion of other noncitizens, with sixteen different states across four regions—East Asia and Pacific, MENA, South Asia, and sub-Saharan Africa—expelling refugee populations *en masse*. The first documented instance of refugee-only expulsion occurred in 1978 in Bangladesh with the forced repatriation of Rohingya refugees to Burma.

One may intuit that the literature has overlooked noncitizen expulsions because these events generally affect fewer people than expulsions involving only citizens. Indeed, mass expulsion episodes targeting fewer than 5,000 persons are overwhelmingly noncitizen-only expulsions (nineteen of the twenty-three cases). However, expulsion episodes that remove 5,000 or more people are relatively evenly distributed between the expulsion of citizens versus noncitizens (see Figure 2.8).

Episodes that expel between 5,000 and 20,000 persons include five citizen-only and eight noncitizen-only events. Those expelling 20,001–50,000 persons are equally split between citizen-only and noncitizen-only episodes (eleven each). And episodes expelling 50,001–100,000 persons (six citizen-only and seven noncitizen-only), 100,001–250,000 persons (fourteen and ten, respectively), and 250,001–500,000 persons (two and four, respectively) are all closely distributed across citizenship status.

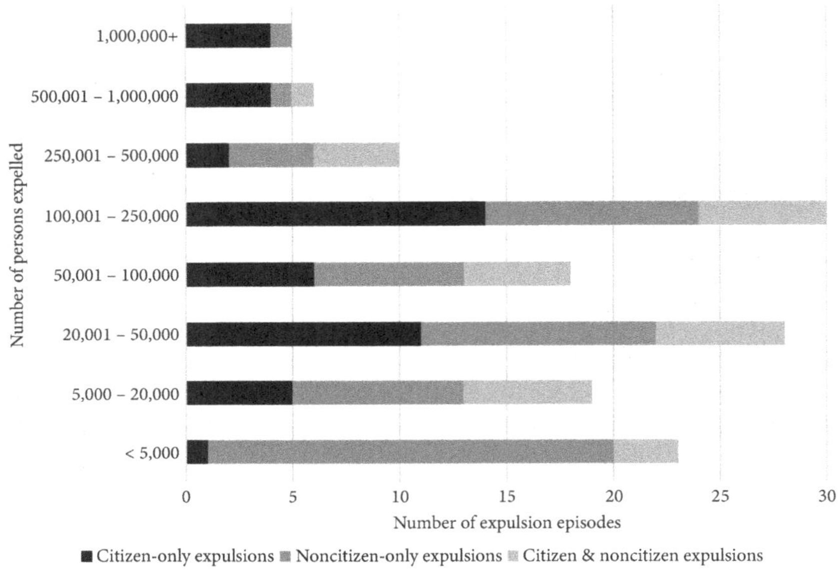

Figure 2.8 Magnitude of expulsion episodes by citizenship status of expellees

Another reason noncitizen expulsions may have been underexamined is because the largest expulsion episodes—those affecting between 500,001 and 1 million persons (or more than 1 million)—tend to be citizen-only expulsions (eight episodes). Nevertheless, there are still incidents of noncitizen-only expulsions targeting more than 500,000 and more than 1 million persons. Similarly, hybrid (citizen and noncitizen) expulsions are evenly distributed across expulsion magnitudes.

2.2.4 What Types of Governments Expel?

Existing explanations of genocide and politicide suggest that autocratic regimes are more likely to engage in eliminationist policies than democratic regimes.[64] Others suggest that rather than autocracies per se, new regimes engaged in the process of democratization, seeking congruence between the nation and the state, are more likely to engage in ethnic cleansing, of which mass expulsion is a component.[65] Using the Polity V data, Figure 2.9 shows

[64] Harff, 2003.
[65] Mann, 2005, p. 4.

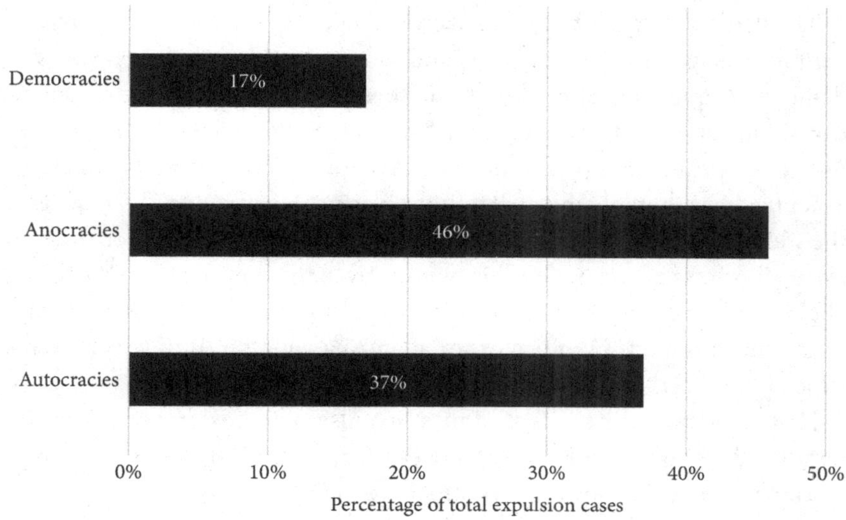

Figure 2.9 Regime type of expelling states (Polity V)

the regime type of the expelling governments across the 139 mass expulsion episodes.[66]

The GSME data support the findings of research on other eliminationist policies that autocracies are indeed more likely to expel than democracies: 37 percent compared to 17 percent of the total cases. The data also substantiate existing theories that checks on executive authority, competitive elections, and respect for minority rights—all features of democratic regimes—are likely to constrain the use of mass expulsion.[67] However, there were still twenty-three instances of democratic regimes that expelled, nearly a fifth of the total sample. Although democracies are less likely to expel than autocracies, they are not immune to this grim practice. Anocracies, defined as mixed regimes with both authoritarian and democratic characteristics, were the regime type most likely to carry out expulsions, accounting for 46 percent of the total caseload. The plurality of expulsionist anocracies fits with existing theories that countries engaged in the process of democratizing are most likely to engage in eliminationist policies.[68]

[66] Marshall, 2021.
[67] Harff, 2003, p. 63; Stanton, 2016, pp. 32–35.
[68] Mann, 2005.

The Polity V data has been criticized by some scholars for its data sources, definitions, aggregation, coverage, and discrimination between degrees of democracy and autocracy.[69] Indeed, three of the four Polity V operational indicators that aggregate into the single Polity score capture features of the executive: competitiveness of executive recruitment, openness of executive recruitment, and constraints on the chief executive.[70] This biases the index to reflect decisional constraints on the executive rather than on broader aspects of democracy.[71] However, given the central role of the ruling elite in deciding and implementing an expulsion policy, the executive bias of the index is a useful indicator for analyzing what kinds of governments expel.

Having defined the concept of mass expulsion and examined the cross-national data on this phenomenon over time, we turn to one of the central research questions: Why do governments expel?

[69] Gleditsch & Ward, 1997; Treier & Jackman, 2008.
[70] Marshall & Gurr, 2020, pp. 14–16.
[71] Gleditsch & Ward, 1997, p. 380.

3

The Logic of Mass Expulsion

Mass expulsion is a distinct concept that has not been comprehensively or systematically examined. As a result, we lack precise explanations about why governments choose this specific policy option. A fertile starting place to begin is the broader literature on the causes of eliminationist policies,[1] more generally, to see whether the factors that drive distinct but related phenomena are relevant to understanding mass expulsion. While no consensus reigns, existing explanations of mass killing, ethnic cleansing, strategic-population displacement, demographic engineering, coercive-engineered migration, and mass immigrant expulsion can be separated into two main categories: (1) war and security/stability rationales and (2) non-war rationales (see Table 3.1). The explanations within these two categories are not mutually exclusive, but each has its exponents.

The dominant narrative in the existing literature is that war and security/stability concerns are the primary drivers of eliminationist policies. These policies are used during war to remove rival groups from strategic territory, or in the immediate aftermath of war to remove "disloyal" groups or those identified as new security threats.[2] This line of argumentation suggests that elimination is motivated by territorial defense/control, particularly when governments have revisionist objectives driven by previous territorial losses.[3] Many wars in the early twentieth century followed the collapse of empires and the rise of ethnonationalism among imperial subjects. Therefore, a large subset of the literature focuses on the creation of modern nation-states and the concomitant desire for ethnic homogeneity as a critical driver of elimination.[4] Some suggest this is the "dark side of democracy" and that democratizing governments are more likely to

[1] Garrity & Mylonas, 2025.

[2] Bulutgil, 2016, p. 3, 2018, p. 1137; Lichtenheld, 2020, p. 3; Mann, 2005, p. 2; McGarry, 1998, p. 615; Mylonas, 2012, p. 41.

[3] Müller-Crepon et al., 2024; Mylonas, 2012, pp. 36–37, 41–43; Valentino, 2004, p. 155.

[4] Lieberman, 2006, p. xi; Marx, 2002, pp. 103–104, 125–126; McGarry, 1998, p. 615; Naimark, 2001, p. 8; Ther, 2014, pp. 1, 5; Zolberg, 1983, p. 30.

Mass Expulsion. Meghan M. Garrity, Oxford University Press. © Oxford University Press (2026).
DOI: 10.1093/9780197829097.003.0003

Table 3.1 Predictions of Existing Explanations

Explanations		*Predictions*
War & Security/Stability Rationales	Territorial defense and control	Governments expel during war to secure strategic territory or, in the immediate aftermath of war, to remove newly identified security threats.
	Democratization and the creation of nation-states	Following the collapse of empires, modern nation-states were founded upon the principle of ethnic homogeneity, leading to the expulsion of ethnic minorities.
	Exclusionary or nationalist ideologies	In the face of political upheaval, elites that espouse exclusionary or nationalist ideologies are more likely to eliminate certain categories of people.
	Foreign policy objectives	Weaker governments use migration, or the threat of migration, to force concessions from stronger powers.
Non-War Rationales	Immigrant scapegoating	During times of economic crisis or deterioration, leaders expel economically dominant immigrant groups.

implement eliminationist policies than stable authoritarian regimes.[5] Closely connected to these explanations is the argument that elites with exclusionary ideologies, that create a hierarchy of peoples within their territories, are more likely to eliminate groups outside of the core political community when threatened.[6] Others argue that eliminationist policies are used as foreign policy instruments. Weaker governments make rational cost-benefit calculations and use the forced removal of populations, or the threat of forced removal, to extract concessions from stronger powers.[7] This puts pressure on neighboring states to achieve a specific foreign policy objective.[8]

The second category of explanations, less prominent in the literature, focus on non-war and non-security rationales. These arguments suggest expulsion is the result of immigrant scapegoating.[9] When an economy is in crisis, or faces a period of decline, governments blame "aliens" and take

[5] Bell-Fialkoff, 1999, pp. 48–49; Mann, 2005, pp. 4, 69.
[6] Harff, 2003, pp. 62–63; Straus, 2015, p. 55–58; Valentino, 2004, p. 155.
[7] Greenhill, 2010, pp. 13–14.
[8] Weiner, 1992, p. 100.
[9] Adepoju, 1984; Adida, 2014; Honig, 2016.

action to remove noncitizens.[10] According to these explanations, those most likely to be targeted for expulsion are immigrant groups that control key sectors of the economy where "native" populations are also active.[11] These arguments suggest governments with ethnic minority elites are more likely to pursue immigrant scapegoating, particularly during economic crises.[12]

While the existing literature on eliminationist policies offers a useful starting point, there are important gaps in our understanding of mass expulsion that remain to be filled. Much of the literature on ethnic cleansing (conceptually distinct, yet related to mass expulsion)[13] focuses specifically on Europe, and thus it remains unknown whether the territorial control arguments travel to other regions. Further, some research on eliminationist policies examines only conflictual contexts or events with extremely high levels of violence (i.e., over 50,000 persons killed). This excludes events that do not occur during war or armed conflict as well as smaller episodes. The analysis here examines these explanations on a wider universe of cases, including all regions, conflictual and nonconflictual contexts, and any episode affecting more than 1,000 persons. Because most existing studies of ethnic cleansing, mass killing, and genocide focus on citizens as the target population, another gap in the literature is how noncitizens are affected by expulsion. As demonstrated in the data analysis in Chapter 2, governments target both citizens *and* noncitizens with expulsion policies. The smaller subset of existing research that argues non-war-related factors drive expulsion does capture the targeting of immigrants, but it excludes the expulsion of citizens and is largely based on research geographically confined to sub-Saharan Africa. This creates another gap regarding the extent to which non-war-related explanations travel to other regions and apply to citizens. To advance a comprehensive theory of mass expulsion, the key dependent variable should be mass expulsion, not mass expulsion conditional on targeting only citizens or only noncitizens. The examination here includes the expulsion of all categories of persons: nationals, foreign nationals, resident aliens, and refugees.

Building on this existing literature, the following two chapters aim to fill these gaps in our understanding of the particular eliminationist policy of mass expulsion. The next section introduces a typology of mass expulsion,

[10] Adepoju, 1984, p. 433.
[11] Honig, 2016, pp. 519–521.
[12] Adida, 2014, pp. 134–136, 144–145.
[13] See Chapter 1, p. 5 and Chapter 2, pp. 20–21.

organizing the phenomenon into two general categories—security and economic—and presents four distinct types of expulsion to address the question: Why do governments expel?

3.1 Typology of Mass Expulsion

Through a detailed examination of mass expulsion events in the twentieth and twenty-first centuries (1900–2020), I have identified four specific types of mass expulsion that under certain conditions incentivize leaders to initiate this policy. These four types can be organized into two general categories: security and economic expulsions. Governments implement mass expulsion to remove target groups they identify as security or economic threats to the state. Security threats concern both territorial and political control. These include challenges to a state's sovereignty or claim to authority, relations between a target group and hostile external powers, interstate disputes, secessionist movements, and militant members of refugee populations known as "refugee warriors." Economic threats, by contrast, concern a target group's control over, or domination of, certain state resources, industries, sectors, or employment opportunities.

The type of threat or risk posed by the target group may be real or perceived. Genuine threats that governments identify may be based on specific actions or plans by members of the target population. Perceived threats are those based on false information or are intentionally manufactured by governing elites. In the latter case, authorities may use propaganda to win internal support for their expulsionist objectives and attempt to persuade domestic public opinion. Regardless, expulsionist governments view the target group's threat as serious enough to merit the use of this eliminationist policy.

The security category is comprised of three types of expulsion: counter-irredentist, counter-subversive, and reprisal. Counter-irredentist expulsions remove a target group with real or alleged ties to an external state in order to resist that state's irredentist claims. This expulsion type aligns with existing arguments that claim expulsion is driven by the desire for territorial control.[14] Expelling the target group eliminates a security threat to the territorial integrity of the state and secures its land for the dominant

[14] Bulutgil, 2016; Lichtenheld, 2020; Mann, 2005; McGarry, 1998; Müller-Crepon et al., 2024; Mylonas, 2012; Valentino, 2004.

group. However, expulsion is not only about territory. Counter-subversive expulsions do not aim to secure territory but instead are driven by the desire for internal political control and stability. These expulsions target groups that support, or are perceived to support, efforts to subvert the existing government or regime. Reprisal expulsions, the third type in the security category, aim to retaliate against an external state. In these cases, governments use expulsion to seek revenge against another government for an unfavorable foreign policy decision, or position, by targeting its co-ethnics.

In line with the existing literature on other eliminationist policies, security/stability rationales are critical drivers of mass expulsion. Nearly two-thirds of the cases in the Government-Sponsored Mass Expulsion (GSME) dataset are motivated by removing groups believed to pose a security threat to the state, albeit in three different forms: counter-irredentism (34 percent), counter-subversion (17 percent), and reprisal (14 percent). Identifying distinct types of expulsion is critical to understanding how this policy option fits within the broader repertoire of eliminationist policies. While much of the existing literature on ethnic cleansing points to territorial concerns as the primary driver of population removal, in only one-third of mass expulsion cases is territory paramount (e.g., counter-irredentist expulsions). Threats, or perceived threats, to political control—in addition to territorial control—is another important aspect of expulsion (e.g., counter-subversive expulsions).

Notably, the occurrence of war and armed conflict is less salient for mass expulsion than other eliminationist policies like mass killing and genocide. Less than a third of expulsions are initiated during war or armed conflict, in comparison to nearly all genocides/politicides and the majority of mass killing events.[15] Thus security concerns, absent active conflict, are critically relevant. The third type of expulsion within the security category, reprisal, highlights a distinction between mass expulsion and the existing literature on "coercive-engineered migration."[16] Unlike coercive-engineered migration, in which weaker states use migration and refugee crises as instruments of persuasion to extract concessions from stronger rivals, reprisal expulsions are typically employed by stronger states against weaker ones, and are less about coercion than retaliation or revenge.

While security concerns are essential in understanding mass expulsion, economic concerns have been largely overlooked, despite motivating a

[15] This is based on Correlates of War and Uppsala Conflict Data Program/Peace Research Institute Oslo data (see Chapter 2, pp. 36–38).
[16] Greenhill, 2010.

significant number of expulsion events in the twentieth and twenty-first centuries. Within the economic category, the fourth type of expulsion is nativism. Nativist expulsions aim to protect the economic interests of indigenous inhabitants of the state by removing groups deemed to be "aliens" or "foreigners." In these expulsions, the dominant core group resents its economic relations with a non-core group,[17] believing that they are usurping their economic rights as natives. While the existing literature has identified economic dimensions of mass expulsion, it has been geographically confined to sub-Saharan Africa and has exclusively focused on the expulsion of immigrants. The nativist expulsion type explained here identifies a much wider phenomenon across regions and across citizenship status, including citizens and noncitizens. It also moves beyond immigrant scapegoating to illuminate other aspects of the nativist motivation, including expulsion in response to a perceived unjust economic hierarchy, foreign competition, and economic/social burdens on the state.

The identification of economic concerns for a significant subset of mass expulsions is a key contribution to our understanding of the dynamics of ethnic violence. Existing arguments emphasizing the importance of resentment in driving ethnic conflict have downplayed the role of economic resentment.[18] While recognizing that economic subordination is present, these arguments suggest political resentment is the more critical driver of violence. However, in the case of mass expulsion, economic resentment is a significant aspect of the phenomenon. More than a third of all mass expulsions from the beginning of the twentieth century were motivated by nativism (35 percent), the largest of the four expulsion types. In these cases, the targeted group does not politically challenge the governing elites, nor do the expulsions exclusively target groups perceived to be higher on the "ethnic hierarchy," as some resentment-based arguments would suggest.[19] Groups below and parallel to the dominant group, in terms of status relations, are also targeted in nativist expulsions.

These expulsions follow a similar logic to Myron Weiner's "sons of the soil" concept, most notably deployed in regard to internal migration[20] and ethnic civil war.[21] However, nativist expulsions extend beyond concerns about

[17] The terms "core group" and "non-core group" are drawn from Mylonas (2012, pp. 23–29).
[18] Horowitz, 1985, pp. 108–124; Petersen, 2002, p. 51.
[19] Petersen, 2002, p. 52.
[20] Weiner, 1978.
[21] Fearon & Latin, 2011.

internal migration to concerns about cross-border or international migration, including the expulsion of citizens who are perceived to be "foreigners" by indigenous groups. Further, nativist expulsions rarely occur during civil war, and the group claiming to be indigenous is the dominant ethnic majority rather than an ethnic minority. In nativist expulsion episodes, the state uniformly supports the dominant majority and expels the targeted non-core group.

Given that existing explanations typically examine different population groups (i.e., war and security arguments examine citizens and non-war explanations examine noncitizens), one may assume that the two overarching categories of mass expulsion—security and economic—are simply an aggregation of these existing explanations. This is not the case. It is true that most economically driven nativist expulsions remove only noncitizens. However, citizens and noncitizens were simultaneously expelled in 24 percent of nativist expulsion episodes. This occurs because governments implementing expulsionist policies seek to remove target groups on the basis of ascriptive characteristics, irrespective of individual documentation status. Thus, the finding that many expulsions are motivated by economic concerns is not exclusively a feature of including noncitizens in the analysis. The GSME data also show that noncitizen-only expulsions occur across all three types of expulsion within the security category (i.e., counter-irredentist, counter-subversive, and reprisal expulsions), challenging the notion that expulsions motivated by security threats are only concerned with citizens. The existing literature's exclusive focus on the elimination of citizens misses these important cases.

In sum, mass expulsion is a distinct eliminationist policy that governments use to remove groups deemed to be security or economic threats, motivated by nativism, counter-irredentism, counter-subversion, or reprisal (see Table 3.2). We now turn to detailed explanations of the four types of mass expulsion.

3.1.1 Nativist Expulsions

Most mass expulsion episodes in the twentieth and twenty-first centuries were motivated by nativism, affecting between 6 and 10.5 million people. These expulsions aim to protect the economic interests of "native-born" or "indigenous" inhabitants of the state by removing groups deemed to be

Table 3.2 Typology of Mass Expulsion

Type	*Motive*	*Description*	*Select Examples: Expelling State (target group, year(s))*
		Economic Mass Expulsions	
Nativist	Indigenous resource control	Expulsion to protect the economic interests of "native-born" or "indigenous" inhabitants of the state by removing a group deemed "alien" or "foreign"	United States (Mexicans/Mexican-Americans, 1929–1939) Uganda (South Asians, 1972) Nigeria (Ghanaians, 1983) France (Roma, 2009–2011)
		Security Mass Expulsions	
Counter-irredentist	Territorial control	Expulsion to counter an external state's irredentist claims by removing a group with real or alleged ties to that state	Turkey (Greek Orthodox Christians, 1923–1926) Czechoslovakia (Germans, 1945–1947) Israel (Palestinians, 1947–1949) Ethiopia (Eritreans, 1998–1999)
Counter-subversive	Internal political control	Expulsion to counter internal efforts to subvert the existing state or regime by removing a group supporting, or perceived to be supporting, those efforts	Dominican Republic (Haitians/Dominico-Haitians, 1937–1938) Burma (Rohingya, 1991–1992) Kuwait (Palestinians/Iraqis, 1991) Tanzania (Rwandans, 1996)
Reprisal	Retaliation	Expulsion to retaliate against an external state for an unfavorable foreign policy decision or position by removing a group tied to that state	Bulgaria (Turks, 1950–1951) Mauritania and Senegal (Senegalese and Mauritanians (respectively), 1989) Gabon (Beninese, 1978) Pakistan (Afghans, 2016)

"aliens" or "foreigners."[22] In nativist expulsions, the target group is perceived to be stifling the economic aspirations of the indigenous population. These expulsions are driven by a resentment of the economic relations between a core group and a non-core (target) group.[23] Typically, in these episodes there is an ethnic or national division of labor,[24] with specific groups

[22] These terms are in quotation marks because the determination of native or indigenous peoples is often made regardless of the temporal arrival in the territory of either the target group or the dominant core group.

[23] This extends the resentment arguments of Petersen (2002) into the economic realm.

[24] Weiner, 1978, pp. 4–5.

dominating commerce, bureaucratic or professional positions (i.e., clerks, doctors, teachers), or sectors of employment desired by the local population. The resentment driving nativist expulsions may be in response to an unjust hierarchy, foreign competition, economic/social burdens on the state, or simply scapegoating. In certain cases, multiple forms of resentment align.

Some nativist expulsions aim to overturn an unjust hierarchy in which the "native" or "indigenous" group, however defined, is in a subordinate position vis-à-vis the target group. The unequal hierarchical relations between the groups may be shopkeeper–customer, lender–lessee, or master–servant. In these cases, the group with the higher economic status is targeted for expulsion. Many of these expulsions occurred in the wake of colonization when economic freedom did not subsequently follow political freedom. Targets of these expulsions included European colonizers, as in the case of Indonesia's expulsion of over 50,000 Dutch nationals in 1957[25] and Libya's expulsion of 20,000 Italians in 1970.[26] More commonly, however, nativist expulsions targeted colonial-era minorities that held key economic positions desired by the local population, such as South Asians in Burma (1962) and Uganda (1972) as well as Beninese in the Republic of Congo (1962) and Côte d'Ivoire (1964).

These colonial-era minorities were brought by Europeans to work in their colonies or migrated within European empires seeking economic opportunities. As part of the colonial divide-and-rule strategy, Europeans preferred "allegedly industrious" outsiders to native inhabitants to keep the majority population economically, and in turn politically, subservient. These "alien" groups, or "strangers" as they were often called, served as intermediaries between the colonizer and the colonized, working as traders or low-level civil servants.[27] In the aftermath of colonial rule, groups that occupied privileged positions, and were perceived to be loyal to the colonial power, were often expelled. In some cases, these expulsions were part of an "economic war," as Ugandan President Idi Amin described the 1972 expulsion of South Asians[28] and as Indonesia declared on the Dutch in 1957.[29] Removing these groups aimed to engender economic decolonization.

In nativist expulsions, the indigenous population may not always be subordinate to the target group but instead may be active in the same sectors.

[25] Henckaerts, 1995; Keesing's Record of World Events, 1957; Palmier, 1961, pp. 24–25.
[26] Legum, 1971, pp. A73–74; Pondi, 1988, p. 141; Winfield, 2009.
[27] Blalock, 1967; Bonacich, 1973.
[28] Amor, 2003, p. 64; Avirgan & Honey, 1982, p. 5; Jamal, 1976, p. 615; Mazrui, 1979, p. 261; Melady & Melady, 1976, p. 44.
[29] Palmier, 1961, p. 25.

In these cases, the expulsion aims to eliminate groups deemed to be foreign competitors to improve conditions for the local population.[30] Throughout the 1930s as part of Cuba's economic nationalization strategy, the government expelled Haitians (1933–1934, 1937–1939) to rid the country of foreigners accused of undercutting the wages of the Cuban working class.[31] Similarly, in 1971–1972 and 1979, Zambia expelled African migrants working in its mines as part of its "Zambianisation" effort to "prepare the ground for all semi- or unskilled jobs to be held by Zambians only."[32]

In addition to foreign competition, the resentment behind nativist expulsions may arise from the perception that a target group is an economic or social burden on the local economy. In 1978, after the Burmese government expelled the Rohingya to Bangladesh (a counter-subversive expulsion), Bangladeshi authorities complained about the economic and social burden that Rohingya refugees placed on the host community.[33] Later the same year, the Bangladeshi government promptly expelled the Rohingya back to Burma.[34] Even the anticipation that a target group might become a burden on the social assistance system may prompt nativist expulsions, as was the case in France's expulsion of over 20,000 ethnic Roma beginning in 2009.[35]

Governments implementing nativist expulsions may falsely accuse a target group of various economic offenses, including undercutting domestic wages (e.g., Mexicans and Mexican–Americans in the United States, 1954), appropriating national wealth (e.g., Chinese in Mexico, 1931; Salvadorans in Honduras, 1969), or taking employment opportunities from natives (e.g., Malians in the Republic of Congo, 1977; Congolese in Angola, 2003). In some of these cases, the target population is scapegoated and branded as exclusively responsible for the fiscal woes of the state in times of economic crisis or decline. During the Great Depression, the US expelled over 500,000 Mexicans, many with American citizenship, accusing the expellees of "taking away jobs from deserving Americans" during a period of extreme economic hardship.[36] Similarly, in Nigeria during the 1980s oil crisis and resulting economic recession, the government expelled over 2 million African migrants,

[30] Honig, 2016, pp. 519–521; Weiner, 1978, p. 7.
[31] Casey, 2017, pp. 235–237; MacLeod, 1998.
[32] Addo, 1982; Henckaerts, 1995; Legum, 1972, p. B264.
[33] Human Rights Watch, 2000; Loescher, 2001, p. 225.
[34] Human Rights Watch, 2000; Piper, 1994; Van Hear, 1998, pp. 93–102.
[35] Human Rights Watch, 2011a, 2011b; Suddath, 2010.
[36] Florido, 2015; Goodman, 2020, pp. 39–46; Lee, 2019, pp. 147–181.

mostly Ghanaians, in the largest twentieth-century expulsion episode on the African continent.[37] Groups are often branded as "illegal aliens" or "illegal immigrants" regardless of their documentation status. Governing elites may promise that nativist expulsions will solve structural domestic economic problems, yet because the root causes are not successfully addressed, the same group is often repeatedly expelled (e.g., Haitian laborers in the Dominican Republic, 1991, 1996, 1999, 2015; Congolese diamond miners in Angola, 2003, 2008, 2011, 2018).

Over one-third (35 percent) of the expulsion cases in the GSME dataset are nativist expulsions (see Table 3.3). It is the only expulsion type that includes episodes in all seven world regions, the most in sub-Saharan Africa (57 percent), followed by Latin America and the Caribbean (16 percent), and the Middle East and North Africa (MENA; 8 percent). Nativist expulsions occur throughout the entire period examined, with the first instance in 1929 (e.g., United States' expulsion of Mexicans) and the most recent in 2018 (e.g., Angola's expulsion of Congolese diamond miners). This type of expulsion is likely to persist, especially during periods of economic decline, when political leaders seek to deflect blame for the country's poor economic performance onto disliked "foreign" groups.

Conditions Under Which Nativist Motivations Emerge

- Resentment of status relations between a dominant core group and a non-core target group in reaction to an unjust hierarchy, foreign competition in key sectors, economic/social burden on the state, or as a scapegoat for economic ills
- Society with an ethnic/national division of labor
- Economic crisis or downturn that intensifies resentment

3.1.2 Counter-Irredentist Expulsions

The most violent mass expulsions, and the type that has affected the largest number of people during the twentieth and early twenty-first centuries, are counter-irredentist expulsions. These expulsions are about territorial

[37] Henckaerts, 1995; Nigerian External Publicity Division, 1983; VanHear, 1998, pp. 72–79.

Table 3.3 Nativist Expulsions[a]

Case Example	*Target Group*	*Number of Persons Expelled*	*Brief Description*
United States (1929–1939)	Mexicans (including Mexican-Americans)	500,000–2,000,000	In response to the Great Depression, government officials launched "repatriation" campaigns targeting Mexicans. Violent raids in workplaces and public places were used to expel Mexicans throughout the US. Efforts did not distinguish between longtime residents, undocumented immigrants, and American citizens of Mexican descent.[b]
Uganda (1972)	South Asians	50,000–80,000	President Idi Amin announced the expulsion of "any person who is of Asian origin, extraction or descent," giving them ninety days to leave the country. In a public address, he stated, "It became obvious to my Government that political independence without economic control of the resources of our Country was of very little use."[c]
Nigeria (1983)	Ghanaians, Nigeriens, Cameroonians, Chadians, Togolese, Beninese	1,500,000–2,000,000	Nigeria's 1980s oil glut led to a severe economic recession, including extremely high unemployment in the lead up to national elections. In response to rising anti-migrant sentiment, the Nigerian government announced all "illegal aliens" must leave the country within two weeks.[d]
France (2009–2011)	Roma	23,000–29,000	French authorities systematically expelled Eastern European Roma on the assumption that they might become a burden on the social assistance system. Despite their EU citizenship allowing freedom of movement throughout the EU, the expellees' cases were not individually evaluated, and the government removal operations used intimidation and force.[e]

[a]The cases listed in Table 3.3, and the rest of the tables in this chapter, are illustrative, not exhaustive examples of each expulsion type. The number of persons expelled includes low- and high-end rounded estimates.
[b]Florido, 2015; Lee, 2019, pp. 147–181; Goodman, 2020, pp. 39–46.
[c]Confidential Memorandum from The Representative, UNHCR Branch Office for Uganda—photostat copies of Decree No. 17 and Statutory Instrument No. 124/72, 14 September 1972; 11/2/64-641.UGA[a] Expulsion and Deportation—Uganda [1972] Volume 1; Series 2, Box 1281; Fonds 11; UNHCR; Pamphlet on "Uganda's Economic War" from the High Commission for the Republic of Uganda in New Delhi, 17 November 1972; 11/2/64-641.UGA[c] Expulsion and Deportation—Uganda [1972–1984] Volume 3; Series 2, Box 1281; Fonds 11; UNHCR.
[d]Nigerian External Publicity Division, 1983; VanHear, 1998.
[e]Suddath, 2010; Human Rights Watch, 2011a, 2011b.

control. Expelling governments target groups that are perceived to pose an existential threat to the territorial integrity of the state. This is often based on the group's real or alleged ties to an external "kin state." The goal is to eliminate irredentism—a desire by one state to annex the territory of another state—and to counter any future irredentist claims, either by the target group itself or by the neighboring state. These expulsions occur simultaneously with the collapse of empires, changes in borders, or shifts in territorial control because of annexation, occupation, cession, liberation, or negotiated peace. They typically occur during or after interstate wars as countries vie for territorial control and adjudicate postwar peace arrangements.

During interstate wars, governments may expel co-ethnics of a neighboring state to solidify control of the territory for "their people." These expulsions often occur in border regions or in territory on the periphery of a state that is annexed or occupied. During the First Balkan War in the early twentieth century, Greece expelled Muslims to the Ottoman Empire to solidify its control of "Greek Macedonia," which was ceded to Greece after the war.[38] Similarly, during the Second Balkan War, Bulgaria expelled Muslims to the Ottoman Empire, and the Ottomans expelled Bulgarians out of Turkish Thrace. These expulsions aimed to solidify control of a 9.3 mile (15 kilometer) area on either side of the new Bulgarian–Ottoman border.[39] Counter-irredentist expulsions are not only confined to Europe. Following the United Nations General Assembly resolution to partition Palestine in 1947, civil war broke out in "Mandatory Palestine," followed by the First Arab–Israeli War between the newly proclaimed State of Israel and Arab armies. By the time the truce was signed in 1949, up to 800,000 Palestinian Arabs had been expelled.[40]

Counter-irredentist expulsions also occur in the aftermath of interstate wars when expulsion is used to "sort" populations along newly established territorial lines to eliminate future irredentist claims. This was the case at the Lausanne Peace Conference in 1923, in which a treaty authorized a "population exchange" between Greece and Turkey facilitating the removal of Muslims and Greek Orthodox Christians from each country, respectively.[41] Postwar expulsions may also be designed to eliminate

[38] Pallis, 1925, p. 317.

[39] Ladas, 1932, p. 19; Mourelos, 1985, pp. 390–391.

[40] de Zayas, 1988, pp. 29–30; Morris, 1999, p. 260; Ther, 2014, pp. 191–198.

[41] League of Nations Archives (LNA), S356, 21/Dossier 5: Convention Concerning the Exchange of Greek and Turkish Populations [Translation reprinted from the British Treaty Series—No.16/(1923).], 30 January 1923; UN Archives at Geneva.

populations perceived to be responsible for, associated with, or supportive of the territorial annexation or occupation that has subsequently been reversed. For example, in 1945 at the Potsdam Conference, the Allied Powers agreed to the mass expulsion of the *Volksdeutsche*—ethnic Germans who lived in Germany's neighboring countries but did not hold German citizenship. Poland, Czechoslovakia, and Hungary expelled their ethnic German populations in retaliation for their support, or alleged support, of the Nazi's annexation and occupation of their territory during World War II.[42]

Governments may use counter-irredentist expulsions to achieve defensive or offensive objectives. Defensive counter-irredentist expulsions occur in response to an external state's invasion or occupation, or the threat of such. In the process of defeating the aggressor, a state may expel co-ethnics of the invading state to deter future irredentist claims (e.g., Turkey's expulsion of Greek Orthodox Christians after Greece's invasion in 1919). Similarly, at the conclusion of an interstate war when territory is liberated from an occupying power, or annexed territory is reclaimed, expulsion may occur to remove co-ethnics of the occupier to deter future land grabs (e.g., Czechoslovakia, Poland, and Hungary's expulsions of ethnic Germans after World War II). Offensive counter-irredentist expulsions, by contrast, seek to overturn existing, or proposed, territorial arrangements to restore the "natural" or "rightful" territorial claims of the expelling state, sometimes despite decades or centuries of status quo borders. In these cases, the expelling state has its own irredentist objectives. In the process of capturing new territory, the perpetrating state expels the target group to preempt, or counter, their irredentist claims or the claims of the state whose territory is being annexed (e.g., Greece's annexation of Ottoman lands and subsequent expulsion of Muslims in 1912; Israel's takeover of land that the UN partition plan had allocated to an Arab state and expulsion of Palestinians in 1947–1949).

The modalities of counter-irredentist expulsions include unilateral force, bilateral "population exchange" agreements, or multilateral "population transfers/exchanges." A slight majority of these expulsions occur unilaterally (51 percent), with the other half occurring through negotiated agreements directly between states (34 percent) or between two (or more) states mediated by a third party or parties (15 percent). The presence of an agreement does not eliminate the use of force or violence in implementation, but it adds

[42] de Zayas, 1977, p. 4; Douglas, 2012; Gilbert, 2009, p. 236; Kulischer, 1948, pp. 284–286; Ther & Siljak, 2001, pp. xii, 87.

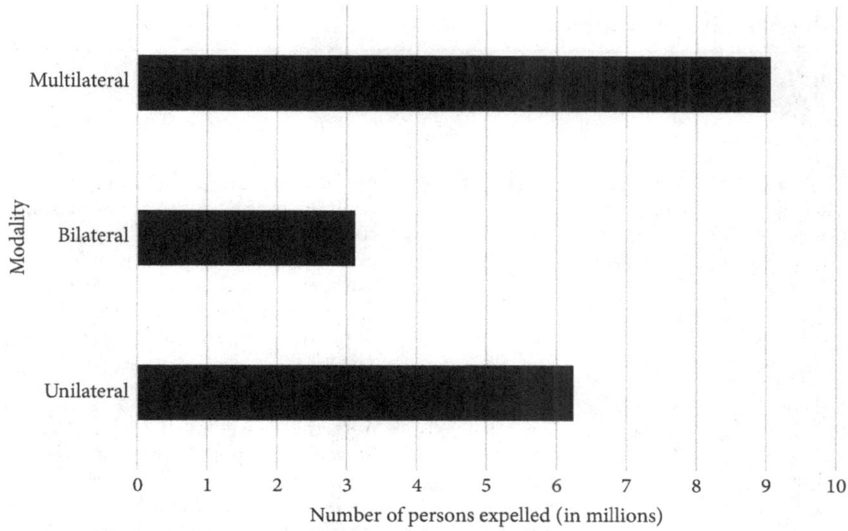

Figure 3.1 Magnitude of different modalities of counter-irredentist expulsion

a cloak of perceived legitimacy to the expelling regime. While multilateral agreements were the smallest of the three modalities of counter-irredentist expulsion (seven of forty-seven episodes), they affected the largest number of people, with over 9 million expelled via multiparty negotiated agreements (see Figure 3.1). This was followed by the modality of unilateral force, expelling over 6 million people, and bilateral agreements affecting just over 3 million.

At the beginning of the twentieth century, particularly after World War I, negotiated treaties to "unmix" populations were widely viewed as the best solution for maintaining international peace and security.[43] However by mid-century, "population transfers" and "population exchanges" fell out of favor and the use of these agreements had drastically declined, although they still have their proponents.

During 1900–2020, there were forty-seven episodes of counter-irredentist mass expulsion—just over one-third of all expulsion events (34 percent)—affecting between 18 and 25 million people (see Table 3.4). Of the forty-seven instances, 89 percent occurred in Europe, with the remainder in MENA (e.g., Israel, 1947, 1967), sub-Saharan Africa (e.g., Ethiopia, 1998;

[43] Frank, 2017, pp. 28–29.

Table 3.4 Counter-Irredentist Expulsions

Case Example	*Target Group*	*Number of Persons Expelled*	*Brief Description*
Greece and Turkey (1923–1926)	Muslims and Greek Orthodox Christians (respectively)	550,000[a]	Negotiated at the postwar peace conference, the Lausanne Convention codified the compulsory "population exchange" between Greece and Turkey. Greek Orthodox Christians in the Ottoman Empire/Turkish Republic were expelled to Greece and Muslims in Greece to Turkey.[b]
Czechoslovakia (1945–1947)	Germans (aka the *Volksdeutsche*)	2,250,000–3,000,000	Article XIII of the Potsdam Agreement, negotiated by the Allied Powers at the post-WWII Potsdam Conference, authorized the "removal of Germans from Poland, Czechoslovakia, and Hungary" and their "transfer" to Germany.[c]
Israel (1947–1949)	Palestinians	600,000–800,000	Following the 1947 UN partition plan for Palestine, civil war broke out in "Mandatory Palestine," followed by the First Arab–Israeli War between the newly proclaimed State of Israel and Arab armies. By the time the truce was signed in 1949, up to 800,000 Palestinian Arabs had been expelled.[d]
Ethiopia (1998–1999)	Eritreans	54,000–75,000	Shortly after Eritrea obtained its independence from Ethiopia, war broke out between the two countries over three disputed border areas. The Ethiopian government expelled thousands of civilians of Eritrean heritage[e] that they accused of supporting the Eritrean war effort, some of whom were Ethiopian citizens.[f]

[a]This number only represents the Muslims and Greek Orthodox Christians that were physically "exchanged" between 1923 and 1926 after the signing of the Lausanne Convention. It does not include the over 1 million Muslims and Greeks who were previously expelled and denied the right to return (more details in Chapter 6).

[b]LNA, S356, 21/Dossier 5: Convention Concerning the Exchange of Greek and Turkish Populations [Translation reprinted from the British Treaty Series—No.16/(1923).], 30 January 1923; UN Archives at Geneva.

[c]de Zayas, 1977, p. 4; Douglas, 2012; Gilbert, 2009, p. 236; Kulischer, 1948, pp. 284–286; Ther and Siljak, 2001, pp. xii, 87.

[d]de Zayas, 1988, pp. 29–30; Morris, 1999, p. 260; Ther, 2014, pp. 191–198.

[e]Simultaneously, the Eritrean authorities expelled 49,000–70,000 Ethiopians.

[f]Abbink, 1998; Amnesty International, 1999; Human Rights Watch, 2003.

Eritrea, 1998), and East Asia (e.g., Vietnam, 1977). One reason for the small number of counter-irredentist expulsions in non-European regions, particularly in sub-Saharan Africa, is the stability of borders in the postcolonial period, stemming from the international legal principle of *uti possidetis*. Most counter-irredentist expulsions occurred in the first half of the twentieth century (79 percent), but this form of mass expulsion may reappear with the creation of new states or changes to existing borders (e.g., Kosovo). A recent instantiation of counter-irredentist mass expulsion occurred in 2020, and again in 2023, with Azerbaijan expelling Armenians after its military forces regained control of the disputed Nagorno-Karabakh enclave.[44]

Conditions Under Which Counter-Irredentist Motivations Emerge

- During interstate wars over territorial control, typically in border regions
- After interstate wars as part of bilateral or multilateral peace negotiations, typically in border regions
- After the liberation of territory from an occupying power, or the cession of territory, as part of an interstate agreement

3.1.3 Counter-Subversive Expulsions

Counter-subversive expulsions are motivated by real or perceived threats to internal political control and stability. They aim to eliminate different forms of subversion through the removal of groups supporting, or perceived to be supporting, such efforts. This includes groups supporting opposition parties or rebels, "refugee warrior" groups,[45] groups supporting a hostile side in an interstate conflict, groups engaged in armed or unarmed government resistance, or groups alleged to be destabilizing border areas. Despite limited participation by members of the target group in the alleged subversion, the entire group is branded as a security threat that must be removed *en masse*.

[44] de Waal, 2023; Edwards, 2023; Hauer, 2021.

[45] "Refugee warriors" refers to refugees that launch military operations from host-state safe havens (Zolberg et al., 1986, pp. 275–278).

While many of these expulsions occur during periods of unrest or civil disturbances, most are not in response to direct armed threats by the target group; and only a quarter occurred during active intrastate armed conflict (from 1900 to 2020). The plurality of counter-subversive expulsions occurred in reaction to a target population's support, or alleged support, of opposition groups within the state. For example, in 1982, Uganda expelled Banyarwanda who supported the opposition Democratic Party and were alleged by President Milton Obote's regime to be involved in "illegal antigovernment activities."[46] In other instances, counter-subversive expulsions target groups engaged in unarmed antigovernment resistance. In 1989, amid growing concerns about the sizable ethnic Nepali population in Bhutan, the government issued "Bhutanization" measures designed to discriminate against Nepalis and to reduce their population in the country.[47] This led to growing unrest and mass demonstrations against the government's coercive assimilation policies, which were met with mass arrest and mass expulsion.[48]

In some of these expulsion episodes, targeted groups directly engaged in armed resistance against the government. For example, in the late 1990s, the Kosovo Liberation Army sought respect for greater political autonomy within the Federal Republic of Yugoslavia. Serbian forces responded with a violent military campaign, during which over 700,000 Kosovar Albanians were expelled, primarily to Albania.[49] Similarly, in 2016, the Arakan Rohingya Salvation Army mounted small-scale attacks against border guard posts in Arakan (Rakhine) State, Burma, killing nine police officers and seizing weapons and ammunition.[50] Burmese authorities responded with disproportionate force over the next two years, killing 12,000 and expelling over 800,000 Rohingya to Bangladesh.[51]

While most counter-subversive expulsions respond to threats to a government's internal control of the state, some have external dynamics. For example, in expulsion episodes targeting "refugee warriors," militant elements within refugee populations engage in cross-border military operations against their home country.[52] Their actions associate the host country with acts of war, creating a security concern for the host state, and in

[46] Coles, 1983, pp. 22–23; de Zayas, 1988, p. 32; Henckaerts, 1995; Mutibwa, 1992, p. 162; Winter, 1983, pp. 28–31.

[47] Human Rights Watch, 2007a, 2008; Van Hear, 1998, pp. 102–109.

[48] Human Rights Watch, 2007a, 2008; Van Hear, 1998, pp. 102–109.

[49] Naimark, 2001, pp. 175–182; Power, 2002, pp. 445, 448–450.

[50] Amnesty International, 2018; Office of the United Nations High Commissioner for Human Rights (OHCHR), 2017; UN Human Rights Council, 2018.

[51] Amnesty International, 2018; OHCHR, 2017; UN Human Rights Council, 2018.

[52] Zolberg et al., 1986, pp. 275–278.

turn, lead to the expulsion of the entire refugee group. In 1996, Tanzania expelled over 250,000 Rwandan refugees after coming under scrutiny for allegedly allowing Rwandan *génocidaires* to use Tanzania as a base to launch renewed attacks against Rwanda.[53] Similarly, in 1979, Thailand expelled over 50,000 Cambodian refugees due to fears about the destabilizing nature of the refugee population along the Thai–Cambodian border.[54]

In other counter-subversive expulsions, governments expel groups that support, or are alleged to support, a hostile side in an interstate conflict. In early 1942, Peru expelled nearly 2,000 Japanese-Peruvian citizens and resident aliens shortly after the Japanese bombardment of Pearl Harbor.[55] Peru's close cooperation with the US encouraged the expulsion of its Japanese population to avert subversive activities and shore up internal security.[56] Likewise, in 1991, the Kuwaiti government expelled over 200,000 Palestinians after the Palestinian Liberation Organization endorsed Iraq's brutal occupation of the country. The government accused Palestinians of collaborating with the Iraqi invaders and expelled them *en masse* in "clean out" operations, confiscating their property.[57]

Counter-subversive expulsions make up 17 percent of the total cases examined (twenty-three episodes) and have affected between 3.5 and 4.6 million people (see Table 3.5). They occur throughout the entire period of study—the first instance in 1937 and the last in 2016—and in six of seven world regions, with the majority in sub-Saharan Africa and East Asia. This type of expulsion is likely to continue as protracted intrastate conflicts persist and as the size and duration of refugee flows increase.

Conditions Under Which Counter-Subversive Motivations Emerge

- When an opposition group or rebel party threatens regime control and a non-core group supports them
- When a refugee population engages in cross-border military operations against their home country or is alleged to support those who do

[53] International Crisis Group, 1999, p. 4; Whitaker, 2002, p. 335.
[54] Amnesty International, 2017, p. 12; Loescher, 2001, pp. 210–213; U.S. Committee for Refugees, 1980, p. 14.
[55] Adachi, 2007, pp. 2–3.
[56] Gardiner, 1975, pp. 83–87.
[57] Henckaerts, 1995; Ibrahim, 1991; Rosen, 2012.

Table 3.5 Counter-Subversive Expulsions

Case Example	*Target Group*	*Number of Persons Expelled*	*Brief Description*
Dominican Republic (1937–1938)	Haitians	10,000–30,000	Dominican troops and sub-municipal political authorities attacked Haitians and Dominico–Haitians in the frontier region in an operation to eliminate threats of alleged military activity and illicit trade and smuggling. During the operation, tens of thousands were forced to flee the country, and thousands were killed.[a]
Burma (1991–1992)	Rohingya	250,000–260,000	The Burmese junta increased its military presence in Arakan (Rakhine) State in response to alleged "insurgent activity" in the area. As part of a "border development programme," they expelled Rohingya and forcibly transferred their land and property to Arakanese (Buddhist) or Burmese settlers to create a "religious and ethnic buffer" along the Burma–Bangladesh border.[b]
Kuwait (1991)	Palestinians, Iraqis	200,000–400,000	Kuwait expelled most of its Palestinian residents after the Palestinian Liberation Organization endorsed Iraq's occupation of the country. The Kuwaiti government launched operations to "clean out" Palestinian neighborhoods, whose residents were accused of collaborating with the Iraqis, and confiscated their property.[c]
Tanzania (1996)	Rwandans	250,000–500,000	In early 1995, northwestern Tanzania hosted nearly 600,000 Rwandan refugees. The Rwandan government regarded the massive refugee camps along its borders as a significant security threat. Rather than risking a Rwandan military attack into its territory, Tanzanian officials launched "Operation Return Refugees" and expelled the "refugee warriors" to Rwanda.[d]

[a] Turits, 2002.
[b] Amnesty International, 1992 (Sept), p. 24; Karens, Nagas report army atrocities; aid urged. *The Nation* (Bangkok) (January 28, 1992). FBIS-EAS-92-019; Piper, 1994, p. 17; Smith, 1994, pp. 56, 82; Van Hear, 1998, p. 99.
[c] Henckaerts, 1995; Ibrahim, 1991; Rosen, 2012.
[d] International Crisis Group, 1999, p. 4; Whitaker, 2002, p. 335.

- When a non-core group actively resists government policies and/or takes up arms, albeit typically limited, against the state
- When a non-core group aligns, or is perceived to align, with an enemy belligerent during an interstate conflict
- When a non-core group, concentrated in a border region, is accused of creating instability

3.1.4 Reprisal Expulsions

Reprisal expulsions have affected the smallest number of people over the twentieth and early twenty-first centuries and have the fewest incidents during the period examined. Governments implement reprisal expulsions in response to foreign policy disputes with the "homeland" state of the target group. These expulsions are motivated by retaliation or revenge. The majority are implemented by stronger states toward weaker ones, and sometimes there is a tit-for-tat dynamic with an expulsion by one state eliciting an expulsion by the other (e.g., Mauritania and Senegal, 1989; Angola and the Democratic Republic of Congo, 2008–2009).

Most reprisal expulsions are sparked by a diplomatic dispute. This may involve a state's relations with an external power or its position on an external conflict. For example, in the early 2000s, political tensions between Russia and Georgia increased as Georgia sought closer relations with the West and NATO.[58] The situation escalated in September 2006 when Georgian authorities detained four Russian military officers on charges of espionage and handed them over to the Organization for Security and Co-operation in Europe.[59] In response, the Russian government systematically rounded up Georgians "living irregularly" in the country, expelling them *en masse* without individual legal evaluation.[60] Other diplomatic disputes may be over an external state's treatment of a specific minority group or opposition movement. In mid-1993, relations between Greece and Albania deteriorated when Albanian authorities deported an Orthodox priest with Greek citizenship, accusing him of fomenting separatism among the Greek community in Albania.[61] Greece retaliated by expelling approximately 30,000 Albanians

[58] BBC, 2006.
[59] Human Rights Watch, 2007b.
[60] BBC, 2006; Radio Free Europe, 2014.
[61] Human Rights Watch, 1994; VanHear, 1998, pp. 122–123.

from Greece. The following year, Greek extremists from the Northern Epirus Liberation Front killed two Albanian soldiers near the Greek–Albanian border. Albania subsequently arrested and charged five leaders of Omonoia, an organization representing the ethnic Greek minority in Albania. The trial and resulting convictions were marred by violations of Albanian and international law.[62] In retaliation, Greece expelled another 70,000 Albanians.[63]

A smaller subset of reprisal expulsions transpire over border disputes that escalate into larger foreign policy clashes. In 1989, Mauritanian border guards shot and killed two Senegalese civilians in response to a dispute between Senegalese farmers and Mauritanian herders.[64] This localized issue quickly expanded into attacks on Mauritanian shops in Dakar, Senegal, and counterattacks against Black Africans in Mauritania, with nearly 300 deaths on each side. In the subsequent weeks, the governments of Senegal and Mauritania each expelled nearly 100,000 Arabs and Black Africans, respectively, in a massive tit-for-tat expulsion involving an international airlift.[65]

In other instances, reprisal expulsion is used in response to feuds between political leaders. A political quarrel in 1978 between Gabon's President Omar Bongo and Benin's President Mathieu Kérékou led to the expulsion of thousands of Beninese foreign nationals from Gabon.[66] The hostility between the two leaders started when a band of mercenaries attempted to overthrow the Kérékou regime.[67] Kérékou blamed Gabonese officials. Then Bongo accused Kérékou of trying to sabotage Gabon's hosting of the upcoming Organization of African Unity (OAU) summit. At the OAU summit, which was moved from Gabon to Sudan, Kérékou reiterated his accusations against Bongo's government, who then retaliated with the mass expulsion of Beninese residing in Gabon.[68]

Reprisal expulsions make up 14 percent of the total cases in the GSME dataset (20 episodes) and have affected between 2.3 and 2.8 million people (see Table 3.6). These instances occur in nearly all regions and are confined to the latter half of the twentieth century, with the first in Bulgaria in 1950.[69] This type of expulsion continues into the present day, with Pakistan

[62] Human Rights Watch, 1994; VanHear, 1998, pp. 122–123.
[63] Human Rights Watch, 1994; VanHear, 1998, pp. 122–123.
[64] Fleischman, 1994, p. 45; Noble, 1989; Tempest, 1989.
[65] Henckaerts, 1995; Noble, 1989; Tempest, 1989.
[66] Coles, 1983, pp. 21–22; Gray, 1998, pp. 396–397; Henckaerts, 1995; Legum, 1980, p. B561.
[67] Gray, 1998, pp. 396–397; Henckaerts, 1995; Legum, 1980, p. B561.
[68] Coles, 1983, pp. 21–22; Gray, 1998, pp. 396–397; Henckaerts, 1995; Legum, 1980, p. B561.
[69] There were no reprisal expulsions in Latin America and the Caribbean or North America during the period examined.

Table 3.6 Reprisal Expulsions

Case Example	*Target Group*	*Number of Persons Expelled*	*Brief Description*
Bulgaria (1950–1951)	Turks	152,000–155,000	In August 1950, the Bulgarian government announced the expulsion of over 150,000 Turks, revoking the special privileges previously granted to the Turkish Muslim minority. Bulgaria was part of the Soviet sphere, and the expulsion retaliated against the Western orientation of the newly formed Turkish government and Turkey's participation in the Korean War.[a]
Gabon (1978)	Beninese	6,000–12,000	A political feud between the leaders of Gabon and Benin led to the expulsion of thousands of Beninese foreign nationals. Benin President Kérékou accused Gabonese officials of supporting mercenaries trying to overthrow his regime. Gabon President Bongo accused Kérékou of sabotaging Gabon's efforts to host an OAU summit. When the summit was moved to Sudan, and Kérékou's accusations continued, Bongo retaliated with the expulsion of Beninese living in Gabon.[b]
Mauritania and Senegal (1989)	Senegalese and Mauritanians (respectively)	150,000–185,000	A border dispute between Senegalese farmers and Mauritanian herders, in which two Senegalese were killed by Mauritanian border guards, led to retaliatory violence on both sides. The rioting led to racially motivated tit-for-tat expulsions of Senegalese and other Black Africans from Mauritania and Arabs from Senegal.[c]
Pakistan (2016)	Afghans	500,000–565,000	In response to deteriorating political relations with Afghanistan—including disputes over Afghanistan's growing trade and development ties with rival India and a deadly border clash between Afghan and Pakistani forces that sparked "anti-Afghan" protests—Pakistani authorities expelled Afghans in what was described as the "largest unlawful mass forced return of refugees and asylum seekers" in recent times.[d]

[a]Bishku, 2003, p. 85; Gökatalay, 2021, p. 921; Kostanick, 1955, pp. 43–44.
[b]Coles, 1983, pp. 21–22; Gray, 1998, pp. 396–397; Henckaerts, 1995; Legum, 1980, p. B561.
[c]Fleischman, 1994; Henckaerts, 1995; Noble, 1989.
[d]Human Rights Watch, 2017, p. 15.

expelling over 300,000 Afghan refugees in 2023 in response to a diplomatic dispute over Afghanistan's failure to crackdown on Taliban militants operating in Pakistan.[70] Additional reprisal expulsions may arise as climate change puts increasing strain on natural resources and territory, resulting in foreign policy disputes over water, grazing rights, and shrinking lands.

Conditions Under Which Reprisal Motivations Emerge

- When interstate tensions are heightened over the outbreak of a diplomatic, border, or leadership dispute
- When a neighboring state pursues, or supports, a foreign policy decision/position that is opposed by the expelling state
- When the expelling state is stronger than the "homeland" state[71]

3.2 Variation in Expulsion Types

Having introduced four types of mass expulsion, it is useful to highlight variation across the types, including expulsion onset, region, magnitude, duration, and target group. Mass expulsion events in the first half of the twentieth century were overwhelmingly motivated by counter-irredentism (thirty-seven of forty-four events), with only seven incidents of the other three types (see Figure 3.2). Motivations changed after World War II. In the second half of the twentieth century, the plurality of expulsions were motivated by nativism (45 percent), with counter-irredentist expulsions much less common (9 percent). All four expulsion types persist in the contemporary period, with new episodes of each occurring in the last decade examined (2011–2020): five nativist, four counter-subversive, two reprisal, and one counter-irredentist.

In terms of geographic distribution, nativist expulsions are the most widespread, with episodes occurring in all seven world regions. By contrast, counter-irredentist expulsions occur almost exclusively in Europe (89 percent), which leads to the predominance of territory-based explanations in the literature on European eliminationist policies. Counter-subversive expulsions are more geographically balanced, with episodes in six

[70] Kugelman, 2023; Noack & Khan, 2023; Sattar, 2023.

[71] In some cases, the expelling state is weaker than the target group's homeland state, but that is the minority share.

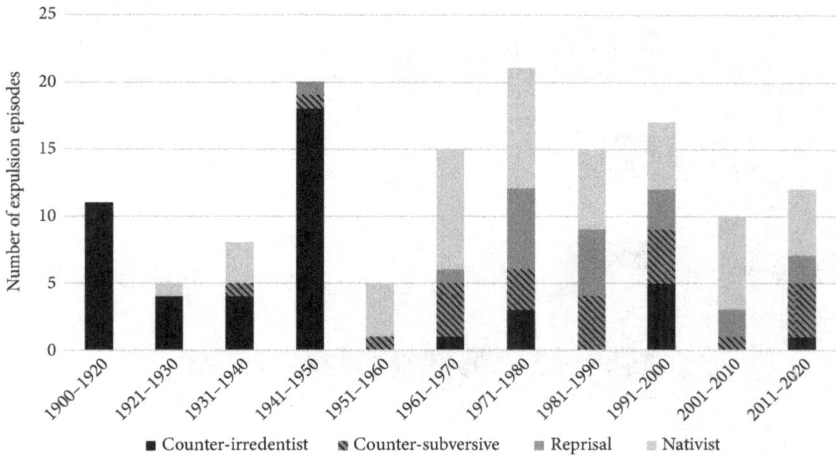

Figure 3.2 Expulsion type by decade of onset (1900–2020)[a]

[a] The first twentieth-century expulsion occurred in 1912, so the first two decades (1900–1910; 1911–1920) are combined.

of the seven regions, mostly in sub-Saharan Africa and East Asia and Pacific. Reprisal expulsions are less regionally dispersed, with most occurring in MENA, followed by sub-Saharan Africa and Europe.

The magnitude of an expulsion event varies considerably by type (see Figure 3.3). Counter-irredentist expulsions have affected the largest number of people: an estimated 18 to 25 million. Nativist expulsions follow, affecting 6 to 10.5 million persons, and then counter-subversive expulsions, generating 3.6 to 4.5 million expellees. Reprisal expulsions affected the smallest total, an estimated 2.3 to 2.8 million. The duration of an expulsion episode is uniformly short across the four types with an average length of 1.6 years—reprisal expulsions are the shortest, on average 1.2 years, and counter-irredentist the longest, at 1.9 years.

All four types of expulsion target citizens and noncitizens, highlighting the importance of comprehensively examining population groups regardless of citizenship status (see Figure 3.4). The forty-seven expulsion episodes that *only* targeted citizens (34 percent) are all confined to the counter-irredentist, counter-subversive, and reprisal types, indicating an important security dynamic for citizen-only expulsions. Because much of the existing literature has excluded noncitizens from its analysis, it is perhaps not surprising that security explanations are predominant. However, hybrid expulsions, targeting citizens and noncitizens, as well as expulsions only targeting noncitizens, are found across all four expulsion types. At least a quarter of nativist

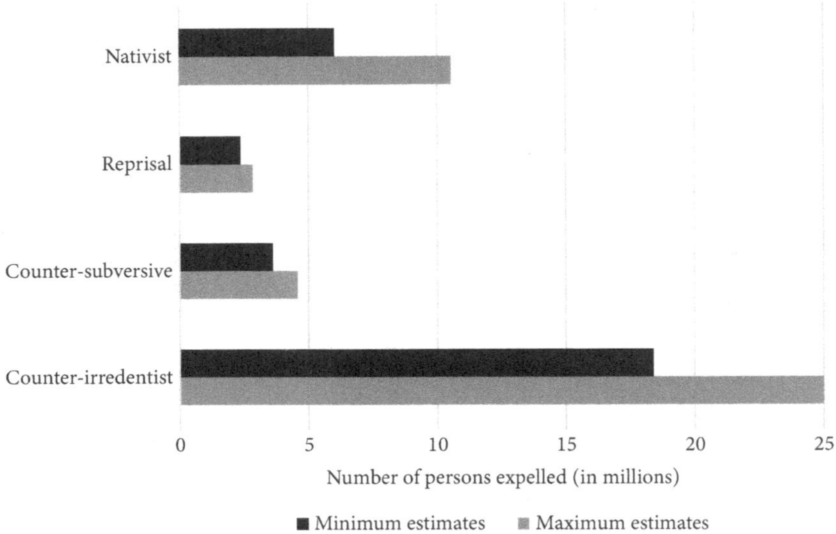

Figure 3.3 Magnitude of expulsion, by expulsion type

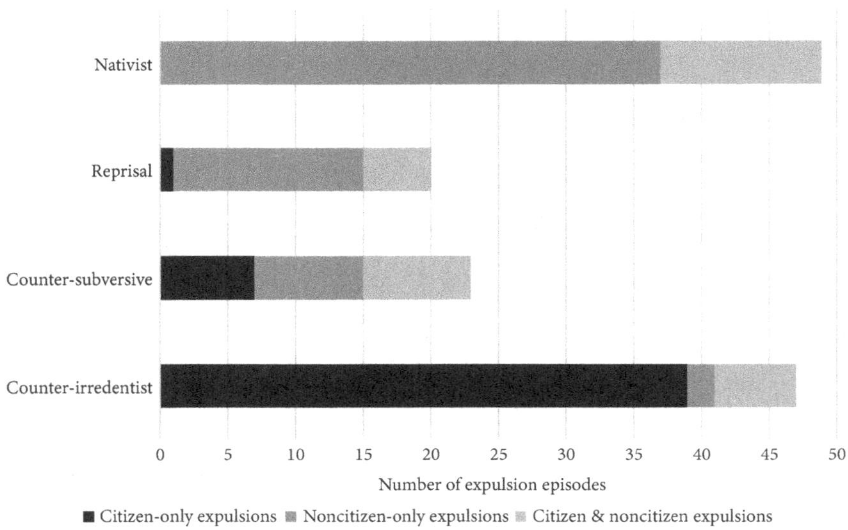

Figure 3.4 Citizenship status of expellees, by expulsion type

(24 percent), reprisal (25 percent), and counter-subversive (35 percent) expulsion episodes are hybrid cases where both citizens and noncitizens were simultaneously expelled. Even counter-irredentist expulsions, which

mostly target only citizens, still include hybrid events (13 percent). Similarly, all expulsion types include episodes of noncitizen-only expulsions with the majority motivated by nativism (76 percent) and reprisal (70 percent), followed by counter-subversion (35 percent). Each of the four expulsion types also includes at least one episode targeting refugee populations, most of which are nativist or counter-subversive. The latter is intuitive given some governments' aim to remove "refugee warrior" groups.

*

The GSME data allow for the systematic classification and categorization of mass expulsion episodes between 1900 and 2020. By isolating this distinct policy of elimination, with the intent to remove groups *en masse*, we can more precisely explain why governments choose mass expulsion. There are two main categories of expulsion—security and economic—with four distinct types. If a government identifies a target group as a security threat to the state, it may turn to counter-irredentist, counter-subversive, or reprisal mass expulsion. Counter-irredentist expulsions seek territorial control, counter-subversive expulsions aim to maintain internal political control, and reprisal expulsions pursue retaliation and revenge. Alternatively, if the target group is identified as an economic threat, governments may implement nativist expulsions, aimed at safeguarding "indigenous" control of state resources by removing alleged "foreigners" or "aliens." Both economic and security concerns are crucial determinants of mass expulsion, with the former needing more careful consideration.

The mass expulsion typology reveals distinct motivations driving this eliminationist policy. With these motivations in mind, we turn to the process of mass expulsion. The next chapter examines how mass expulsion unfolds, explaining the broader context in which it occurs and how government motivations are transformed into action.

4

A Theory of Mass Expulsion

Armed with an understanding of the different types of expulsion, this chapter introduces a theoretical framework to explain the process of mass expulsion. The theory identifies key structural, proximate, precipitating, and intervening factors that critically shape the environment and increase the likelihood of expulsion.[1] It also explains why some governments—facing similar contexts, conditions, and motivations—may refrain from expelling populations. Similar to other eliminationist policies, mass expulsion is not a single moment or decision, but rather a process, a sequence of events that culminates in the removal of groups *en masse*.[2]

The process of mass expulsion begins with a status quo relationship between the target group, let's call them Group X, and the state. These relations may be accommodating, with the group being left on its own to reside within the state without much, or any, interference. Or the relations may be conflictual, with the state targeting Group X with different forms of discrimination and repression, but not the use of eliminationist policies. Then a shock to the existing status quo changes the dynamics in the country. These structural shock factors, derived from the geopolitical environment or macro political economy, increase the possibility of expulsion. They may include the dissolution of multinational empires and the creation of new nation-states, the outbreak of interstate or intrastate wars, or regime change, all of which impact the stability of the state and alter the status quo. Similarly, postcolonial independence or major financial crises rearrange structural hierarchies and impact the existing environment, increasing the possibility of expulsion.

The relevant shock to the status quo changes relations between Group X and the state, shifting the government's view of the target group. This is where the four types of mass expulsion outlined in Chapter 3 emerge. In the new environment, the government identifies Group X as a security or

[1] The theoretical framework draws on Nicholas Van Hear's integrative approach in explaining the dynamics of mass exodus and forced migration more generally (1998, pp. 14–21).

[2] Rosenberg, 2012; Stanton, 1996.

Mass Expulsion. Meghan M. Garrity, Oxford University Press. © Oxford University Press (2026).
DOI: 10.1093/9780197829097.003.0004

economic threat to the state. The proximate factors—counter-irredentism, counter-subversion, reprisal, or nativism—are derived from the consequences of the change in structural features and bear more immediately on expulsion.

At this point, the government must assess the suitability of mass expulsion: Is this eliminationist policy appropriate to deal with the threat identified? Four important elements increase the likelihood of mass expulsion and can be understood as preconditions for expulsion. The first is the government's conception of the nation. This precondition builds on existing arguments about the importance of exclusionary ideologies as it relates to eliminationist policies.[3] Governments that view the nation as having a dominant core group, and identify Group X as outside of the ethnonational identity of the state, are more likely to consider an expulsion policy. The rhetoric of exclusionary ideologies includes populist refrains such as "Turkey for the Turks" or "Africa for Africans."

The second precondition is the nature of the group's threat. Will Group X continue to pose a threat to the state if they are removed outside of the state's boundaries? This is particularly relevant for expulsions within the security category (e.g., counter-irredentist, counter-subversive, and reprisal). If the government believes the group's removal from the territory would solve the real or perceived threat, it may view expulsion as a suitable policy option. However, if Group X is anticipated to continue to pose a threat to the state, even if removed, then alternative eliminationist policies, such as mass killing or genocide, are more likely to be considered.[4] For expulsions within the economic category (e.g., nativist), the removal of Group X typically resolves the concerns of the dominant core group. Key jobs, sectors, and positions abandoned by expellees are acquired by "indigenous" or "native" people, eliminating the economic threat and satisfying this precondition.[5]

A third precondition for expulsion is the presence or construction of an alternative "homeland" where Group X "belongs." In cases of mass expulsion, governing elites identify a "homeland," real or constructed, where they argue the group should be instead of their current location. Officials contend that they came from elsewhere and need to go back regardless of their migration or origin story. In expulsion episodes targeting noncitizens, the

[3] Harff, 2003; Straus, 2015.

[4] Valentino, 2004, p. 157.

[5] As noted in Chapter 2, this theory pertains to cross-border mass expulsions where the target group is removed outside the boundaries of the state. It assumes that the expelling government does not aim to eliminate the threat by moving the target group internally, distinguishing the concept of mass expulsion analyzed here from internal expulsion or displacement.

"homeland" is the group's state of citizenship. For example, the "homeland" of Ghanaians expelled from Nigeria in 1983 was Ghana. In cases where citizens are expelled, the alternative "homeland" is the state where the government alleges the expellees should reside. Greek Orthodox Christians in Turkey were believed to "belong" in Greece, despite many speaking only Turkish and having never lived in the Greek nation-state. South Asians expelled from Uganda were similarly argued to "belong" in the United Kingdom or India, despite most never having lived in either country. The presence or construction of an alternative "homeland" is a critical component of mass expulsion, differentiating it from other eliminationist polices. In cases without an alternative "homeland," other eliminationist policies may be considered.

The fourth precondition is a government's capacity to carry out the expulsion. Does the state have the capability to remove Group X by force or the threat of force? Can the gendarmerie, police, or other paramilitary groups feasibly corral the target group to the border region and force them into a neighboring state? Or does the government have the capability to incite Group X to flee by engendering fear of the consequences if they do not leave "voluntarily." In many instances of expulsion, the threat of force or the use of limited force encourages the departure of the larger group. Importantly, when forceful coercion is used or threatened, it does not constitute "voluntary" departure, despite claims to the contrary by the expelling regime. Features of the group, particularly those that are relatively small, identifiable, and geographically concentrated, lower the level of state capacity required.[6] Governments with these capabilities may consider expulsion a viable policy.

If the four preconditions for expulsion are in place—a governing elite with an exclusionary ideology, a target group whose threat would be neutralized if removed, an alternative "homeland," and a state with adequate capabilities for removal—a government may determine that expulsion is a suitable policy to eliminate the threat posed by Group X. The governing elites, and sometimes the public, begin calling for Group X's removal.

Next in the process of mass expulsion are the precipitating factors that trigger expulsion. These factors answer the question "why now?" For expulsions within the security category (e.g., counter-irredentist, counter-subversive, and reprisal), the precipitating factors are usually clear and observable events, such as an external attack on the state, a postwar treaty, an internal

[6] Stanton, 2016, pp. 10, 26; Straus, 2015, pp. 76–77.

uprising threatening the regime, or a border clash. The trigger may not be as obvious for expulsions in the economic category (e.g., nativist). Sometimes an impending critical election may spur an economically motivated expulsion, but in these cases the proximate factors may, on their own, be enough to stimulate the decision to expel.[7]

Up to this point, the theoretical framework presented here may seem deterministic. With the appropriate structural, proximate, and precipitating factors in place, we should expect a mass expulsion. However, it is essential to emphasize that this is a probabilistic, not a deterministic, theoretical framework. Each of the factors described, along with the preconditions, ripens the environment for expulsion, making the use of this policy option more likely but not certain. Most importantly, even if a government determines that mass expulsion is a suitable eliminationist policy to address the problem at hand, there is still the question of feasibility.

Key intervening factors influence whether a government with the motivation to expel, where the preconditions are in place, will move forward with expulsion. These critical enabling and restraining/constraining factors[8] include the ruling elites' alliances, the "homeland" state of the target group, and pertinent international organizations. The impact on and relations between these three actors and the expelling government, as well as the actors' response, or anticipated response, to an expulsion affect the outcome. In line with existing scholarship on atrocity restraints,[9] each of these factors can individually influence expulsion decisions; however, when they operate in combination, they are most effective. The relative strength of the restraints/constraints, and whether they can be successfully overcome, is key to understanding a government's decision to expel.

4.1 Alliances

One of the first considerations for a government contemplating expulsion is the effect of the policy on its key allies—domestic and transnational. How will expulsion impact political parties, military co-ethnics, the business community, and trade unions? If the ruling elites' key domestic partners

[7] Van Hear, 1998, p. 20.

[8] Restraints connote measures or conditions of self-control that indicate internal moderation of behavior. Constraints indicate limitations or restrictions placed on something to inhibit actions or behavior, more aligned with external factors.

[9] Stanton, 2016, p. 42; Straus, 2012, p. 345.

would directly benefit, politically or economically, from removing the target group, expulsion becomes more likely. Benefits of expulsion include political gains from eliminating a security threat to the ethnonational state or removing internal opposition. Economic gains include appropriating the assets and income of an economically dominant group, as well as opening new employment opportunities by removing a group concentrated in a specific sector or that holds key positions in the bureaucracy or desirable skilled trades.

These benefits may assist governing elites in building a new nation-state or in consolidating their rule. They may also generate political goodwill in advance of critical elections. If the ruling elites believe expulsion will strengthen their domestic alliances via these political or economic gains, then this policy option becomes more attractive. In other cases, the interests of the executive's core domestic allies might be harmed by expelling the target group—affecting a critical source of revenue, cheap labor supply, political buffer, or future bargaining chip. In these situations, altering the existing political or economic status quo is too costly for the government's domestic partners, restraining the decision to expel.

The effect of expulsion on transnational alliances is another determining factor in government expulsion decisions. Transnational alliances may be formal (e.g., treaties, agreements, defense pacts) or informal (e.g., strong trade relations, preferential arms sales, intelligence sharing). Governments with core transnational allies that support or ignore their expulsion policies are more likely to expel. These allies may support expulsion when they have a common interest in removing the target group from a given territory, or they may ignore expulsion, preferring to simply "look the other way" and continue business as usual. Alternatively, transnational allies may actively oppose an expulsion policy. Those committed to human rights norms are more likely to oppose an ally's violation of those norms,[10] although these commitments alone are often inadequate, as even democratic regimes have facilitated expulsion. Their opposition to expulsion may arise because of economic, security, or reputational costs resulting from an expulsion, or costs stemming from the ally's perceived support for the policy. Or, they may simply want to ensure stability in the country or region, and hence will actively deter an allied government from implementing a policy that might compromise stability. Concerns that expulsion may jeopardize critical

[10] Salehyan et al., 2014.

transnational alliances act as a restraint on a government's decision to expel. The joint dynamics of domestic and transnational alliances greatly influence government expulsion decisions and either enable or constrain their policy choices.

The critical role of alliances, particularly domestic alliances, builds on existing literature that emphasizes the importance of cross-cutting cleavages as a key domestic factor in restraining mass violence.[11] While cross-cutting cleavages are relevant in some expulsion cases, the lens of domestic alliance patterns is wider and, as such, encompasses cases where there are no cross-cutting cleavages between the ruling elites and the target group, yet where expulsion is still restrained by the potential harm to domestic allies. The broader lens of alliances also allows for the consideration of internal and external allies.

The role of transnational allies in expulsion decision-making outlined here is distinct from existing explanations about the role of interstate relations. These existing arguments stress that the source and level of external country support to a target group are key to restraining eliminationist policies.[12] However, in many expulsion cases, crucial transnational allies have neither a direct relationship nor a perceived relationship with the target group. Instead, what is salient is not the transnational ally's patronage or protection of the group, but how their interests may or may not be affected by the removal of the group, as well as their views of expulsion as a viable policy option. Shared interests with the expulsionist government may take precedence and lead the ally to ignore the expulsion. This aligns with emerging literature on the importance of regional, or great power, competition in motivating patron states to restrain eliminationist policies, like genocide, by withdrawing military assistance.[13]

4.2 "Homeland" State(s) of the Target Group

In addition to assessing the effect of expulsion on its alliances, governments motivated to expel consider the effect on the target group's "homeland" state(s). How will the "home" country of the expellees react and respond to

[11] Bulutgil, 2016, p. 2; Chirot & McCauley, 2006, p. 133; Harff, 2003, p. 67; Jha, 2013, p. 806; Mann, 2005, p. 5.

[12] Butt, 2017, pp. 39–41; Mylonas, 2012, pp. 36–37.

[13] Nanlohy, 2024.

an expulsion policy? The critical role of the "homeland" state extends findings from the existing literature on national minorities regarding the role of external national "homelands" and kin-state politics.[14] Because expulsion policies target citizens, noncitizens, and sometimes both simultaneously, the conception of "homeland" proposed here is broader than that in the national minorities literature. Here "homeland" is conceptualized as states of citizenship, states with co-ethnics, and states with alleged or fabricated co-ethnics.

When noncitizens are expelled, the "homeland" state is simply the expellees' state of citizenship (e.g., Tunisia in the case of Libya's 1985 expulsion of Tunisians). When citizens are expelled, the "homeland" state follows Rogers Brubaker's concept of external national "homeland"—a state with ethnic co-nationals (e.g., Germany in the case of the 1945 expulsion of the Sudeten Germans from Czechoslovakia). Brubaker's concept assumes the "homeland" state takes a political interest in protecting its co-ethnics who possess a different citizenship and reside in another state.[15] That is not always the case when it comes to mass expulsion. Rather than an active external patron, in some expulsion cases the "homeland" is merely the recipient of expellees (e.g., Haiti in the case of the Dominican Republic's expulsion of Haitians and Dominico–Haitians in the 1990s, or Mexico when the United States expelled Mexicans and Mexican–Americans in 1929 and 1954). The "homeland" state can also be the country that the expelling regime alleges, or falsely asserts, that the target group "belongs" to despite no actual ties. For example, Idi Amin proclaimed that the UK was responsible for all South Asians expelled from Uganda, even those with Ugandan citizenship, because of its colonial ties to the Indian subcontinent. Yet, most South Asians had no co-ethnic connections to Britain. In Burma, the Tatmadaw asserted that expelled Rohingya were "illegal Bengalis" and "belonged" in their alleged "homeland" of Bangladesh—this despite generations of Rohingya residing in Burma's Arakan (Rakhine) State. The broader three-part conceptualization of "homeland" used here encompasses external states affected by expulsion policies targeting ethnic groups with varying legal statuses and varying ties to those states.

There are two important considerations regarding the effect of expulsion on the "homeland" state. The first is the strength of ties between the

[14] Brubaker, 1996; Waterbury, 2020.
[15] Brubaker, 1996.

government contemplating expulsion and the "homeland" state. Governments that have strong ties with the "homeland" of the target group may be concerned that expulsion could jeopardize that relationship, restraining their decision to expel. Conversely, if a government's ties with the target group's "homeland" are weak, there are fewer concerns about damaging the relationship, which removes internal restraints. The second consideration is the response, or anticipated response, of the "homeland" state to an expulsion policy. A "homeland" state that the government believes will acquiesce to the expulsion and resettle expellees is more likely to enable the policy, whereas a state that is believed to resist by denying entry to expellees restrains the policy implementation. Importantly, the ability of a "homeland" state to deny entry to expellees is contingent on state capacity and the geography of the border region. Governments faced with the combination of strong "homeland" state ties and "homelands" that resist and deny entry to expellees are the most likely to be constrained. In other instances, the two aspects of the "homeland" state factor are in tension. There may be strong ties but the "homeland" is anticipated to acquiesce, or weak ties but the "homeland" is anticipated to deny entry to expellees. In these cases, the combination of other intervening factors must be considered to assess the likelihood of expulsion.

More than one "homeland" state may be affected by an expulsion episode—for example, the UK and India in the case of Uganda's 1972 expulsion of South Asians, or Ghana and other West African states in Nigeria's 1983 expulsion of African migrants. In these cases, government decisions are based on the "homeland" state of the majority of the expellees. Since most South Asians expelled from Uganda in 1972 held British nationality, the effect on Britain was more of a factor in the Ugandan government's decision than the effect on India, which only had 6,000 citizens expelled.

The first aspect of the "homeland" state factor, the strength of ties, builds on the existing literature that suggests interstate relations—alliance or rivalry—are crucial to determining the difference between strategies of exclusion and accommodation.[16] However, while groups targeted for expulsion may or may not have external power backers, or the perception of external support, they always have a "homeland" state (real or constructed). The broader framing of the "homeland" state factor captures the targeting of groups that do and do not have external backers (i.e., "homelands" that do

[16] Mylonas, 2012.

and do not support the group targeted for expulsion). Additionally, because mass expulsion policies remove the target group from the territory of the expelling state, the policy's physical ramifications are thrust on the state where expellees are forcibly sent "home." Therefore, in contrast to eliminationist policies more generally, the "homeland" state is a critical factor enabling or constraining mass expulsion.

4.3 International Organizations

International organizations (IOs) are the third intervening factor that influence a government's expulsion calculus. The relationship with, and the response or anticipated response of, pertinent IOs enables or constrains expulsion decisions. Here pertinent IOs include the United Nations (UN), its precursor the League of Nations, UN agency affiliates (i.e., the United Nations High Commissioner for Refugees [UNHCR] and the International Organization for Migration [IOM][17]), the International Committee of the Red Cross (ICRC), and regional bodies such as the Organization of African Unity (now the African Union) and the Association of Southeast Asian Nations (ASEAN). Since this analysis begins in 1900, before the creation of the League of Nations and the multitude of post–WWII international organizations that exist today, this factor also includes the "Great Powers" of the early twentieth century. In the absence of an institution of member nation-states, the Great Powers acted like an international decision-making body at conferences such as the Paris Peace Conference in Versailles, France (1919–1920), and the Lausanne Peace Conference in Lausanne, Switzerland (1922–1923), just before and after the emergence of the League of Nations.

Similar to the "homeland" state factor, governments with strong ties, or desiring to cultivate strong ties, with IOs are more likely than those with weak ties to be restrained in their expulsion decisions. Strong ties with the UN or regional bodies may restrain governments from implementing an expulsion policy because of concerns about damaging relations with, or their standing within, these organizations. This restraint is operative when a government believes that membership and status within these institutions convey important legitimacy and prestige to their domestic constituents,

[17] The IOM was previously known as the Intergovernmental Committee for European Migration (1952–1980) and the Intergovernmental Committee for Migration (1980–1989). It became a UN agency in 2016.

as well as regionally and abroad. Governments uninterested in cultivating these ties and unconcerned with maintaining international norms will not be restrained. Thus, weak ties with IOs will ease the decision to expel.

The response of IOs to an expulsion episode, or the government's anticipation of their response, also affects expulsion decisions. These organizations may enable expulsion by supporting, facilitating, or ignoring the policy, or they may constrain expulsion by resisting and pressuring governments to change course. Overt IO support most often appears in facilitating or backing bilateral or multilateral "population transfer" or "population exchange" treaties.[18] It also materializes in the physical extraction of expellees from a territory on behalf of an expelling government.[19] Indirectly, IOs signal support by ignoring expulsion decrees and small-scale expulsions that may test the waters for larger episodes or by turning a blind eye as expulsions unfold and staying mum on the matter. Conversely, IOs may play a critical constraining role through resistance in the face of imminent or planned expulsion decisions using sanctions, travel bans, and the withdrawal of diplomatic, military, or financial support.[20]

The IO factor presented here bridges competing literatures that argue IOs enable eliminationist policies[21] or that IOs restrain their implementation.[22] The arguments that IOs enable these policies largely focus on indifference or inaction in the face of atrocities.[23] This is relevant to mass expulsion, as IOs have ignored expulsion policies, but notably they have also supported or facilitated expulsion on behalf of expelling regimes—an important aspect of this factor. However, IOs have also played a key constraining role, deterring mass expulsion through diplomacy, mediation, and negotiation. The ability of IOs to constrain is highly dependent on their relationship with the expelling government. Their resistance to expulsion will be much less effective if the government that is motivated to expel does not have or want to cultivate strong ties with IOs. A government content to ignore international rules and norms and to spurn dialogue with the UN or regional organizations greatly diminishes this factor's constraining power. In these cases, the

[18] Examples include "population transfers" from Czechoslovakia to Germany (1945) and "population exchanges" between Bulgaria and Greece (1919), among many others.

[19] The UNHCR, ICEM, and ICRC helped to do this in 1972 Uganda, and the UNHCR oversaw the same in Bangladesh in the early 1990s.

[20] Stanton, 2016; Straus, 2015.

[21] Bass, 2013; Power, 2002.

[22] Jo & Simmons, 2016; Robinson, 2010; Stanton, 2016; Straus, 2015.

[23] Bass, 2013; Midlarsky, 2005, pp. 392–393; Power, 2002, p. xxi.

other two intervening factors—alliances and "homeland" states—are more critical.

A few additional clarifications are needed regarding the role of IOs in mass expulsion. Undoubtedly, IOs are not homogenous institutions. Those pertinent to constraining expulsion include a diverse group of actors from the UN Secretariat to the UNHCR to regional organizations, each with their own views and bureaucracies.[24] In some cases, IOs are aligned. For example, the UNHCR, the Intergovernmental Committee for European Migration (ICEM), and the ICRC jointly facilitated the removal of South Asians from Uganda in response to Idi Amin's expulsion decree. Similarly, the "Great Powers" at the Lausanne Conference all advocated for the Greek Orthodox Christians of Istanbul to be exempted from the "population exchange." In other cases, IOs have conflicting stances or internal disagreements over the organization's position. In 1992, the UN and UNHCR were adamantly against the expulsion of the Rohingya from Burma, while ASEAN took a position of noninterference. Within ASEAN, Muslim-majority Indonesia and Malaysia condemned Burma's expulsion, while other members urged the organization to pursue "constructive engagement," refusing to publicly condemn the Tatmadaw's human rights violations.[25]

In cases where IOs are united, this factor exerts a strong influence on the decision whether or not to expel. When there is divergence, particularly when some IOs condemn and others ignore the policy, this factor is less likely to constrain. In these cases, the key determinant is the strength of ties between IOs and the government motivated to expel.

Another point of note is the dramatic changes from 1900 to the present in the composition, influence, size, scale, and norms of IOs. One of the tradeoffs in examining a phenomenon over the *longue durée* is the evolution of institutions and norms.[26] The IO factor examined here cannot be held constant when investigating expulsion events in the early twentieth century and those in the early twenty-first century. While this inhibits holding the IO factor constant across cases, it can be controlled when examining expulsions that took place during the same period or within a single country at one point in time.

[24] Barnett & Finnemore, 2004.

[25] ASEAN called to act on Burmese situation. *The Nation* (Bangkok), (March 5, 1992). FBIS-EAS-92-044; Asia Watch (1992, May 7), p. 22.

[26] Finnemore, 2003.

The three intervening factors—alliances, "homeland" states, and international organizations—are crucial in understanding the implementation of this eliminationist policy. They help to explain why mass expulsion does not occur more frequently, given the many governments motivated to expel. Each factor may individually influence an expulsion decision, but they are most effective when operating in combination.

Having presented a theory of mass expulsion, including the typology of expulsion motivations and the process of expulsion, Chapters 5–7 examine three historical case studies. Each chapter features a different expulsion type—nativist, counter-irredentist, and counter-subversive.[27] The case study chapters apply the theoretical framework to demonstrate the process of mass expulsion, including crucial negative cases to explain why governments equally motivated to expel may refrain.

We begin in 1970s Uganda under the infamous regime of Idi Amin.

[27] Reprisal expulsions are not included, as they are the least frequent of the four expulsion types and affect the smallest number of people.

PART II
EMPIRICS

5

Nativist Expulsion: South Asians in Postcolonial Uganda and Kenya

On August 4, 1972, President Idi Amin gave a speech to the Tororo Airborne Regiment in eastern Uganda. He told his troops there was no place "for the over 80,000 Asians . . . who are sabotaging Uganda's economy and encouraging corruption."[1] Instead, Uganda's economy should be in the hands of indigenous Africans. Five days later, Amin announced that South Asians[2] had ninety days to leave the country.[3] His decree set off an international scramble to remove tens of thousands of people, with the United Kingdom both leading the efforts and deflecting responsibility to absorb 50,000 of its own nationals of South Asian descent residing in the country. Although the expulsion order targeted South Asians with foreign citizenship,[4] Amin declared that the government would "double check" the citizenship of South Asians who were registered as Ugandan citizens.[5] Through the citizenship verification process, many South Asians had their legitimate claims rejected.[6] International organizations coordinated the documentation, transportation, and resettlement of approximately 23,000 South Asians who had Ugandan

[1] Patel, 1972, p. 17.

[2] During the 1960s and 1970s, the South Asian population in East Africa (i.e., people with ethnic/familial ties to contemporary India, Pakistan, or Bangladesh) were collectively referred to by the governing authorities, media, and public as "Asians" or "Indians." This chapter uses the terms "South Asian," "East African Asian," and "Asian" interchangeably for ease of reading.

[3] Statement by H. E. The President of Uganda Concerning the Status of the Asian Community in Uganda, 09 August 1972; 11/2/64-641.UGA[c] Expulsion and Deportation—Uganda [1972–1984] Volume 3; Series 2, Box 1281; Fonds 11; UNHCR.

[4] Official Decree 17 stated that "any person of Asian origin" from the UK, India, Pakistan, or Bangladesh must leave, extending the expulsion to all Asians with foreign citizenship, not just to British Asians.

[5] Daily Telegraph newspaper article, "Expulsion decree by Amin after 'divine message'"; 10.08.1972; 11/2/10-100.UGA.ASI[a], Refugees from Asia in Uganda [Volume1-1.UGA.ASI]; Series 2, Box 204; Fonds 11; UNHCR.

[6] *East Africa Standard.* (1972, August 20). Now all Ugandan Asians are ordered out. In Z. Lalani (1997), *Ugandan Asian expulsion: 90 days and beyond through the eyes of the international press* (pp. 25–26). Expulsion Publications.

Mass Expulsion. Meghan M. Garrity, Oxford University Press. © Oxford University Press (2026).
DOI: 10.1093/9780197829097.003.0005

citizenship but were left de facto stateless by the expulsion order. Within three months, only 1,500 South Asians remained.[7]

5.1 Background Context: South Asians in East Africa

South Asian traders facilitated the exchange of goods along the East African coast in the Indian Ocean corridor centuries before the arrival of Europeans.[8] In the nineteenth century, the UK established two protectorates in East Africa[9] and brought South Asians deeper inland as indentured laborers to build the railway network from Mombasa, Kenya, to the White Nile in present-day Uganda.[10] These laborers originated from the Indian states of Gujarat and Punjab, as well as from what was then the Portuguese colony of Goa.[11] Most of the laborers either returned home to India at the end of their contract, were repatriated due to illness, or died in Africa; only a few thousand permanently settled on the continent.[12]

A second wave of Asians arrived in the 1920s and 1930s.[13] These voluntary immigrants, often called *dukawallahs*,[14] sought economic opportunities in small-scale trade, cotton ginning, transportation, and clerical services for the colonial administration.[15] Most were male, and they rarely stayed for long, coming to work and then returning home in a circular migration pattern. These immigrants extended the monetary economy into previously subsistence areas. They brought consumer goods to rural indigenous populations and served as the main outlet for surplus produce from African farmers, controlling most of the import-export trade.[16]

The Asians in Uganda and Kenya lived a much higher quality of life than their kin on the Indian subcontinent. Their population numbers steadily

[7] Hoagland, Jim. (1972, November 13). Kampala exodus: Asian quarter like a ghost town. *Washington Post*. In Z. Lalani (1997), *Ugandan Asian expulsion* (pp. 138, 140).

[8] Herzig, 2006, p. 10.

[9] The Protectorate of Uganda was established in 1894. The British East Africa Protectorate (later Kenya) followed in 1895, and in 1920 was transformed into a Crown colony directly administered by imperial officials, becoming a site of significant European settlement.

[10] Mattausch, 1998, p. 122.

[11] Herzig, 2006, p. 15.

[12] O'Brien, 1972, p. 16.

[13] O'Brien, 1972, p. 16.

[14] *Dukawallah* comes from the Swahili word "*duka*," meaning shop (from the Hindi word "*dukaan*" for store) and the Hindi word "*wallah*" meaning owner (Ghai & Ghai, 1971, p. 6; Herzig, 2006, p. 19, footnote 9; Tandon & Raphael, 1978, p. 17, footnote 4).

[15] Tandon, 1972, p. 3.

[16] Ghai & Ghai, 1965, p. 37.

Table 5.1 South Asian population in Uganda (1910–1972)[a]

Year	1910	1921	1935	1948	1959	1969	1972
Population	2,000	5,000	15,000	34,000	69,000	70,000	74,000

[a]Adapted from text in Jamal, 1976, p. 613 and Uche, 2017, p. 823.

Table 5.2 South Asian population in Kenya (1911–1969)[a]

Year	1911	1921	1931	1948	1962	1969
Population	11,787	25,253	43,623	97,687	176,613	139,037

[a]Adapted from data in Herzig, 2006, p. 30 and Nowik, 2015, p. 121.

increased between the 1910s and 1960s, particularly after World War II, driven by a combination of family reunification and high birth rates (see Tables 5.1 and 5.2).[17] Despite similar stories of arrival, the East African Asian community was far from homogenous. They were divided by caste, religion, occupation, and, after the partition of India in 1947, nationality. Most were Hindus of the Lohana or Patidar caste, but there were also Muslims (largely Ismailis), Sikhs, and Catholics.[18]

During the colonial period, the British institutionalized a tripartite separation of races.[19] There were three segregated hierarchical groups—Europeans, Asians, and Africans—with minimal economic, social, or political integration. Europeans controlled political power and owned the major industries, including financial institutions and many of the larger distribution enterprises. Asians filled middle-class functions. In the public sector, they worked in skilled and semi-skilled positions, especially the railways and schools, and in clerical and secretarial roles in the civil service. In the private sector, they worked as professionals—doctors, lawyers, teachers—or provided technical services to European firms as clerks, accountants, or sales assistants.[20] They also dominated retail and wholesale trade.[21] Africans worked mostly in agriculture but also as wage laborers, taxi drivers, and domestic workers.[22] Segregation manifested in separate schools, hospitals,

[17] Mattausch, 1998, p. 128.
[18] Mamdani, 1975, p. 32; Parson, 1973, p. 63.
[19] Mattausch, 1998, p. 128.
[20] Ghai & Ghai, 1971, p. 9.
[21] Maxon, 1995, p. 112.
[22] Mattausch, 1998, p. 129.

residential areas, and social spaces.[23] Most Asians lived in urban centers, whereas the majority of Africans resided in rural areas.[24] Asian immigrants also maintained close connections to their relatives in India, and endogamy was commonplace.[25]

Colonial policies, by design, favored Asian businesses to the exclusion of Africans. An alien mercantile class ensured that Africans could not easily obtain the resources or skills to organize against colonial rule. These policies also facilitated the circulation of goods within the British Empire as Asian traders imported British iron and cotton from India to sell in Uganda and Kenya, and exported domestic African cash crops to the metropole.[26] The daily African–Asian, buyer–seller interactions reinforced colonial hierarchies, deepening resentment and frustration. The Asians near monopoly on medium-sized commerce and industry constrained the entrepreneurial aspirations of the African population.[27]

Inequality during the colonial period was stark, marked by vast disparities in wealth and income between Europeans and Asians and between Asians and Africans. In Kenya, the colonial government paid Asian workers an average of 400 shillings per month, compared to 56 shillings per month for Africans. Although Asians typically held more skilled positions, income disparities also existed at the same level.[28] The private sector was no exception, with 18 percent of Asians earning more than £750 per year, compared to 1 percent of Africans earning £600 per year.[29] Inequalities in education existed as well. By the early 1960s, 59 percent of Asians had received at least nine years of schooling compared to 4 percent of Africans.[30] Low levels of education, in turn, reduced employment opportunities, with 23 percent of Asian adult males holding technical positions compared to only 1 percent of African males.[31]

In 1959, in response to Uganda's unequal trading relations, Baganda businessman Augustine Kamya organized a boycott of non-African traders.[32] Though the boycott was directed at all non-African shops, Asians were the

[23] Herzig, 2006, p. 18.
[24] O'Brien, 1972, p. 9; Sharma & Woolridge, 1974, p. 397.
[25] Mattausch, 1998, p. 130; O'Brien, 1972, p. 13.
[26] Mamdani, 1975, pp. 31–32.
[27] Mattausch, 1998, pp. 131–132.
[28] Aiyar, 2015, p. 231.
[29] Aiyar, 2015, p. 267.
[30] Aiyar, 2015, p. 266.
[31] Aiyar, 2015, p. 266.
[32] Ghai, 1970, pp. 755–759.

primary target. Their shops were burned, rudimentary bombs were thrown into stores and public areas, thousands of coffee farms were laid waste, and dozens were assaulted.[33] Africans who violated the boycott faced violence and intimidation.[34] While the boycott was regionally confined to Uganda's historically powerful Buganda kingdom, it revealed the extent of intergroup tensions in the country—tensions that, though provincially concentrated, were a harbinger of things to come.

5.2 Structural Factors: Decolonization

The external shock to the status quo in the case of Uganda and Kenya was their independence from British rule. As the two countries gained their freedom, Africans harbored deep skepticism about the South Asian community's commitment to the new order and were resentful of their presence. Asians were accused of bribery, evading taxes, inflating prices, falsifying accounts, suppressing African commerce, and remitting all their savings to India.[35] Dishonest business practices took on a racial dimension because of the high concentration of Asians in trade. Many Africans saw Asians as the immediate obstacle to their participation and success in commerce. They hoped the structural privileges previously enjoyed by Europeans and Asians would be abolished in the postcolonial period in favor of the native population. The dissolution of the UK's East African territories left those expectations wanting.

During the postcolonial transition, a key political issue was the question of citizenship. The Ugandan and Kenyan governments wanted automatic citizenship for indigenous Africans and contingent citizenship for non-Africans (including Asians). In contrast, Britain wanted the countries to provide automatic citizenship to Africans *and* Asians, to avoid the possibility of resettling tens of thousands of their former South Asian subjects in the UK. The political compromises on this question had critical implications for the fate of the South Asian communities.

After obtaining its independence in October 1962, Uganda's new constitution stated that all persons born in Uganda, with at least one parent who was

[33] Ghai, 1970, pp. 757–758.
[34] Ghai, 1970, p. 756.
[35] O'Brien, 1973, pp. 92–93; Seidenberg, 1996, pp. 187–188; Tangri, 1966, p. 121.

also born in Uganda, would automatically become Ugandan citizens.[36] All others had a two-year period to apply for citizenship.[37] The new provision had varied effects on South Asians in Uganda, who possessed a range of legal statuses. The majority were Citizens of the UK and Colonies (CUKCs)[38]—those born in British India (i.e., pre-1947 India/Pakistan) or whose parents were born in British India. Some were British protected persons (BPPs), typically those born to parents from the Indian Princely States.[39] Others held Indian or Pakistani citizenship. Consequently, at independence, most Asians had two choices: retain their foreign citizenship (or foreign nationality in the case of BPPs) or naturalize and adopt Ugandan citizenship. The majority chose to retain their existing citizenship, particularly the CUKCs, lacking confidence in the new Ugandan government.[40] Even among those who obtained Ugandan citizenship, most had at least one family member with an alternative passport as an insurance policy.[41]

For Asians who chose to adopt Ugandan citizenship, the Uganda Citizenship Ordinance stated that after registering as a Ugandan citizen, one had to renounce any other nationality and take an oath of allegiance within three months of approved registration.[42] Uganda did not permit dual nationality; therefore without this renunciation, one's Ugandan citizenship was invalid. Ignorant of this clause, or not realizing its importance, some Asians did not submit evidence of their renunciation or the British government did not process their renunciation on time.[43] This was acutely problematic for BPPs who lost their BPP status on the acquisition of Ugandan citizenship,[44] and thus were particularly vulnerable after the 1972 expulsion

[36] Memorandum, Ugandan Asians—Statelessness, 22.09.1972; 11/2/10-100.UGA.ASI[b]—Refugees from Asia in Uganda [Volume 2-1.UGA.ASI]; Series 2, Box 204; Fonds 11; UNHCR.

[37] Sharma & Woolridge, 1974, p. 398.

[38] CUKC was a legal status created in 1948 under the British Nationality Act for British subjects of New Commonwealth countries (e.g., India, Pakistan) (Cosemans, 2021, p. 6; Uche, 2017, p. 824).

[39] BPP was a legal status given to people born in colonies that Britain indirectly administered (e.g., the Indian Princely States, semiautonomous monarchies in India during British rule, as well as Zanzibar and Tanganyika). BPPs were not eligible for CUKC status in 1948 and thus were British nationals without citizenship (Cosemans, 2018, pp. 103–104, 2021, pp. 5–7; Sharma & Woolridge, 1974, p. 398).

[40] Amor, 2003.

[41] Cosemans, 2021, pp. 8–9; Jørgensen, 1981, pp. 246–247; Sharma & Woolridge, 1974, p. 399.

[42] Sharma & Woolridge, 1974, p. 399.

[43] O'Brien, 1972, p. 7; *Times Newspaper Limited, London*. (1972, August 16). Kampala fear that more will become stateless. In Z. Lalani (1997), *Ugandan Asian expulsion* (pp. 19–20).

[44] Under UK law, British subjects were permitted to hold dual citizenship (i.e., CUKCs), although this was prohibited under Ugandan law. Consequently, if their Ugandan citizenship was revoked or rejected—as occurred during the 1972 expulsion—they could still rely on their British citizenship. In contrast, the holders of BPP status could not.

decree.[45] Five years after independence, 10,527 Asians were still waiting for their Ugandan citizenship applications to be processed.[46]

A year after Uganda, Kenya obtained its freedom from Britain in 1963. Its citizenship scheme was similar to Uganda's, granting automatic citizenship to all those born in Kenya, including non-Africans, if at least one parent had also been born in Kenya.[47] Under this provision, 48,000 South Asians automatically qualified for Kenyan citizenship, approximately 30 percent of the total South Asian population.[48] Those who did not automatically qualify had two years to apply, but few took advantage of this opportunity.[49] As in Uganda, South Asians were uncertain about the new Kenyan government and wanted to keep their British (CUKC) or other citizenship as a backup. By the 1965 deadline, an estimated 20,000 of the 130,000 noncitizen Asians had applied for Kenyan citizenship.

South Asian uncertainty about the postcolonial African regimes was not the only reason for the low number of citizenship applications; the process was also expensive and cumbersome. Many could not afford the £200 security deposit per applicant and the required bond from a Kenyan citizen with immovable property within the country. For an average family of five or six, the cost would have been £1000–£1200, out of reach for most petty traders.[50] Additionally, many Asians did not have the necessary documentation required to apply, such as a birth certificate. Even those who did obtain citizenship were often branded by locals as "economic" or "paper" citizens.[51]

5.3 Proximate Factors: Nativist Motivations Emerge

5.3.1 Nativism in Uganda

In 1969, seven years after independence, Ugandan President Milton Obote introduced a series of Africanization initiatives designed to improve the country's economic conditions.[52] These culminated in his socialist

[45] Memorandum, Ugandan Asians—Statelessness, 22.09.1972; 11/2/10-100.UGA.ASI[b]—Refugees from Asia in Uganda [Volume 2-1.UGA.ASI]; Series 2, Box 204; Fonds 11; UNHCR.
[46] Mamdani, 1975, p. 52.
[47] Hansen, 1999, p. 825.
[48] Rothchild, 1970a, p. 28.
[49] Rothchild, 1970a, p. 11.
[50] Aiyar, 2015, p. 279.
[51] Confidential Report: The Asians in East Africa, B. Sjollema, World Council of Churches, 30.04.1969; 11/1-1/0/KEN/ASI, Refugees situation—Refugees from Asia in Kenya; Series 1, Box 26; Fonds 11; UNHCR.
[52] Uche, 2017, p. 828.

"Move to the Left" policies, which included plans to nationalize large sectors of the economy in a 60:40 division between state and private ownership.[53] Obote advocated for Africanization, and partial nationalization, but he did not initially expel noncitizens as other newly independent African countries were doing at the time (e.g., Gabon, 1962; Republic of Congo, 1962; Côte d'Ivoire, 1964; Sierra Leone, 1968, Ghana, 1969). Through these maneuvers, Obote stifled the emergence of an African merchant class, allowing Asians and Europeans to continue to dominate the commercial and industrial sectors, respectively, while tightening state control.[54] In preserving the South Asians as a buffer class, Obote was able to exclude his main ethnic rival, the Baganda,[55] from obtaining economic dominance. However, the status of the Asians was not secure.

In the summer of 1970, the first population Uganda targeted for expulsion was not South Asians, but fellow Africans. On July 10, the Ugandan minister of labor announced the wage-earning sector was comprised of too many non-Ugandans[56] and that their positions needed to be "Ugandanized" within two months.[57] Approximately 20,000–30,000 Kenyan Luos were subsequently expelled across the border to Kenya.[58] President Obote initially distanced himself from the expulsion, but when outrage rose in Kenya over Uganda's actions, he defended the decision and stated he did not want unemployed Kenyan workers to be exported to Uganda because of Kenyan President Jomo Kenyatta's failed capitalist policies.[59] The Luo expulsion was news for a day but then largely forgotten.

The following year, on January 25, 1971, while Obote attended a Commonwealth Conference in Singapore, the Ugandan Armed Forces overthrew his government in a military coup.[60] That evening, a radio broadcast announced that the authority previously vested in the president would

[53] O'Brien, 1972, p. 11; Republic of Uganda, 1970, pp. 41–43.

[54] Jørgensen, 1981, pp. 246–248; Kasozi, 1994, p. 92.

[55] The first president of Uganda was the *Kabaka*, or king, of Buganda province. In 1966, Prime Minister Obote ordered the military, headed by Colonel Idi Amin, to take over the presidential palace and remove the Kabaka, who fled to Britain while many of his supporters in Uganda were killed. Obote then declared himself president of Uganda (Amor, 2003, p. 57; Kasozi, 1994, pp. 82–87; Leopold, 2020, pp. 141–142).

[56] The Uganda Ministry of Labor estimated 285,000 persons were employed in the wage-earning sector, of whom 80,000 (approximately 28 percent) were non-Ugandan (Mazrui, 1979, p. 262).

[57] Mazrui, 1979, p. 262.

[58] Kasozi, 1994, p. 120; Leopold, 2020, p. 166; Mazrui, 1979, p. 262.

[59] Mazrui, 1979, p. 272.

[60] Kasozi, 1994, p. 103; Keesing's Contemporary Archives, 1971–1972, pp. 24450–24451; Leopold, 2020, pp. 178–189.

now reside with Major General Idi Amin.[61] Amin dissolved parliament and declared that the new government would legislate by decree, with advice from the cabinet.[62] Despite seizing power undemocratically, Amin was heralded by many inside and outside Uganda. Local African and Asian traders, along with foreign governments—Britain, Israel, Ethiopia, and South Africa—hoped Amin would steer the state toward capitalism and rescind Obote's socialist policies.[63] Neighboring African countries were not as sanguine. Neither Kenya nor Tanzania recognized Amin's government.[64] Tanzanian President Julius Nyerere offered refuge to Obote and his political allies, and Zambian President Kenneth Kaunda discouraged Western leaders from recognizing Amin's new government.[65]

In the aftermath of the coup, the South Asian community was enthusiastic about Amin's takeover. They were hopeful he would pursue trade liberalization and continue to renew their trade licenses.[66] That optimism was short-lived. In October 1971, Amin called for a census of all Asians, which Obote had announced the year before.[67] Asians were required to participate in the census or forfeit any claims to live in Uganda. During the process, many had their Ugandan passports confiscated.[68] After the census, Asians were obligated to carry green passes to indicate that they had been counted, without which their movement was restricted.[69] Although results of the census were not made public until after the expulsion the following year, many suspected Amin was not happy with the results, which indicated 23,242 Asians held Ugandan citizenship.[70]

Shortly after the census, in response to public statements and letters complaining about the Asian population, Amin convened an "Indian Conference" for December 7–8, 1971.[71] South Asians from across the country traveled to the capital, Kampala, to attend. Amin opened his address by situating the conference in the context of a series of meetings the government was conducting with "different groups of persons," such as the Muslim

[61] Keesing's Contemporary Archives, 1971–1972, p. 24450; Leopold, 2020, p. 182.
[62] Keesing's Contemporary Archives, 1971–1972, p. 24451.
[63] Jørgensen, 1981, pp. 271–272; Leopold, 2020, p. 202.
[64] Country Status Report on Uganda, 15.03.1971; 11/2/10-100.GEN.UGA, Refugees from Uganda—General; Series 2, Box 34; Fonds 11; UNHCR.
[65] Keesing's Contemporary Archives, 1971–1972, p. 24450; Mutibwa, 1992, p. 87.
[66] Gitelson, 1977, p. 364; Jørgensen, 1981, p. 271; Leopold, 2020, p. 199; O'Brien, 1972, p. 12.
[67] Leopold, 2020, pp. 228–229; O'Brien, 1972, pp. 12–13.
[68] Sharma & Woolridge, 1974, p. 400.
[69] Tandon, 1972, p. 5.
[70] O'Brien, 1973, p. 93; Tandon, 1972, p. 5.
[71] O'Brien, 1972; Patel, 1972, p. 13.

Leaders Conference and the Church of Uganda Leaders Conference.[72] Amin stated, "My aim is to ensure that, like a father in a family, understanding and unity between the different communities in this country are established on a permanent basis."[73] His speech began with praise for the South Asian community's contributions to commerce and trade, job creation, education, healthcare, and various government sectors. However, after a few pleasantries, the speech took a negative turn. Amin criticized the Asians for their disloyalty, refusal to integrate, commercial malpractice, and citizenship choices.[74] He further announced the cancellation of 12,000 pending Asian[75] citizenship applications.[76] While the conference concluded without any specific policy changes, it foreshadowed events to come.

5.3.2 Nativism in Kenya

In the aftermath of colonial rule, the Kenyan government pursued several Africanization measures to assert native control of the economy. It began with land redistribution. The indigenous African population was largely agricultural, and access to land had been a key demand of the anti-colonial Mau Mau rebellion.[77] Asians could not own land under the colonial administration, so they were unaffected by these initial actions. After land redistribution, attention shifted to the civil service as the next priority area. Table 5.3 shows the demographic composition of the Kenyan Civil Service in 1962, shortly before independence. Europeans dominated the senior functions, with Asians and Africans concentrated in lower-tiered positions. Asians comprised an estimated 29 percent of the civil service workforce despite making up less than 2 percent of the total population. The Kenyan African Civil Servants Union demanded the removal of all non-Africans from the civil service.[78] By 1965, most of the

[72] O'Brien, 1972, p. 25.
[73] O'Brien, 1972, p. 25.
[74] O'Brien, 1972, pp. 25–31.
[75] Keesing's Contemporary Archives, 1971–1972, p. 25023; O'Brien, 1972, p. 17; Tandon & Raphael, 1978, p. 10.
[76] Ironically these were the Asians who were trying to become "loyal" Ugandan citizens, undermining Amin's critique.
[77] Cable, 1969, p. 231.
[78] Himbara, 1994, p. 115.

Table 5.3 Demographics of the Kenyan Civil Service (1962)[a]

Position	*European*	*African*	*Asian*	*Total*
Upper administration	71	18	—	89
Provincial administration	193	181	—	374
Professional and senior technical staff	2,820	180	—	3,000
Clerical	—	2,600	2,100	4,700
Secretarial	—	1	417	418
Total	3,084	2,980	2,517	8,581

[a]Adapted from data in Himbara, 1994, p. 115.

administrative positions were filled by Africans, and by mid-1967, 91 percent of the civil service was Africanized.[79]

This phase of Kenya's Africanization also included a significant expansion of the public service.[80] Between 1963 and 1969, the total number of public service employees increased from approximately 160,000 to over 237,000.[81] Many Africans coveted these positions because they were well compensated, offered excellent benefits, and provided job security.[82] The Africanization of the public service, including the civil service, resulted in the first wave of South Asian emigration. Between 1963 and 1969, an estimated 4,500 Asians lost their jobs affecting 22,500–27,000[83] persons, with others departing in anticipation of future Africanization measures.[84]

When it came to the private sector, President Kenyatta's Africanization efforts relied more on rhetoric than policy change. Kenyatta and his cabinet showed no interest in nationalizing industry or creating a state-dominated economy as Obote had tried in Uganda. Kenya's minister of economic planning and development, Tom Mboya, developed *Sessional Paper No. 10, African Socialism* to articulate the government's economic vision. The policy paper's stated goals were rapid economic growth, a commitment to

[79] Himbara, 1994, p. 116; Maxon, 1995, p. 113.

[80] The public service consisted of government positions that provided services of general interest such as courts, schools, electricity, railways, telecommunications, the military, the police, and healthcare. It included the civil service, although the civil service was a distinct component.

[81] Vinnai, 1974, p. 182.

[82] Mueller, 1984, p. 418.

[83] These calculations are based on an estimated average household size of five to six persons (Confidential Report: The Asians in East Africa, B. Sjollema, World Council of Churches, 30.04.1969; 11/1-1/0/KEN/ASI, Refugees situation—Refugees from Asia in Kenya; Series 1, Box 26; Fonds 11; UNHCR).

[84] Ghai & Ghai, 1971, p. 19; Vinnai, 1974, p. 183.

nonalignment, Africanization of the economy and public service, and building the Kenyan nation.[85] Section 53 of *Sessional Paper No. 10* summarized these aims:

> The most important of these policies is to provide a firm basis for rapid economic growth. *Other immediate problems such as Africanization of the economy*, education, unemployment, welfare services, and provincial policies *must be handled in ways that will not jeopardize growth*. The only permanent solution to all of these problems rests on rapid growth. . . . Growth, then, is the first concern of planning in Kenya" [emphasis added].

In May 1965, parliament unanimously voted to approve *Sessional Paper 10* as the blueprint for Kenyan development.[86]

However, five years after independence, many Kenyans were frustrated that they had not seen the economic fruits of postcolonial governance. Although the government had announced some restrictions on certain kinds of trade and business, South Asians continued to dominate commerce and petty trade. Adding pressure was Kenya's rapid population growth, which created chronic unemployment. Approximately 80,000 students entered the job market annually, with only a fraction absorbed into the formal labor market.[87]

In the absence of structural changes to the Kenyan economy, anti-Asian sentiment rose and continued to grow among officials within the ruling Kenya African National Union (KANU) Party and the public. Paul Ngei, a member of parliament, articulated these frustrations, stating that "the Indian monopoly on trade was compromising Kenya's independence," while other MPs referred to Asians as "blood suckers" and "devils."[88] The Kenyan government-run Voice of Kenya radio station broadcast, "Indians [are] a hangover from the colonial past . . . [they are] onerous to the nation. . . . The 'lip service' they had paid to integration . . . [was] evidence of their continuing 'racist' and 'exploitative' colonial attitudes."[89] Even Mboya described the Asians as "neocolonialist" who were impeding Kenya's "national integration and economic growth."[90] Kenyatta himself announced that "*uhuru*

[85] Republic of Kenya, 1965.
[86] Maloba, 2017, p. 86.
[87] Cable, 1969, p. 227.
[88] Aiyar, 2015, p. 270.
[89] Aiyar, 2015, pp. 269–270.
[90] Aiyar, 2015, p. 267.

would be complete only when economic power, not just political power, was in African hands," calling on Asians "who were unwilling to work with Africans to 'pack their bags and go.'"[91] Nativist sentiment was strong in both Uganda and Kenya, with considerable popular and elite pressure to push the Asians out.

5.4 Preconditions for the South Asian Expulsion

The newly independent Ugandan and Kenyan regimes were both autocracies.[92] Although regime type is distinct from the precondition that governing elites hold exclusionary ideologies, officials within authoritarian governments are far more likely to espouse such views. In the case of Uganda, the exclusionary ideology held by the Obote and Amin regimes was evident. Both viewed their ethnic group as superior and tried to eliminate and suppress their ethnic rivals. In the case of Obote, the key outgroup was the Baganda; for Amin, it was the Langi and Acholi.[93] Kenyatta, by contrast, seemed to promote an inclusive ideology. When he assumed the presidency in 1964, he urged his fellow countrymen to start anew and "erase all the hatreds and the difficulties . . . which now belong to history."[94] He called on Kenyans to unite under the slogan "*harambee*," Swahili for "all pull together," and put aside differences to focus on the common goal of nation-building. Yet his rhetoric belied his actions in which he maintained full control of the state to the benefit of his ethnic kin, the Kikuyu.[95] When it came to their South Asian populations, the Ugandan and Kenyan governments both viewed them as inferior to and outside of the Black African majority. In short, the ruling elites in both Uganda and Kenya held exclusionary ideologies, satisfying a key precondition for expulsion.

[91] Aiyar, 2015, p. 270.

[92] The Polity V Project assigned both governments a polity score of −7, and the Varieties of Democracy (V-Dem) electoral democracy index ranked them both in the lowest quartile: 0.085 (Uganda, 1972) and 0.217 (Kenya, 1967-69 average). A Polity V score of −10 is the most autocratic and +10 the most democratic. The V-Dem electoral democracy index scores countries on a continuum from 0.0, indicating no attainment of the relevant attributes, to 1.0, indicating the full realization of electoral democracy. Since the Kenya case looks at events from 1967 to 1969, the Polity V scores during this time were −1 (1967), −1 (1968), and −7 (1969). While in 1967 and 1968 Polity V codes the country as an "anocracy," the −7 score ("autocracy") in 1969 shows that President Kenyatta's policies became increasingly authoritarian during the period examined (Coppedge et al., 2020; Marshall, 2021).

[93] Avirgan & Honey, 1982, p. 7; Jørgensen, 1981, pp. 229–231; Kasfir, 1976, pp. 200–201, 212–213, 219–220; Kasozi, 1994, p. 111.

[94] Aiyar, 2015, p. 263.

[95] Aiyar, 2015, p. 263.

Because the Ugandan and Kenyan governments sought to restore indigenous control over the economy—and were motivated by economic and not security concerns—there were no fears that the Asian target group would remain a threat to the state after their removal. The threat the South Asians posed to indigenous economic control would have been eliminated via expulsion, satisfying another precondition. There was also an alternative "homeland" where both governments could send the expelled Asians, and where they believed they rightfully "belonged." The Ugandan and Kenyan governments viewed the UK, as the metropole of the British Raj, along with the nation-states that emerged from the Indian subcontinent (i.e., India, Pakistan, Bangladesh), as the Asians' "home." Governing authorities maintained the Asians should return to their "place of origin." Finally, both Uganda and Kenya had large military and police forces with the ability to physically remove the South Asian populations from their territories. All four preconditions for expulsion were met in both cases.

Some may suggest that the individual characteristics of the leaders—Amin and Kenyatta—may be driving the variation between these two cases. Amin was a brutal dictator, and some contend that he expelled the Asians from Uganda simply because he was a vicious, unpredictable tyrant who lashed out as part of his violent rule. Proponents of this theory often highlight Amin's mental state, pointing to his announcement that the Asian expulsion was inspired by a dream.[96] None would disagree that Amin was a personalist autocrat who repressed many populations within Uganda: African and non-African, citizen and noncitizen. Nonetheless, there are reasons to be skeptical of this simplistic rationale.

While autocracies are more likely to expel populations than democracies, brutal dictatorships are neither a necessary nor sufficient condition for mass expulsion. During this period, there were other brutal leaders on the African continent, such as President Francisco Macías Nguema of Equatorial Guinea, known as the "Hitler of Africa," who did not implement expulsion policies. President Kenyatta of Kenya did not eliminate his ethnic rivals like Amin did, but by the late 1960s, he wielded dictatorial powers. These included discretion over detention without trial, emergency powers, censorship, control of the press, and the denial of opposition party organization.[97]

[96] Melady & Melady, 1976, p. 8.

[97] Gertzel, 1970, pp. 147, 152; Ghai, 1967, p. 12; Keesing's Contemporary Archives, 1965–1966, pp. 21525, 21718; Mueller, 1984, p. 408.

This culminated in banning the opposition Kenya People's Union (KPU) Party in October 1969 and imprisoning its leaders.[98] Political assassinations of high-level officials, such as Pio Pinto, a Kenyan Asian and KANU left-wing supporter, were blamed on Kenyatta, although never proven.[99] This is not to equate the brutality of the Kenyatta and Amin regimes, but to highlight that the years of the Kenyatta regime examined here were also authoritarian and similarly served to benefit his ethnic kin to the exclusion of others.

It is also important to note that the early years of Amin's regime were less brutal than his rule in the mid-to-late 1970s. It is these later years that often bias the retrospective view of Amin. In the lead up to the expulsion, Amin had the backing of Western powers, including Britain and the United States, who were actively courting him as a viable partner. Estimates of the total persons killed in Uganda in the early 1970s vary dramatically. Most of the figures available are aggregated over Amin's eight-year rule,[100] with approximations of those killed in 1971 in the thousands.[101] These arguments in no way attempt to diminish the atrocities committed by Amin. It is simply to suggest that the brutality Amin is infamous for was not as extreme in 1972 and is not sufficient to explain the divergent outcomes in Uganda and Kenya.

5.5 Uganda's Mass Expulsion of South Asians (August–November 1972)

The South Asian community, foreign governments, and international organizations (IOs) were all surprised by President Amin's August 4, 1972, expulsion announcement. Given his history of erratic behavior, many were not convinced that he would follow through with the expulsion.[102] It was also unclear from Amin's initial pronouncement whether the Asians to be expelled referred to all the Asians in the country or only to those

[98] Mueller, 1984, p. 415; Ochieng, 1995, p. 100.

[99] Cullen, 2017b, p. 793.

[100] Jørgensen, 1981, pp. 314–315; Kasozi, 1994, p. 104; Leopold, 2020, pp. 239, 250–253; Posner, 1974, p. 61.

[101] Posner, 1974, p. 33.

[102] ACICR B AG 252 152-001; Confidential Report on the Current Situation in Uganda, 05.10.1972.

with British passports, who were accused of "sabotaging the economy and encouraging corruption."[103] The release of Official Decree 17 clarified and formalized what Amin had first announced to his troops in Tororo:

> On and after the commencement of this Decree, every entry permit or certificate of residence issued or granted under the provisions of the Immigration Act, 1969, to any person who is of Asian origin, extraction or descent and who is a subject or citizen of any of the countries specified in the Schedule to this Decree shall cease to have any validity whatsoever.[104]

The schedule of countries in the decree included the United Kingdom of Great Britain and Northern Ireland, the Republic of India, the Republic of Pakistan, and the Republic of Bangladesh. This extended the expulsion to South Asians holding citizenship of states formed from British India[105] as well as to those with UK passports.

Nevertheless, the South Asian community and the British government took limited action for nearly six weeks, hoping that Amin would change his mind.[106] He did not. Amin continued to ratchet up his rhetoric: "I must emphasize that after the 90-day period has expired, any of these people still in Uganda will face the consequences. They will be sitting on a fire and they will not sit comfortably."[107] It was not until mid-September, over a month after the initial announcement, that evacuations began in earnest.[108] Before departure, Asians were required to declare all their assets and liabilities to the Register of Properties and Businesses[109] and complete income tax and foreign exchange clearances at the Bank of Uganda.[110] They were only allowed

[103] Patel, 1972, p. 17.

[104] Confidential Memorandum from the Representative, UNHCR Branch Office for Uganda—photostat copies of Decree No. 17 and Statutory Instrument No. 124/72, 14 September 1972; 11/2/64-641.UGA[a] Expulsion and Deportation—Uganda [1972] Volume 1; Series 2, Box 1281; Fonds 11; UNHCR.

[105] India, Pakistan, and Bangladesh were all independent countries in 1972, although they were all former British colonies.

[106] Tandon & Raphael, 1978, p. 13.

[107] Harper, Stephen. (1972, August 10). Cold-comfort curry: Amin asks Asians to lunch, then issues new threat. *Daily Express London*. In Z. Lalani (1997), *Ugandan Asian expulsion* (pp. 9–10).

[108] O'Brien, 1973, p. 96.

[109] Confidential Memorandum Regarding the Legal and Policy Aspects of Compensation Claims, 17.04.1974; 11/2/66-660.1[a], Compensation Claims of Ugandan Asians in any Country [Volume 1]; Series 2, Box 1293; Fonds 11; UNHCR.

[110] ACICR B AG 232 152-002.04; United Nations Centre IPS Building Kampala: Important Notice, 30.10.1972.

to take £50 per person[111] and a maximum of 485 pounds of personal effects out of the country.[112]

Although the official expulsion decree targeted South Asian noncitizens, Amin announced in a presidential statement on the same day that the government would "double check" the citizenship of Asians who were registered as Ugandan citizens in the 1971 census.[113] On August 14, a spokesman for the Ministry of Internal Affairs instructed Asian citizens to report to the Immigration Office in Kampala by September 10 to verify their documents; otherwise, they would be considered noncitizens.[114] He emphasized that all documentation must be original—no duplicates, photocopies, or carbon copies would be accepted.[115] The stated purpose of the verification campaign was to eliminate "false citizens" who illegally obtained citizenship or who held dual citizenship, which was illegal under Ugandan law. After the exercise began, Amin stated, "If all of them go I'll be very, very happy."[116]

Correspondence between UN officials indicated concern that the citizenship verification exercise was a façade: "We suspect that the scrutiny of citizenship will be used as a means of rejecting the bulk of the Asian community holding Ugandan citizenship. The [Asian] community leaders fully share our views."[117] Through the verification process, many of the 23,000 Asians claiming Ugandan citizenship had their legitimate claims rejected. There were four main modes of rejection: lack of renunciation of secondary citizenship or delayed renunciation;[118] photocopies or carbon copies of documents; omission of Ugandan Central Registry page numbers on birth certificates; and the destruction or confiscation of documents

[111] ACICR B AG 252 152-001; Confidential Report on the Current Situation in Uganda, 05.10.1972.

[112] Munnion, Christopher. (1972, September 1). Asians searched to skin by Uganda customs. In Z. Lalani (1997), *Ugandan Asian expulsion* (p. 43).

[113] *Daily Telegraph* newspaper article, "Expulsion decree by Amin after 'divine message,'" 10.08.1972; 11/2/10-100.UGA.ASI[a], Refugees from Asia in Uganda [Volume1-1.UGA.ASI]; Series 2, Box 204; Fonds 11; UNHCR.

[114] Document from UNHCR/Kampala: Uganda Asians, 09.10.1973; 11/2/60-600.UGA[a]; Series 2, Box 1012; Fonds 11; UNHCR.

[115] *Uganda Argus*. (1972, August 15). These Asians are required to report. In Z. Lalani (1997), *Ugandan Asian expulsion* (pp. 15, 18).

[116] *Times Newspaper Limited, London*. (1972, August 16). Kampala fear that more will become stateless. In Z. Lalani (1997), *Ugandan Asian expulsion* (pp. 19–20).

[117] Confidential Cable from UNHCR Branch Office Kampala, 24.08.1972; 11/2/64-641.UGA[a] Expulsion and Deportation—Uganda [1972] Volume 1; Series 2, Box 1281; Fonds 11; UNHCR.

[118] Many Asians whose citizenship was invalidated on this criterion blamed the British Home Office, which took several months (more than the ninety days allowed) to process the renunciation papers. Most were unaware that their renunciation had not gone through.

by officials—an allegation Amin vehemently denied.[119] Verified Asian citizens were required to purchase special identification cards to facilitate their continued stay and movements.[120]

More confusion ensued on August 16 when Amin rescinded Statutory Instrument No. 124—an addendum to the initial expulsion decree that had exempted Asian civil servants and professionals from expulsion.[121] This was significant. Asian sources estimated that 10,000 people qualified to stay under this provision, accounting for roughly 13.5 percent of the total Asian population.[122] Amin explained the change stating, "They [the Asians] could not serve their country with a good spirit after the departure of the other Asians."[123] All Asian government workers and professionals were now to be expelled. Adding to the chaos, three days later at a mass rally in Rukungiri in southwestern Uganda, Amin stated that Ugandan Asian citizens would also have to leave.[124] He additionally ordered all refugees residing in Uganda to return home, including an estimated 100,000 refugees from Rwanda, 80,000 from southern Sudan, 30,000 from Zaire, and others from Burundi.[125]

Student leaders from Makerere University protested Amin's decision to expel South Asian citizens of Uganda.[126] They were joined by some members of the cabinet and regional African leaders.[127] Amin shifted course again, returning to his previous position that Asian citizens would not be expelled

[119] *Times Newspaper Limited, London.* (1972, August 16). Kampala fear that more will become stateless. In Z. Lalani (1997), *Ugandan Asian expulsion* (pp. 19–20).

[120] Pamphlet on "Uganda's Economic War" from the High Commission for the Republic of Uganda in New Delhi, 17.11.1972; 11/2/64-641.UGA[c] Expulsion and Deportation—Uganda [1972–1984] Volume 3; Series 2, Box 1281; Fonds 11; UNHCR.

[121] Confidential Memorandum from the Representative, UNHCR Branch Office for Uganda—photostat copies of Decree No. 17 and Statutory Instrument No. 124/72, 14.09.1972; 11/2/64-641.UGA[a] Expulsion and Deportation—Uganda [1972] Volume 1; Series 2, Box 1281; Fonds 11; UNHCR.

[122] *Daily Telegraph* newspaper article, "Expulsion decree by Amin after 'divine message'"; 10.08.1972; 11/2/10-100.UGA.ASI[a], Refugees from Asia in Uganda [Volume1-1.UGA.ASI]; Series 2, Box 204; Fonds 11; UNHCR.

[123] News compilation. (1972, August 19). Asians queue to beat citizenship deadline. In Z. Lalani (1997), *Ugandan Asian expulsion* (p. 21).

[124] *East Africa Standard.* (1972, August 20). Now all Ugandan Asians are ordered out. In Z. Lalani (1997), *Ugandan Asian expulsion* (pp. 25–26).

[125] Coded cable from UNHCR High Commissioner to Secretary General OAU, 20.08.1972; 13/1/3-129; Series 3, Box 31; Fonds 13, Sub-Fonds 1; UNHCR; *East Africa Standard.* (1972, August 20). Now all Ugandan Asians are ordered out. In Z. Lalani (1997), *Ugandan Asian expulsion* (pp. 25–26).

[126] Memorandum from Frank A. Bauman, Representative UNHCR Branch Office for Australia and New Zealand to UNHCR/HQ Geneva—Newspaper Clippings, "Asian Airlift to Britain Soon," 25.08.1972; 11/2/64-641.UGA[a] Expulsion and Deportation—Uganda [1972] Volume 1; Series 2, Box 1281; Fonds 11; UNHCR.

[127] Jørgensen, 1981, p. 287.

if they could prove their citizenship status; he also said the refugees could stay, but should return home as soon as possible.[128] Not fully acceding to the student demands, Amin noted a "second phase operation" would look at the remaining Asian citizens.[129] Much of the confusion during this period stemmed from the fact that Amin's personal declarations often contradicted or preempted official policy decisions. This left Asians and government officials guessing which declarations would become official decrees and which were simply musings from the president.

Taking advantage of the chaos, on September 17, 1972, former President Obote's supporters invaded Uganda from Tanzania.[130] Local newspapers reported that Tanzanian troops captured three towns and advanced within 100 miles of Kampala. Tanzania distanced itself from the fighting, claiming the conflict was between Amin's troops and dissidents from the Uganda "People's Army" (i.e., Obote's troops backed by Tanzania).[131] The government of Uganda accused Britain of supporting the invasion, but Amin successfully repelled the attack.

Having suppressed this attempted external invasion, Amin further expanded the scope of the expulsion decree in October, announcing that South Asians with Kenyan, Tanzanian, and Zambian citizenship would also be expelled because of the "continued sabotage by the Asians" and allegations that Asian citizens of neighboring countries were helping Ugandan Asians smuggle property out of the country.[132] With less than a month remaining, it was clear that all South Asians in the country would be expelled. As the November deadline approached, most Asians departed Uganda on commercial flights or with support from IOs.

Another surprise came on November 2, 1972. Amin announced that any Asian citizens remaining in Uganda after the expulsion deadline would have to leave the towns and move to the rural villages.[133] Amin directed the minister of public service and local administrations and the minister of internal

[128] *East African Standard*. (1972, August 23). Gen. Amin relents on expulsion of citizens. In Z. Lalani (1997), *Ugandan Asian expulsion* (p. 29).

[129] Memorandum from Frank A. Bauman, Representative UNHCR Branch Office for Australia and New Zealand to UNHCR/HQ Geneva—Newspaper Clippings, "Asian Airlift to Britain Soon," 25.08.1972; 11/2/64-641.UGA[a] Expulsion and Deportation—Uganda [1972] Volume 1; Series 2, Box 1281; Fonds 11; UNHCR.

[130] Uche, 2017, p. 832.

[131] News Compilation. (1972, September 18). Uganda claims "invasion by Tanzania." In Z. Lalani (1997), *Ugandan Asian expulsion* (p. 63).

[132] Keesing's Contemporary Archives, 1971–1972, p. 25599.

[133] Confidential Cable from Kampala, 02.11.1972; 11/2/64-641.UGA[c] Expulsion and Deportation—Uganda [1972] Volume 2; Series 2, Box 1281; Fonds 11; UNHCR.

affairs to count all Asians remaining in Uganda beginning on November 9.[134] Amin believed this forced resettlement to rural areas would facilitate Asians mixing with Africans and allow the commercial sector to be taken over by indigenous African Ugandans. UN officials in Kampala expressed skepticism about Amin's order: "It is reasonable to believe that President Amin is whipping up fear among the remaining Ugandan Asians to force them to leave the country and claim later that Ugandan Asians left on their own. It is unlikely, for the time being, that he will implement his threats."[135] His threats were effective because many of the remaining Asian citizens did leave after this announcement for fear of being forced to move to the countryside. In the final twenty-four hours before the expulsion deadline, 2,000 stateless Asians departed on a dozen flights, the highest number in a single day since the beginning of the Asian airlift; another 800 departed the day after, on Friday, November 10.[136] After the expiration of the ninety-day timeline, an estimated 1,500 Asian citizens remained in Uganda. They were counted and had their citizenship verified again at special registration centers.[137]

Despite Amin's assurances that the expelled Asians would be fully compensated, they were not. Over the weekend of December 16, a Ugandan government spokesman announced that properties left behind, as well as other assets, would be taken over by the government without compensation.[138] The Asian middle class was replaced by an aspirant Nubian, Muslim, West Nilotic middle class, one ethnic monopoly for another.[139] The unequal asset redistribution left the poorest income groups in Uganda—peasants, pastoralists, and urban workers—in the same difficult economic state as before. Africans who had supported Amin's expulsion soon complained that the newly enriched African traders were worse than the South Asians, calling them "Black Asians" or "Black Patels."[140]

[134] *Uganda Argus.* (1972, November 7). Asians to be counted—person by person. In Z. Lalani (1997), *Ugandan Asian expulsion* (p. 125).

[135] Confidential Memorandum Between Mr. A. Komorsky and Mr. R. Mkanda, 14.12.1972; 11/2/10-100.UGA.ASI[d]—Refugees from Asia in Uganda [Volume 4-1.UGA.ASI]; Series 2, Box 205; Fonds 11; UNHCR.

[136] Kaipe, Michael. (1972, November 9). Only 800 stateless Asians left as Amin deadline expires. *Times Newspaper Limited, London.* In Z. Lalani (1997), *Ugandan Asian expulsion* (pp. 127–128).

[137] Hoagland, Jim. (1972, November 13). Kampala exodus: Asian quarter like a ghost town. *Washington Post.* In Z. Lalani (1997), *Ugandan Asian expulsion* (pp. 138, 140).

[138] Confidential Memorandum from the Representative, UNHCR Branch Office for Kampala, 18.12.1972; 11/2/64-641.UGA[c] Expulsion and Deportation—Uganda [1972–1984] Volume 3; Series 2, Box 1281; Fonds 11; UNHCR.

[139] Mutibwa, 1992, pp. 115–116.

[140] Jørgensen, 1981, p. 293.

5.6 Kenya as a Negative Case: The "Asian Exodus" (1967–1969)

From a methodological standpoint, Kenya is a "hard case" in that intuitively it should have been more likely to expel its South Asian population. Unlike Uganda, which had a peaceful transition from colonial rule, Kenya had a violent anti-colonial struggle. The British killed thousands of Kenyans in the Mau Mau rebellion, imprisoned and exiled future President Kenyatta as the alleged head of the insurgency, and incarcerated tens of thousands of Kikuyu in camps or reserves.[141] Given this experience, one might have expected the Kenyan government to retaliate against the British and the comparatively privileged colonial-era South Asian minority. But the Kenyan government did not expel its Asians, which makes this paired comparison even more puzzling.

Though the ruling KANU Party agreed on the nationalist slogan "Africa for Africans," parliamentarians disagreed about the means to achieve it. The unanimous endorsement of the government's economic vision in *Sessional Paper No. 10* belied internal discord. The policy paper was not submitted to the party for review and feedback,[142] and it was an open secret that it was penned by a single man: Minister of Economic Planning and Development Tom Mboya. Many within the party, particularly KANU's left-wing faction, disagreed with its core message. Vice President Jaramogi Oginga Odinga, leader of KANU's left wing, advocated for the removal of nonindigenous control of the economy—through industrial nationalization, state-mandated racial preferences, and the exclusion of South Asians from managerial positions.[143] Urban workers, trade unions, and students supported these policies. The trade unions were particularly frustrated with the African socialism outlined in *Sessional Paper No. 10* and spoke out in favor of "real socialism."[144]

In March 1966, internal KANU disagreements reached their apogee, and KANU's left-wing faction formally split from the party and formed the KPU, led by Vice President Odinga. The KPU advocated socialist policies, seeking economic independence for the people of Kenya.[145] In their

[141] Anderson, 2005, pp. 4–5; Elkins, 2005, pp. xiv, 358; Walton, C., 2013, p. 237.

[142] It was shared with both the cabinet and the Cabinet Development Committee, but this was a small select group (Mohiddin, 1969, p. 10).

[143] Aiyar, 2015, p. 271; Gertzel, 1970, p. 51; Gertzel et al., 1969, p. 30.

[144] Maloba, 2017, p. 90.

[145] Ochieng, 1995, p. 98.

war of words from 1966 to 1969, the KPU consistently described KANU's "African socialism" as merely a guise for tribalism and capitalism.[146] KANU's right-wing faction, supported by President Kenyatta and led by Mboya, preferred piecemeal policies rather than major structural change, advocating for Kenyanization of the economy (really partial Kenyanization) targeting select noncitizens.[147]

In the face of growing pressure, in 1967 the government passed two pieces of legislation focused on Africanization of the economy: the Immigration Bill (July) and the Trade Licensing Bill (October). The Kenyan government believed these two legislative actions would create 20,000 private sector jobs.[148] The Immigration Bill cancelled permanent residency certificates that allowed noncitizens to work in Kenya and replaced them with work permits.[149] Work permits were now required for all licensed businesses and were only issued to businesses that employed and trained Kenyan citizens.[150] Certain skilled and semiskilled workers were also affected—including bank clerks, secretaries, and carpenters—whose employers had to apply for work permits on their behalf.[151] The process was costly. Each application cost £25, required a £150 security bond, and the permits were only issued for a limited duration of three to six months.[152]

The Trade Licensing Bill, passed three months later, required all businesses to apply for new trade licenses and restricted the trade of basic goods—sugar, posho, and other staples—to Kenyan citizens.[153] It also restricted the areas of the country where South Asians could trade, designed to remove Asian traders from rural areas, although this was only an estimated 10 percent of the total population.[154] Importantly, the trade licensing legislation did not apply to manufacturing licenses, a sector dominated by Asians and a major source of revenue for Kenya.[155] These two pieces of legislation deeply affected noncitizen Asians, many of whom were permanent residents and worked in occupations restricted by the new laws.

[146] Ochieng, 1995, p. 100.
[147] Aiyar, 2015, p. 269; Branch & Cheeseman, 2006, p. 21; Gertzel, 1970, p. 54.
[148] Aiyar, 2015, p. 276.
[149] Aiyar, 2015, p. 276; Maxon, 1995, p. 114.
[150] Aiyar, 2015, p. 276.
[151] Aiyar, 2015, p. 276.
[152] Aiyar, 2015, p. 283.
[153] Himbara, 1994, pp. 59–60; Rothchild, 1970a, p. 12.
[154] Cable, 1969, p. 229.
[155] Himbara, 1994, pp. 63–65; Rothchild, 1970b, p. 750.

In reaction to Kenya's private sector Africanization efforts, the UK's opposition Conservative Party strongly lobbied the British government to restrict the entry of Asians holding British passports.[156] In 1960s Britain, racial tensions were high with the arrival of approximately 750,000 non-white Commonwealth citizens[157] between 1962 and 1968.[158] Fearing both Kenya's new legislation and the possibility of limited UK immigration access, South Asians in Kenya with British citizenship rapidly fled the country, with 13,600 arriving in the UK by the end of 1967.[159] Thus began the "Asian exodus." This was not an expulsion, but it is a useful comparison, as it could have devolved into *en masse* forced population removal.

Some argue that it was not Kenya's legislative action but rather the impulsive and imprudent British immigration policy that led to the large-scale emigration of South Asians from Kenya. UK Labour Home Secretary Roy Jenkins, a liberal in the cabinet, argued that the threat of British legislation was causing the exodus.[160] For its part, the Kenyan government denied responsibility for the surge in emigration, instead blaming the British government and its hastily enacted immigration policies for prompting Asians to depart before the Kenyan legislation came into force.[161] According to Kenya's Attorney-General Charles Njonjo:

> There was "no intention on the part of the Kenya Government to, irrationally, throw these British nationals out of the country." . . [instead] what they sought was a smooth transition to full African participation, not a hasty change-over which would have adverse effects upon the country's growth prospects or relationships to the Western capitalist market.[162]

Since a hasty removal of Asian traders would have negatively impacted Kenya's growth, it is plausible to believe Njonjo that increased out-migration was not the government's intent. The Trade Licensing Bill was passed in October 1967, but it did not come into force until January 1969, almost a year after the UK Commonwealth Immigration Act.

[156] Aiyar, 2015, p. 285.
[157] These included British citizens from new Commonwealth countries in the West Indies, India, Pakistan, and East Africa (e.g., Kenya, Uganda, Tanganyika).
[158] Memorandum from UNHCR London Representative to High Commissioner for Refugees, Geneva, 24.01.1969; 11/1-1/0/KEN/ASI, Refugees situation—Refugees from Asia in Kenya; Series 1, Box 26; Fonds 11; UNHCR.
[159] Cullen, 2017a, p. 163; Hansen, 1999, p. 818.
[160] Aiyar, 2015, p. 286.
[161] Rothchild, 1973, p. 385.
[162] Rothchild, 1973, p. 385.

By mid-1969, after the dust had settled from the "Asian exodus," the Kenyan government enforced its Trade Licensing Act and withdrew, or did not renew, 3,000 licenses affecting approximately 15,000 Asians.[163] It is difficult to precisely determine how many Asians left Kenya in the late 1960s due to the politicized nature of the figures. However, combining public sector Africanization data with emigration statistics from 1967 to 1969 suggests an estimated 39,000–45,000 South Asians left Kenya between independence and 1969.[164] Rather than carrying out a mass expulsion, the government used legal, legislative tools to selectively remove individual noncitizens—particularly those working in specific sectors and locations or those who failed to employ and train Africans in their businesses. While South Asians were disproportionately affected by the new legislation—largely because they were permanent residents and dominated the trading sector—their cases were evaluated on an individual basis. If they met the new requirements, by purchasing work permits and/or employing Kenyans in their businesses, they could remain in Kenya. These legislative maneuvers did not affect South Asians with Kenyan citizenship, nor noncitizen South Asian manufacturers who were crucial for the continued growth of the Kenyan economy. Despite a similar nativist motivation to assert indigenous control of the economy, the Kenyatta regime did not resort to the mass expulsion of its Asian minority. The next section examines why.

5.7 Intervening Factors

Nativism centered on the resentment of an "alien" outgroup perceived to be suppressing the economic aspirations of the indigenous population is not unique to Uganda or Kenya. Many former European colonies had "middlemen minorities" that controlled key sectors of the economy or held coveted positions in the civil service. Yet not all newly independent states expelled these economically dominant minority populations, as demonstrated in the negative case of Kenya. Three pivotal intervening factors help to explain the divergence between the two cases. In Uganda, Amin's regime

[163] Confidential Report: The Asians in East Africa, B. Sjollema, World Council of Churches, 30.04.1969; 11/1-1/0/KEN/ASI, Refugees situation—Refugees from Asia in Kenya; Series 1, Box 26; Fonds 11; UNHCR.

[164] Ghai & Ghai, 1971, p. 21; Hansen, 1999, p. 818; Rothchild, 1973, pp. 374–375.

overcame the restraints of its alliances, the "homeland" states of the target group, and IOs. While in Kenya, the restraints outweighed the enablers, deterring expulsion despite strong elite and public motivation to remove the Asians.

5.7.1 Alliances

Domestic Alliances

After taking power in Uganda in January 1971, Idi Amin's main concern was consolidating control and purging any traces of the previous regime. He placed his ethnic kin into key military positions and killed Obote loyalists, including Langi, Acholi, and Teso members of the armed forces, intelligence services, and police.[165] Amin further expanded the size of the military from 7,680 to 20,000 persons (by 1974) and more than tripled defense expenditures by the end of his first year in power.[166] He used military patronage to buy loyalty and maintain his rule.

To gain legitimacy, Amin first turned to the Baganda—the largest and formerly most powerful ethnic group in the country, and Obote's main ethnic rival.[167] Amin quickly restored their power and status, which had been diminished under Obote.[168] He made a series of concessions, including releasing Baganda detainees, holding a state funeral for the late Baganda king, and renaming districts that were previously part of the Buganda kingdom, from East and West Mengo to East and West Buganda.[169] Despite these changes, the Baganda made further demands for the Africanization of trade.

Amin was initially cautious about making economic policy changes. If the Baganda became economically powerful, political aspirations would likely follow. During an August 1971 meeting, Amin argued that "the Baganda were already advancing rapidly in trade and warned that Ugandanisation of commerce and industry must not lead to tribal discrimination."[170] Like Obote, Amin was hesitant to replace the South Asian commercial monopoly

[165] Kasfir, 1976, pp. 219–220; Kasozi, 1994, pp. 110–111; Leopold, 2020, pp. 202, 214; Mutibwa, 1992, p. 88; Posner, 1974, p. 32;
[166] Avirgan & Honey, 1982, p. 7; Jørgensen, 1981, pp. 274–275.
[167] Avirgan & Honey, 1982, p. 5; Kasfir, 1976, pp. 216–217.
[168] Kasfir, 1976, pp. 216–217; Leopold, 2020, pp. 192, 199.
[169] Kasfir, 1976, pp. 216–217; Leopold, 2020, pp. 192, 199.
[170] Jørgensen, 1981, p. 285.

with a Baganda monopoly. Though he refused Baganda calls to Africanize the economy, he took other actions to appease them, including conducting a South Asian census, holding the "Indian Conference" in which he outlined public grievances against the South Asian community, and canceling 12,000 South Asian citizenship applications.[171]

While Amin desired Baganda political support, his core domestic allies were his military co-ethnics: West Nilotics, including Kakwa,[172] Madi, Lugbara, Alur, and Nubians, as well as co-ethnic foreign nationals from Zaire and Sudan.[173] This domestic alliance eliminated Amin's military rivals and strengthened his rule. By the summer of 1972, Amin had been in power for over a year, and violence against his domestic African rivals continued. The dramatically expanded military size and spending required liquid financial resources to reward his loyal supporters and continue his patronage system. The appropriation of Asian assets and income was the most expeditious means to achieve his aims. Expulsion of the Asians would open a windfall of new economic assets and opportunities for his co-ethnics, strengthening his domestic alliance.

The political elites who may have been able to persuade Amin to reconsider his expulsion decision were not consulted. The civil service and the Baganda aristocracy were as surprised as the Asians when they heard the news.[174] Some domestic restraints on Amin's expulsion decision are seen in the issuance of Statutory Instrument No. 124, which exempted South Asian professionals and government workers.[175] Though mass expulsion was popular among the Ugandan public, many bureaucrats and cabinet officials favored granting broad exemptions from Amin's initial announcement, particularly for skilled Asians in the civil service and the professions.[176] While advocating for exemptions is not the same as contesting or resisting the expulsion decision, this addendum to the official expulsion decree indicates some influence by Ugandan civil servants to restrain Amin. Yet, shortly after Statutory Instrument No. 124 was released, Amin rescinded it, demonstrating his disregard for any dissenting opinions within his inner circle.

[171] Keesing's Contemporary Archives, 1971–1972, p. 25023; Leopold, 2020, pp. 228–229; O'Brien, 1972, p. 25; Sharma & Woolridge, 1974, p. 400.

[172] Arbitrary colonial borders divided the Kakwa—a Sudanic group closely related to the Bari, in what was then southern Sudan—across Uganda, Sudan, and Zaire (Woodward, 1978, p. 154). This helps explain why Amin drew military support from Sudanese and Zairean soldiers.

[173] Avirgan & Honey, 1982, p. 7; Kasfir, 1976, p. 220; Kasozi, 1994, p. 111.

[174] Melady & Melady, 1976, p. 7.

[175] Jørgensen, 1981, p. 287; O'Brien, 1973, p. 95.

[176] Jørgensen, 1981, p. 286.

Amin's domestic allies were the main beneficiaries of the expulsion.[177] Civilian business allocation committees (BACs) distributed Asian properties, allocating large technical companies to parastatal corporations and the rest to African traders, civil servants, and soldiers. However, the BACs were quickly coopted by the military because of alleged delays in allocating properties, and most Asian businesses were divided among Amin's military allies and their families.[178] The spoils included 5,655 firms, factories, ranches, and agricultural estates, along with all the abandoned Asian assets—vehicles, homes, household goods—neatly registered as part of their exit clearance process.[179] Through this maneuver, Amin economically marginalized the Baganda while creating opportunities for military loyalists and their families to fill middle-class economic functions. The strength and maintenance of Amin's regime relied on ethnic military patronage; thus, the benefits of the expulsion to his domestic allies were a critical enabling factor in the Uganda case.

In Kenya, President Kenyatta was similarly focused on maintaining control of the Kenyan state, including resource distribution to his Kikuyu co-ethnics. He cultivated domestic alliances that ensured the stability and continuity of his rule.[180] After the British transferred power to Kenya in 1963, an African elite inherited the top positions in the independent government. Kenyatta developed a tripartite alliance with wealthy conservative KANU Party members and the provincial administration.[181] These officials, both in Nairobi and in the countryside, enriched themselves and their allies by extracting rents from state programs and through the allocation of government contracts. They saw no issue with continued foreign economic dominance, believing the solution to low levels of African economic participation was expanded commercial and industrial opportunities, which required private, usually foreign, capital investment.[182] Kenyatta needed the economy to continue functioning smoothly, which included South Asian dominance of commerce and manufacturing.[183]

Although the parliamentary debate around Africanization of the economy and the fate of the Asian minority was robust and public, the Kenyan legislative institution lacked teeth.[184] It was a colonial artifact, "verbally vigorous

[177] Kyemba, 1977, p. 64.
[178] Jørgensen, 1981, p. 289; Leopold, 2020, p. 232.
[179] Jørgensen, 1981, p. 289.
[180] Parsons, 2007, p. 57.
[181] Branch & Cheeseman, 2006, pp. 20–22.
[182] Rothchild, 1970b, p. 747; Tignor, 1998, p. 384.
[183] Rothchild, 1970a, p. 750.
[184] Branch & Cheeseman, 2006, pp. 23–24; Gertzel et al., 1969, p. 10; Ghai, 1967, p. 11.

but politically impotent."[185] Kenyatta and the majority KANU right-wing faction resisted demands by party leftists for structural economic changes that would have threatened their position.[186] Instead, they responded to the internal opposition with the Africanization of the civil service and an expansion of the public sector, but not robust Africanization of the private sector. Even the title of their capitalist development plan—*African Socialism and its Application to Planning in Kenya*—was a rhetorical sleight of hand.[187] By coopting and repackaging the socialist language of the left wing, Kenyatta and the conservative faction outwardly projected concessions and compromise, while maintaining the economic status quo. Members of Kenyatta's tripartite alliance would have been harmed by expelling the Asians. Thus, despite internal KANU opposition, and popular pressure to remove the Asian minority, domestic alliances restrained expulsion in Kenya.

Transnational Alliances

In the early 1970s, Uganda was neither economically nor militarily self-sufficient. The country received an estimated $25.5 million per year in aid from the Organization for Economic Cooperation and Development (OECD) countries and multilateral institutions.[188] Much of that aid came from the UK, Israel, and the US, all of whom ignored Amin's anti-democratic seizure of power and repression of domestic opponents.[189] In July 1971, amid local massacres, Britain signed a £2 million defense contract with Uganda to provide military training and armored personnel vehicles, and the following month offered a three-year £10 million loan.[190] British–Ugandan military cooperation continued into 1972[191] with a visit to the UK by Ugandan Defense Minister Charles Oboth-Ofumbi in January to purchase additional equipment and armored cars.[192] Israel also increased its in-kind support after the coup, and Amin's first international visit was to Israel. The country

[185] Mueller, 1984, pp. 401, 405.
[186] Branch & Cheeseman, 2006, p. 25; Mueller, 1984, pp. 405–406.
[187] Atieno-Odhiambo, 1987, p. 196.
[188] Jørgensen, 1981, p. 307.
[189] Curtis, 2004, p. 254; Leopold, 2020, p. 196; Martin, 1974, p. 164; Walton, C., 2013, p. 273.
[190] Curtis, 2004, pp. 254–255.
[191] It was not until June 1972, two months before the South Asian expulsion decree, that the British government considered pausing military support and hesitated in sending additional military trainers. This was not because of Amin's human rights abuses, but rather his anti-imperialist statements and naval cooperation with the Soviets (Curtis, 2004, pp. 258–259).
[192] Curtis, 2004, pp. 256–257.

agreed to continue, and even augment, its military and economic support to Uganda, including £1 million worth of arms, tanks, aircrafts, military trainers, and technical advisors.[193] In addition, the US provided over $2.1 million in grants for technical assistance in education, agriculture, and healthcare.[194] The risk of alienating these transnational allies should have acted as a significant constraint on Amin's decision to expel.

As part of Amin's strategy of purging any traces of the previous regime, he requested funds and equipment from these allies to invade Tanzania, where Obote had sought refuge after the coup.[195] When they denied his request, Amin began looking for alternative sources of support. In February 1972, Amin sent his minister of education, Abu Bakr Mayanja, to Egypt to meet with Egyptian President Anwar Sadat.[196] Sadat could not offer any support, given Egypt's financial strain, but he referred Mayanja to Libyan President Muammar Gaddafi.[197] Gaddafi was willing to assist Amin, a fellow Muslim, as part of his larger pan-Islamic, anti-Israel strategy on the continent.[198] But his aid was conditional on aligning with the Arab cause, severing diplomatic ties with Israel, and expelling Israelis from Uganda.[199] Eager for financial and military support, Amin complied with Gaddafi's requests, and in March 1972, Uganda expelled an estimated 700 Israelis—military advisors, diplomats, and their families.[200]

After meeting with Gaddafi, Amin visited seven Arab states, including Morocco, Sudan, Syria, and Jordan, and he sent his foreign minister to Iraq and Somalia—Amin even went on the Hajj pilgrimage to Mecca.[201] In addition to Libya, Saudi Arabia and Kuwait became key donors, pleased with Amin's militant anti-Israel position and support for pan-Islam. Libya and the Palestinian Liberation Organization swiftly replaced the military aid and training gap left by the Israelis.[202] By the summer of 1972, Uganda was no

[193] Bishku, 2017, p. 83; Oded, 2006, p. 72.

[194] Welles, 1972, p. 4.

[195] Avirgan & Honey, 1982, p. 11; Bishku, 2017, p. 84; Gitelson, 1977, pp. 366, 376; Leopold, 2020, pp. 209–210; Martin, 1974, pp. 161–162; Oded, 2006, pp. 72–73; Pondi, 1988, p. 142.

[196] Avirgan & Honey, 1982, p. 11; Bishku, 2017, pp. 84–85; Martin, 1974, pp. 161–162; Oded, 2006, p. 73; Pondi, 1988, p. 142.

[197] Oded, 2006, p. 73.

[198] Gitelson, 1977, p. 377; Lemarchand, 1988, p. 11; Pondi, 1988, pp. 141–142.

[199] Lemarchand, 1988, p. 11; Martin, 1974, p. 163; Oded, 2006, p. 73.

[200] Keesing's Contemporary Archives, 1971–1972, p. 25236; Leopold, 2020, pp. 226–227; Oded, 2006, p. 75; Tandon, 1972, p. 6.

[201] ACICR B AG 252 152-001; Confidential Report on the Current Situation in Uganda, 05.10.1972; Gitelson, 1977, p. 378.

[202] ACICR B AG 232 152-002.03; Frank Schmidt, Rapport de mission Ouganda, 25.11.1972; Foltz, 1988, p. 62; Jørgensen, 1981, p. 316; Oded, 2006, p. 76.

longer reliant on its previous transnational allies. Amin received substantial economic and military support from Arab states.[203]

Consequently, any economic leverage the UK and other Western countries might have had to persuade Amin to repeal or modify his expulsion decision had vanished. Amin was immune to the retaliatory actions of the UK and the US, which suspended loans of £10 million[204] and $3 million, respectively, in response to his expulsion decree. He had already replaced the $25.5 million in Western support with an estimated $26-33 million from Arab states and the Organization of the Petroleum Exporting Countries.[205] Amin's new transnational allies had no concerns about expulsion as a viable policy option.[206] In fact, in 1970, shortly after coming to power in a coup like Amin's, Gaddafi had expelled 20,000 Italians from Libya.[207] The shift in Amin's transnational alliances opened alternative sources of financial and military support and overcame this potential constraint on the decision to expel. These new allies ignored the Asian expulsion, further enabling the policy implementation.

In 1960s Kenya, Cold War rivalries ran high, and Kenyatta leveraged transnational alliances with Eastern and Western states to secure the best deals and the most support.[208] Britain was Kenya's main transnational ally, delivering £50 million in both grants and loans for civil and defense programs, including capital development, arms, equipment, vehicles, aircraft, and British military trainers.[209] Postcolonial Africa was not only underdeveloped, requiring large economic investments, it was also politically precarious, with coups and mutinies threatening new leaders. Kenya was not immune.

In January 1964, mere weeks after independence, army mutinies swept across East Africa, originating in Zanzibar and spreading to Tanganyika, Uganda, and Kenya.[210] Kenyatta immediately turned to Britain for military support, and British soldiers quickly suppressed the small-scale mutiny.[211]

[203] Foltz, 1988, p. 62; Martin, 1974, p. 163.
[204] Gitelson, 1977, p. 370; Leopold, 2020, p. 235; News Compilation. (1972, August 30). Britain freezes £10 million loan to Uganda. In Z. Lalani (1997), *Ugandan Asian expulsion* (p. 39).
[205] Jørgensen, 1981, p. 307; Oded, 2006, p. 74; Welles, 1972, p. 1.
[206] Although a small portion of the Uganda Asians were Muslim, they were Ismaili Shias and thus not a concern of Amin's Sunni Arab transnational alliance.
[207] Martin, 1974, p. 165; Pondi, 1988, p. 141.
[208] Cullen, 2017a, p. 149; Keesing's Contemporary Archives, 1963–1964, p. 20128.
[209] Keesing's Contemporary Archives, 1963–1964, p. 20128.
[210] Clayton, 1986, p. 222; Parsons, 2007, p. 51.
[211] Cullen, 2017a, p. 115; Parsons, 2007, pp. 51, 62.

Afterward, Kenya signed a major defense agreement with Britain, including military equipment, arms, technical assistance, and the continued presence of 160 British troops to assist in "dealing with internal disturbances."[212] Britain's military support also extended to intelligence collaboration. Kenyatta and his inner circle regularly received detailed British intelligence reports, and Kenyatta retained MI5's colonial-era Nairobi-based security liaison officer as an advisor.[213] Kenyatta deployed the same colonial intelligence apparatus once used against him to surveil the activities of his political rivals.[214]

Along with Britain, Israel was another vital transnational partner, providing critical economic and intelligence support, and was the first to build an embassy in independent Kenya.[215] Kenyatta collaborated closely with Israel's intelligence agency, meeting with the head of Mossad as early as 1962. Nairobi, Kenya's capital, became Mossad's East Africa hub.[216] Israeli intelligence was vital to Kenya's internal security, including in the war against Somali separatists in Kenya's Northern Frontier District. The destabilizing effects of an expulsion of South Asians would have harmed Kenya's transnational allies by jeopardizing investor confidence, hindering economic growth, and risking military and intelligence support.

The counterfactual question then arises: If Kenya was similarly reliant on transnational alliances, like Uganda, why couldn't Kenyatta have identified new allies and alternative resources like Amin? Some options were not open to Kenyatta. First, Amin was Muslim, which opened the door to Islamic sources of funding with pan-Islamic and anti-Israel objectives that were not readily available to Kenyatta. Second, Kenya was closely aligned with Israel, and Israel's strongest African partner was Ethiopia. In 1963, Kenya and Ethiopia signed a mutual defense pact because both countries were battling Somali insurgencies.[217] The Shifta War against Somali nationals fighting to secede and join "Greater Somalia" was one of Kenya's most significant domestic-cum-foreign policy issues at the time.[218] The agreement with

[212] Cullen, 2017a, p. 125; Cullen, 2018, p. 46; Keesing's Contemporary Archives, 1963–1964, p. 19964; Parsons, 2007, p. 67.
[213] Walton, C., 2013, p. 271.
[214] Walton, C., 2013, p. 272.
[215] Bishku, 2017, pp. 77, 80; Naim, 2005, p. 79.
[216] Bishku, 2017, pp. 81–82; Jacob, 1971, p. 178; Naim, 2005, pp. 78–79.
[217] Bishku, 2017, p. 82; Howell, 1968, p. 40; Keesing's Contemporary Archives, 1963–1964, p. 19809.
[218] The British also signed a military agreement with Kenya in 1966–1967 regarding support for the Shifta War (Cullen, 2017a, p. 156).

Ethiopia was a crucial insurance policy. The destabilizing consequences of an expulsion would likely have harmed relations with Israel, which, in turn, could have negatively impacted relations with Ethiopia—a risky prospect.[219] Kenya's direct ties with Israel for economic and military support, as well as its indirect ties through Ethiopia, meant alternative funding from Arab states was not a viable option.

Two other possible alternative transnational allies were the Soviets or the Chinese. Kenya had relationships with, and received financial support from, both countries. However, in 1965, rumors spread about a planned coup against Kenyatta headed by Odinga with Soviet support.[220] Although many scholars retrospectively agree these rumors were unfounded, both Kenyatta and the British took them seriously at the time. At Kenyatta's request, Britain made plans to intervene if necessary.[221] The Soviets also provided significant financial support to Somalia—an estimated $30 million in 1963—against whom Kenya was fighting in its border region.[222] Kenyatta's capitalist leanings and Soviet support for the Kenyan opposition, internally and externally, ruled out an alternative alliance with the Soviets.

Relations with communist countries further deteriorated in 1967 when the Chinese chargé d'affairs was ordered to leave Kenya after the Chinese Embassy made statements attacking Mboya, one of Kenyatta's closest advisors.[223] Although outwardly committed to a policy of nonalignment, the Kenyatta regime had clearly chosen sides. Its relationship with the West, especially Britain, was prioritized.[224] Given this context, Kenyatta had no viable alternative transnational allies to whom he could turn. Considering that removing the Asians *en masse* would have jeopardized Kenya's alliance with Britain and Israel, which was essential for maintaining the economic status quo and safeguarding Kenyatta's rule, mass expulsion was further constrained.

5.7.2 "Homeland" State(s) of the Target Group

Uganda's South Asian community was composed of an estimated 55,660 noncitizens—50,000 with British citizenship and 5,660 with Indian

[219] Cullen, 2017a, p. 118; Howell, 1968, pp. 37–38.
[220] Cullen, 2017b, p. 791.
[221] Cullen, 2017b, p. 792.
[222] Cullen, 2018, p. 42.
[223] Cullen, 2018, p. 47; Keesing's Contemporary Archives, 1967–1968, p. 22280.
[224] Cullen, 2018, p. 46.

citizenship—as well as 23,000 citizens.[225] Consequently, the two key "homeland" states of concern were the UK and India, neither of which shared a border with Uganda. After the expulsion announcement, Kenya and Tanzania, two of Uganda's neighbors, immediately closed their borders, eliminating proximate exit routes to countries with Asian co-ethnics, which further complicated the implementation of the expulsion.[226]

Uganda's relationship with the first "homeland" state, Britain, was tense, and in early 1972, Amin's government began reducing its dependence on its former colonizer. Just over a month after the expulsion announcement, Uganda's Defense Council gave Britain's military training mission four days to leave the country.[227] Amin balked at British threats to rescind aid, saying that he was "not at all worried."[228] Accordingly, this potential restraint was no longer operative, as Amin was not concerned about damaging relations with the UK.

After the expulsion announcement, the UK "lived in a twilight period of false optimism," taking limited action and hoping Amin would change his mind.[229] They doubted he would follow through with the expulsion.[230] After realizing Amin would not relent, the UK government launched overt and covert operations to pressure him to change course.[231] British officials' main concern was the anticipated domestic backlash to the absorption of 50,000 non-white immigrants and the possibility that Kenya and Tanzania might follow Amin's lead and expel their Asian populations.[232] The UK lobbied Tanzania, Kenya, India, and Pakistan to convince Amin to reverse his decision.[233] Tanzanian President Nyerere condemned Amin's actions, calling him an animal and accusing him of "racialism." But he also called on Britain to accept responsibility for its citizens and to stop "pursuing racist immigration policies."[234] In contrast, Kenyan Vice President Moi announced his support for Amin's expulsion decision, and while President

[225] Cosemans, 2018, pp. 101–102; Jørgensen, 1981, pp. 287–288; Melady & Melady, 1976, p. 1; Memorandum, Asians in Uganda—Statistics, 07.09.1972; 11/2/10-100.UGA.ASI[b]—Refugees from Asia in Uganda [Volume 2-1.UGA.ASI]; Series 2, Box 204; Fonds 11; UNHCR.

[226] Patel, 1972, p. 18.

[227] *The Times of India*, 1972.

[228] *Uganda Argus*. (1972, August 7). Asians milked the cow: They did not feed it—Gen. Amin. In Z. Lalani (1997), *Ugandan Asian expulsion* (p. 5).

[229] Tandon & Raphael, 1978, p. 13.

[230] ACICR B AG 252 152-001; Confidential Report on the Current Situation in Uganda, 05.10.1972.

[231] Uche, 2017, pp. 819, 829–830.

[232] Uche, 2017, p. 830.

[233] Uche, 2017, pp. 829–830.

[234] Memorandum from Frank A. Bauman, Representative UNHCR Branch Office for Australia and New Zealand to UNHCR/HQ Geneva—Newspaper Clippings, "Black Africa Reacts at Last

Kenyatta did not endorse Moi's statement of support, he refused the UK's requests to intervene with Amin.[235]

When bilateral efforts failed, the UK took its case to the UN General Assembly, advocating for an assembly debate on Uganda's "arbitrary and inhumane" policy and stating that it was ready to table a resolution.[236] It urged member states to convince Amin to at least extend the ninety-day deadline and to help resettle Asian expellees.[237] The irony of the UK accusing an African state of racial discrimination was not lost on Grace Ibingira, Uganda's permanent representative to the United Nations (UN). He pointed out the hypocrisy of the UK's concerns: "Britain had never protested when East African countries expelled black Africans from neighboring countries in the early postcolonial era."[238] The UK dropped its request for a UN debate after an African initiative sent Zaire's[239] President Mobutu Sese Seko to negotiate with Amin. When Mobutu's efforts failed, the UK acquiesced and resettled most of its citizens with assistance from the UN.[240]

Uganda's ties with India—the other "homeland" state of concern—were moderate, which could have constrained Amin's decision to expel the approximately 6,000 Asians holding Indian citizenship. More importantly, India's foreign policy strategy would have signaled to Amin that any backlash was unlikely. When African states achieved their independence, then Indian Prime Minister Jawaharlal Nehru had encouraged Indians abroad to adopt local citizenship and integrate with indigenous Africans. He stated that they should "cease to seek a separate and better destiny from their fellow countrymen."[241] Therefore, the August 11 statement from the Lok Sabha, India's lower house of parliament, came as no surprise: "The Government of India recognized the right of the Ugandan government to regulate their internal affairs according to their best judgement."[242] India's foreign policy was focused on the Non-Aligned Movement among former colonies, and the

to Asian Expulsion," 23.08.1972; 11/2/64-641.UGA[a] Expulsion and Deportation—Uganda [1972] Volume 1; Series 2, Box 1281; Fonds 11; UNHCR.

[235] Uche, 2017, p. 830.

[236] Shannon, Don. (1972, September 28). Britain seeks U.N. help for Uganda Asians. *Los Angeles Times*. In Z. Lalani (1997), *Ugandan Asian expulsion* (p. 88).

[237] Shannon, Don. (1972, September 28). Britain seeks U.N. help for Uganda Asians. *Los Angeles Times*. In Z. Lalani (1997), *Ugandan Asian expulsion* (p. 88).

[238] Shannon, Don. (1972, September 29). Uganda hits plea for U.N. debate on Asians. *Los Angeles Times*. In Z. Lalani (1997), *Ugandan Asian expulsion* (pp. 89–90).

[239] In 1971, Mobutu changed the name of the Democratic Republic of Congo to Zaire.

[240] Jørgensen, 1981, p. 288; Mattausch, 1998, p. 134; Tandon, 1972, p. 1.

[241] Gupta, 1974, p. 317; Lall, 2001, p. 89.

[242] Lall, 2001, p. 117.

government was not willing to risk those ties on behalf of Indians living in Uganda.[243] The Indian government acquiesced to Amin's expulsion decision, swiftly repatriating its citizens. Thus, the two principal "homeland" states further enabled expulsion in Uganda.

In the case of Kenya, the South Asian community was slightly larger than in Uganda, but it was composed of a similar proportion of noncitizens and citizens: approximately 115,000 with British citizenship, 4,500 with Indian citizenship, and 68,000 with Kenyan citizenship.[244] Therefore, the UK and India were the pertinent "homeland" states, with most of the potential target group holding UK citizenship. Given that Kenya is a negative case, there was no expulsion decree to which the "homeland" states could respond. Examining their response to the 1967–1969 "Asian exodus" is a useful parallel to see how things may have unfolded.

In an attempt to halt the "exodus" of South Asians from Kenya, the UK cabinet sent its special representative in East Africa, Malcolm Macdonald, to meet with Kenyatta. In their Nairobi meeting in February 1968, Macdonald tried to persuade Kenyatta to put a stop to the rapid emigration of Asians from Kenya.[245] Kenyatta refused. Thus on March 1, 1968, the UK Parliament passed the Commonwealth Immigrants Act, which imposed an immigration quota for British citizens without at least one parent or grandparent born or naturalized in the UK.[246] This law directly targeted former colonial subjects and restricted Asian immigration to the UK to 1,500 heads of households and their dependents per year—approximately 6,000–7,000 persons, half the number that had arrived in the months before.[247] Through this legislation, the UK effectively barred additional Asians in Kenya from moving to Britain. Unlike in Uganda, where the UK eventually acquiesced and resettled many of its expelled nationals, it resisted and denied entry to its Asian citizens in response to Kenya's actions. Sensing that it would become a dumping ground for denied UK immigrants, and dismayed at Britain's abdication of its responsibility toward its citizens, India announced that it would not resettle Asians with British passports.[248]

[243] Gupta, 1974, p. 317; Lall, 2001, p. 90.

[244] Rothchild, 1973, p. 408. There were also an estimated 500 Pakistani citizens.

[245] Hansen, 1999, p. 820.

[246] Mattausch, 1998, p. 132.

[247] Hansen, 1999, p. 821.

[248] Lall, 2001, p. 100; Mattausch, 1998, p. 133. By the summer of 1968, the UK and India agreed that some of Kenya's Asian UK passport holders could enter India temporarily if the British High Commission ensured they would be admitted to the UK (Gupta, 1974, p. 319; Lall, 2001, p. 100).

Back in Kenya, President Kenyatta did not bend to the UK's requests to rescind the economic Africanization legislation, nor did he openly encourage Asians to remain. He did not object to the new British legislation, and he indicated to various British representatives that their new immigration policy would not damage Kenya–British relations.[249] Kenyatta announced that Kenya's Africanization legislation would be gradually phased in over a two-year period and that the government would not "endanger the buoyant state of the economy by forcing the pace of localization."[250] Vice President Moi further clarified that this gradual implementation would only affect certain positions where unemployed Kenyan citizens had the skills to replace noncitizens—a low percentage given high rates of illiteracy and low levels of education among Africans at the time. Both the strong ties between Kenya and the UK, and the UK's fierce resistance to the effects of Kenya's Africanization legislation, constrained expulsion when it seemed most likely.

5.7.3 International Organizations

In 1972, Uganda's ties with IOs, like the UN, were extremely weak. Amin was not concerned about the effect of expulsion on Uganda's relations with IOs, nor did he anticipate their strong resistance. Amin's disposition toward the UN is evident in a telegram he sent to UN Secretary-General (UNSG) Kurt Waldheim and Israeli Prime Minister Golda Meir after the September 1972 Munich Olympic massacre. In it, he praised the killings of Israeli athletes. He stated that Germany was the appropriate site for the attack given Hitler's murder of more than 6 million Jews and that Hitler "knew that the Israelis are not a people who work for humanity."[251] At the regional level, after overthrowing regionally well-liked Obote, Amin's presidency was initially not recognized by the Organization of African Unity (OAU).[252] This led to tense relations between Uganda and the organization and was unlikely to restrain Amin's decision to expel.

In addition to weak ties between Uganda and IOs, recent history would have reinforced Amin's lack of concern about any response from these

[249] Cullen, 2017a, pp. 164–165.
[250] Aiyar, 2015, pp. 291–292.
[251] Martin, 1974, p. 11; Oded, 2006, p. 75; Welles, 1972, p. 1.
[252] Cervenka, 1972, pp. 34–35; Gitelson, 1977, p. 365.

organizations to his expulsion decree. There had been no reaction at the UN or regional level to Obote's expulsion of Kenyan Luos in 1970, nor to other African expulsions throughout the continent in the 1960s and early 1970s.[253] In fact, the OAU Charter explicitly prohibited interference in the internal affairs of member countries, and as a result, the organization rarely condemned human rights violations during this period.[254] Nearly a month after Uganda's expulsion announcement, UNSG Waldheim told reporters at a press conference in Vienna that "Uganda had declared the matter an internal one and Article 2, para. 7 of the Charter[255] forbade Unations [sic] to intervene in domestic affairs. However Unations [is] always ready to help in humanitarian matters."[256] IOs were neither an internal restraint nor an external constraint on Amin's decision to expel.

Although they were a minority of the total expellees, nearly 23,000 South Asians held Ugandan citizenship and were rendered stateless by Amin's expulsion decree. IOs played a critical role in facilitating their departure. In a two-day meeting on October 24 and 25, 1972, the UN and the Ugandan Ministry of Foreign Affairs[257] discussed the modalities of international assistance to facilitate the removal of Asians of "undetermined nationality."[258] It was agreed that the United Nations Development Program would have overall responsibility for the operation, with the International Committee of the Red Cross (ICRC) providing travel documentation,[259] the United Nations High Commissioner for Refugees (UNHCR)

[253] Umozurike, 1979, p. 199.

[254] Ojo & Sesay, 1986, pp. 89–92; Umozurike, 1979, pp. 197–198.

[255] Article 2(7): "Nothing contained in the present Charter shall authorize the United Nations to intervene in matters which are essentially within the domestic jurisdiction of any state or shall require the Members to submit such matters to settlement under the present Charter; but this principle shall not prejudice the application of enforcement measures under Chapter VII" (United Nations, 1945).

[256] Incoming Cable from UNHCR/New York, 31.08.1972; 11/2/10-100.UGA.ASI[b]—Refugees from Asia in Uganda [Volume 2-1.UGA.ASI]; Series 2, Box 204; Fonds 11; UNHCR.

[257] Incoming Cable from UNHCR/New York, 26.10.1972; 11/2/10-100.UGA.ASI[c]—Refugees from Asia in Uganda [Volume 3-1.UGA.ASI]; Series 2, Box 205; Fonds 11; UNHCR.

[258] The UNHCR used the language "undetermined nationality" because it did not want to make legal status determinations. In most cases, the British government claimed that persons were Ugandan citizens, while the Ugandan government claimed they were British citizens. The UNHCR could not adjudicate who was right, and since neither government claimed them as citizens, they were de facto stateless (Document from UNHCR/Kampala: Uganda Asians, 09.10.1973; 11/2/60-600.UGA[a]; Series 2, Box 1012; Fonds 11; UNHCR).

[259] ICRC travel documents are internationally recognized travel papers, valid for three months, that allow undocumented refugees to travel to a transit center or resettlement country. Upon arrival, the refugees must obtain permanent documentation. The travel papers are then returned to the ICRC (ACICR B AG 232 152-002.02; Communiqué de presse No 1139, 27.10.1972).

organizing resettlement, and the Intergovernmental Committee for European Migration (ICEM)[260] facilitating transportation.[261] Given that the UK only accepted 27,000 of its 50,000 citizens,[262] the UNHCR also negotiated resettlement for the remaining British Asians, as well as those of "undetermined nationality." These Asians were resettled across numerous countries, including Canada, India, the US, Pakistan, Sweden, the Netherlands, Austria, Belgium, Norway, New Zealand, the Gulf States, Iran, and throughout Latin America.[263]

Although IOs did not endorse or approve of the Asian expulsion, they facilitated their removal with minimal resistance or pressure applied to the Ugandan government to reconsider or modify its decision. In an internal cable from UNHCR Deputy High Commissioner Charles Mace to the director of the Protection Division, Mace gently suggested "it might be relevant to mention" Uganda's obligations under the 1954 Convention Relating to the Status of Stateless Persons.[264] Article 31 of the convention states, "The Contracting States shall not expel a stateless person lawfully in their territory save on grounds of national security or public order."[265] But rather than condemning the Ugandan government, the UN praised its cooperation. A cable from the UNHCR/New York office stated, "The Government of Uganda has been most cooperative in working with the United Nations Officials involved."[266]

The day after the expulsion deadline, on November 10, the UN held a press briefing in New York in which Under Secretary-General Bradford Morse stated:

> The operation on behalf of the Asians of undetermined nationality in Uganda had been successfully concluded. . . . We have had in the last several weeks the full co-operation of the Ugandan Government. . . . The President of Uganda has gone out of his way to express his respect for

[260] The ICEM is now the International Organization for Migration (IOM).

[261] Incoming Cable from UNHCR/New York, 26.10.1972; 11/2/10-100.UGA.ASI[c]—Refugees from Asia in Uganda [Volume 3-1.UGA.ASI]; Series 2, Box 205; Fonds 11; UNHCR.

[262] Jørgensen, 1981, p. 288; Mattausch, 1998, p. 134.

[263] ACICR B AG 234 019-003, Statistical Report on the Departure of Stateless Asians from Uganda to Overseas Countries, 10.11.1972; Cosemans, 2018, p. 102.

[264] Outgoing Cable from UNHCR Deputy High Commissioner, Mace, to Dadzie, UNHCR Director Protection Division, 05.09.1972; 11/2/10-100.UGA.ASI[b]—Refugees from Asia in Uganda [Volume 2-1.UGA.ASI]; Series 2, Box 204; Fonds 11; UNHCR.

[265] United Nations, 1954.

[266] Incoming Cable from UNHCR/New York, 26.10.1972; 11/2/10-100.UGA.ASI[c]—Refugees from Asia in Uganda [Volume 3-1.UGA.ASI]; Series 2, Box 205; Fonds 11; UNHCR.

> the Secretary-General's part in this and for other elements of the United Nations family which did participate.[267]

Read out of context, this statement could be confused with a successful UN partnership with a democratic government jointly responding to a natural disaster, rather than the UN aiding a military dictatorship to expel an ethnic group *en masse*.

The ICRC, by contrast, questioned its involvement in the operation, albeit in hindsight. Frank Schmidt, ICRC regional delegate for East Africa, expressed concern about assisting Amin to "finish his dirty work." In the conclusion of his final report, dated November 25, 1972, after the expulsion was complete, he wrote:

> From a humanitarian point of view our intervention is not without ambiguity. *In the end we have helped Amin finish his dirty work on time.* So far no one has reproached us, not even the concerned Asians, and our action is perfectly defensible from the point of view of ICRC doctrine. However, documenting these families, some already separated, and sending them to distant, unknown and cold countries has not been a perfectly positive achievement [emphasis added].[268]

There may have been a high level of anxiety among IOs about what may have happened without their intervention, although this is not documented in the archives. Nevertheless, the absence of IO resistance to the expulsion decree, followed by their assistance to the government in removing the Asians from the country, was a significant enabling factor in the Uganda case.

Unlike Uganda, the Kenyan government maintained strong ties with both the UN and the OAU, which served as an important restraint on the decision to expel. Kenyatta was keen to play a part on the global stage and to be recognized by IOs.[269] Supporting the UN and its founding principles was a key component of Kenyan foreign policy, and Kenya had achieved "a steady growth in prestige abroad."[270] At the regional level, Kenyatta was a

[267] Cable from New York to UNHCR/Geneva, 10.11.1972; 11/2/64-641.UGA[c] Expulsion and Deportation—Uganda [1972] Volume 2; Series 2, Box 1281; Fonds 11; UNHCR.

[268] ACICR B AG 232 152-002.03; Rapport de mission Ouganda, Frank Schmidt, 25.11.1972 (translated from the French original).

[269] Howell, 1968, pp. 34–35; Mazrui, 1964, p. 517.

[270] Howell, 1968, pp. 32, 34.

prominent figure in the OAU as a well-respected nationalist leader. He was selected chairman of the Congo Conciliation Commission in 1964 and was the diplomatic leader of the African Commonwealth.[271] The Kenyan government's stability, amid much turmoil and leadership changes across the continent, was another reason Kenya played a vital role in the OAU.[272] Given Kenyatta's desire to be prominent on the international stage and his championing of the human rights of small states, the country's strong ties with IOs restrained the implementation of a policy that could have damaged its reputation or contradicted its stated goals.

Because Kenya is a negative case, it is not possible to conclusively determine how IOs would have responded to a Kenyan expulsion. Kenya pursued a legal, legislative approach that individually targeted South Asian noncitizens, so there was nothing for the UN or the OAU to resist. Nevertheless, in the 1960s, expulsion was widespread across sub-Saharan Africa,[273] including eight expulsion events between 1962 to 1969, with little outcry at the UN. As previously noted, the OAU Charter prohibited intervention in the internal affairs of member countries. This suggests that IOs would likely have ignored an expulsion policy, given their apathy toward other expulsions elsewhere in Africa—a critical enabling factor. Instead, the pertinent restraint associated with this intervening factor was Kenya's strong ties with IOs and the desire to maintain those relations.

5.8 Conclusion

The motivation to remove the South Asian minority as the last vestiges of colonial rule and to restore indigenous control over the economy, combined with a conducive enabling environment, led to Uganda's mass expulsion of its Asian population. The government viewed the Asians as an economic threat to the country's full independence. To combat this perceived threat, the government launched an "economic war."[274] As Amin told reporters after the expulsion announcement, "Uganda will not be independent until the Asians have gone. . . . I want to see all Ugandan African faces in Kampala

[271] Howell, 1968, pp. 46–47.

[272] Howell, 1968, pp. 46, 48.

[273] E.g., Gabon, 1962; Republic of Congo, 1962; Niger, 1963; Democratic Republic of Congo, 1964; Côte d'Ivoire, 1964; French Somaliland, 1967; Sierra Leone, 1968; Ghana, 1969 (Garrity, 2022).

[274] Amor, 2003, p. 64; Avirgan & Honey, 1982, p. 5; Jamal, 1976, p. 615; Mazrui, 1979, p. 261; Melady & Melady, 1976, p. 44.

streets and offices."[275] In a speech on September 21, 1972, Amin stressed the themes of economic control and independence in describing the motivation for the expulsion:

> Our policy is designed purely and simply to place the economy of this Country in the hands of the nationals of Uganda. We know that in 1962 we got political independence from Britain. We also know that despite that political independence, *the economy of the Country remained under the control of foreigners*, as it had been for all the years during colonial rule. It became obvious to my Government that *political independence without economic control of the resources of our Country was of very little use.* We therefore took a decision which we are determined to implement, and that is to *transfer the economy of this country firmly into the hands of the nationals* [emphasis added].[276]

Even the International Commission of Jurists, a human rights nongovernmental organization, seemed to sympathize with the Ugandan government's motive, if not the policy of expulsion. In a September 4, 1972, press release, they stated: "The Commission recognizes that the motive of this decision stems from the legitimate aspirations of freedom and independence of Africans. Like many other countries, Uganda does not want its economy to be owned or controlled by foreigners."[277] Although the organization deplored President Amin's racist statements, it understood its logic. While Uganda's domestic and transnational allies, and the UK as the primary "homeland" state of the Asians, initially constrained the decision to expel, over the course of 1971 and the first half of 1972, Amin gradually overcame these constraints, enabling the expulsion decision.

The negative case of Kenya presented a government that similarly sought to Africanize its economy and replace the South Asian commercial hierarchy with an African petit bourgeoise. However, key constraints prevented Kenyatta's administration from pursuing mass expulsion. Kenyatta's domestic allies preferred the postcolonial economic status quo, which relied

[275] *Daily Telegraph* newspaper article, "Expulsion decree by Amin after 'divine message,'" 10.08.1972; 11/2/10-100.UGA.ASI[a], Refugees from Asia in Uganda [Volume1-1.UGA.ASI]; Series 2, Box 204; Fonds 11; UNHCR.

[276] Pamphlet on "Uganda's Economic War" from the High Commission for the Republic of Uganda in New Delhi, 17.11.1972; 11/2/64-641.UGA[c] Expulsion and Deportation—Uganda [1972–1984] Volume 3; Series 2, Box 1281; Fonds 11; UNHCR.

[277] Communiqué de Presse, Commission Internationale de Juristes, 04.09.1972; 13/1/4-18, Uganda Asians [Volume 2]; Series 4, Box 43; Fonds 13, Sub-Fonds 1; UNHCR (translated from the French original).

on continued economic growth largely dependent on Asian commerce and manufacturing. Its close transnational alliances with Britain and Israel, provided crucial economic, military, and intelligence support, which restrained a policy that would have harmed those relationships. The "homeland" state of Britain, with its fierce resistance to Kenya's Africanization measures in 1967 and to the subsequent "Asian exodus," constrained expulsion in Kenya when it seemed most possible. Furthermore, Kenyatta's goals of augmenting the international standing of the new Kenyan state, at both the global and regional levels, restrained an eliminationist policy that may have damaged its reputation within these international institutions. Instead, Kenya reduced its noncitizen Asian population through legal, legislative maneuvers, while leaving the Asians with Kenyan citizenship untouched.

We next turn to a mass expulsion motivated by security concerns and examine the counter-irredentist expulsion of Greek Orthodox Christians in the Ottoman Empire.

6

Counter-Irredentist Expulsion: Greek Orthodox Christians in the Ottoman Empire

Over the course of a decade, from 1913 to 1923, the Ottoman Empire reduced its Greek Orthodox Christian population from approximately 1.75 million[1] to less than 500,000.[2] The mass expulsion of the Greek Orthodox population coincided with the collapse of over 600 years of Ottoman rule and the birth of the Turkish Republic.[3] Their removal spanned four wars—the First and Second Balkan Wars, World War I, and the Greco–Turkish War—and culminated in the first internationally sanctioned compulsory "population exchange." In the 1923 exchange, religion was used as the demarcation criterion: Greek Orthodox Christians were forced from their homes in Turkey to Greece, and Greek nationals of the Muslim faith were forced from Greece to the new Turkish nation-state. In addition, refugees from Greece and Turkey who had fled the two countries over the preceding decade were prevented from returning to their homes and were required to adopt the citizenship of their country of refuge. According to the Great Powers, the 1923 "population exchange" was necessary to

[1] The size of the Greek Orthodox Christian population in the Ottoman Empire during this period was estimated to be 1.5–2 million (Akçam, 2012, pp. 262–263 (cites Karpat, 1985); Emin, 1930, p. 210; Karpat, 1985, p. 45; Ladas, 1932, p. 14; Macartney, 1931, p. 81; Morris & Ze'evi, 2019, p. 24; Pentzopoulos, 1962, pp. 29–30 (cites Polybius, 1918, p. 44)).

[2] There are no precise figures of how many Greek Orthodox remained in the Turkish Republic in 1923. Ladas claims that 189,916 Greeks were expelled by the Lausanne Convention between 1923 and 1926 (1932, pp. 438–439). Estimates of the Greek Orthodox in Istanbul, who were exempted from the exchange, are around 300,000 (Lausanne Conference on Near Eastern Affairs 1922–1923: Records of Proceedings and Draft Terms of Peace, 1923 (hereafter, Lausanne Conference on Near Eastern Affairs), p. 318). Adding these two figures together gives a rough estimate of just under 500,000 Greek Orthodox remaining in Turkey at the end of 1923 (including the 189,916 expelled in the subsequent three years).

[3] The Turkish Republic was officially declared in October 1923, with Mustafa Kemal serving as its first president.

Mass Expulsion. Meghan M. Garrity, Oxford University Press. © Oxford University Press (2026).
DOI: 10.1093/9780197829097.003.0006

bring sustainable peace. For those expelled from their ancestral homelands, never to return, it was an unjust sacrifice.

6.1 Background Context: Greek Presence in Asia Minor

The Greek presence in Asia Minor spanned millennia. For our purposes, a brief historical overview beginning in the fourth century AD must suffice. The Byzantine Empire, also known as the Eastern Roman Empire, ruled over Asia Minor for 1,123 years, from 330 until 1453.[4] It emerged when Constantine the Great, emperor of Rome, established a second or "Eastern Rome" with a new capital named in his honor: Constantinople. Byzantium's first great defeat came over 700 years after its founding in 1071 to the Seljuk Turks, foreshadowing events to come.[5] In 1453, the expanding "House of Othman," which gave its name to the Ottoman Empire, captured Constantinople, and what remained of the Byzantine Christian Empire fell into Muslim hands.[6] For the next four and a half centuries, the Ottomans ruled over large portions of Asia, Europe, and North Africa, forming a powerful multi-confessional empire.

To govern its diverse population, the Ottomans established the millet system for *People of the Book*—followers of Abrahamic, monotheistic religions. All pagans or nonbelievers had the Manichaean choice of conversion or the sword.[7] Each millet—the three largest were the Rum,[8] Armenian, and Jewish—was ruled by its respective religious authority. In return for ensuring that their populations remained obedient to the sultan, they were given complete autonomy over their religious institutions, civil courts, education systems, cultural associations, and tax collection, a portion of which was paid to Ottoman authorities.[9] Greek Orthodox Christians were members of the Rum millet, a reference to Rome as the seat of Christianity, and were referred to as Rum or Romios. The word "Greek," *Yunanli*, had no national significance until Greece gained its independence from the

[4] Norwich, 2013, p. xxxvii.
[5] Norwich, 2013, p. xxxvii.
[6] Norwich, 2013, p. xxxvii.
[7] Karpat, 1982, p. 148; Psomiades, 1968, p. 17.
[8] The Rum millet came under the jurisdiction of the Greek patriarch but included Greeks, Bulgarians, Serbians, Albanians, Wallachians, Moldavians, Ruthenians, Croatians, and Arab Christians, among others (Karpat, 1982, p. 146).
[9] Alexandris, 1983, p. 24; Psomiades, 1968, pp. 15–16.

Ottoman Empire in 1830. Thereafter, *Yunanli* was used to describe citizens of the newly independent Greek state, and Rum continued to refer to Greeks, or Hellenes, living outside of Greece who were not Greek citizens, including those residing in the Ottoman Empire.[10]

Since Islamic law discouraged Muslims from engaging in commerce and banking, Christians and Jews dominated the empire's economic and industrial sectors.[11] The Greeks were prominent in commerce, shipping, manufacturing, banking, and foreign trade.[12] In the second half of the nineteenth century, trade with Europe increased significantly, augmenting the size of coastal trading hubs along the Aegean and Black Sea littorals.[13] During this period, many Greeks emigrated from the independent Kingdom of Greece to the Ottoman Empire, as it offered more economic and entrepreneurial opportunities than the new Greek nation-state.[14] Ottoman railway concessions to the Great Powers further opened the interior of the empire, and Ottoman Greeks set up trading posts and small shops along the rail lines, serving as agents for the influx of foreign capital.[15] Although the Ottoman Greeks maintained cultural ties with their co-ethnics in Greece, they traced their historical lineage back to Romano-Byzantine Constantinople[16] and politically were content within the Ottoman Empire.[17]

While the Greeks living in the Ottoman Empire may have been satisfied with the political status quo, some politicians in Greece were not. In the early nineteenth century, Greece fought a nearly decade-long war (1821–1829) to gain independence from the Ottoman Empire. Out of this victory, and the long historical presence of Greeks in Asia Minor, emerged a Pan-Hellenic nationalist idea known as the "*Megali Idea*" or Great Idea. The core aim of this foreign policy position was to unite all Hellenic people within a single Greek state, essentially reviving Christian Byzantium. Its territorial scope included Epirus,[18] Macedonia, Thrace, western Anatolia, and the Aegean Islands, all of which were under Ottoman control before 1912. The culmination of the Megali Idea would be the recapture of Istanbul (Constantinople)

[10] Hirschon, 2003, p. xii; Oran, 2003, p. 98.
[11] Naimark, 2001, p. 19.
[12] Alexandris, 1982, p. 138.
[13] Morris & Ze'evi, 2019, p. 21.
[14] Alexandris, 1983, p. 49; Clogg, 1982, p. 195.
[15] Llewellyn-Smith, 1998, pp. 25–27.
[16] Oran, 2003, p. 98.
[17] Morris & Ze'evi, 2019, p. 25.
[18] Epirus is a historical region in the Balkans, now divided between Albania and Greece.

and its return to a Christian city.[19] The advocates of this policy had a stronger emotional connection with Byzantium than to ancient Athens.[20] However, by the early twentieth century, the Megali Idea was far from being realized—in 1910, only 37 percent of the estimated 7 million Greeks lived in Greece.[21]

6.2 Structural Factors: Collapse of the Ottoman Empire & Interstate Wars

Throughout the nineteenth century, the Ottoman Empire acquired the unfortunate sobriquet "sick man of Europe."[22] Its territory contracted and it lost much of its political status.[23] Serbia (1817) and Greece (1821) were among the first to revolt and declare their independence, inspiring nationalist sentiment throughout the Balkans.[24] The Russo–Turkish War (1877–1878) led to further Ottoman territorial losses.[25] Ottoman Sultan Abdülhamid II responded to these defeats with an iron fist, overturning the constitution, dissolving parliament, and resorting to repression.[26]

The despotic Sultan Abdülhamid II was not well liked by the army. He ignored its basic needs and young cadets began mobilizing against him. These cadets were well educated, having received military training abroad, and were largely from the Ottoman Balkan territories. They believed that the Ottoman army was out of date and were concerned about the shrinking empire and its weak defenses.[27] Their frustrations bubbled over in 1908 with a series of army mutinies and strikes across the empire.[28] The primary aim of these revolutionaries, who came to be known as the "Young Turks," was to save the Ottoman Empire by restoring its sovereignty and protecting its territory.[29] In restoring the constitution, the Unionist

[19] Alexandris, 1982, p. 137.
[20] Pentzopoulos, 1962, p. 26.
[21] Pentzopoulos, 1962, p. 27.
[22] This first appeared in print on May 10, 1860, in a *New York Times* article titled "Austria in Extremis" attributing the reference to Nicholas I of Russia (Austria in Extremis, 1860; Mylonas, 2012, p. 67).
[23] Naimark, 2001, p. 20.
[24] Ladas, 1932, pp. 5–6.
[25] Morris & Ze'evi, 2019, pp. 17–18.
[26] Morris & Ze'evi, 2019, p. 39.
[27] Lewis, 2002, p. 206.
[28] Lewis, 2002, p. 207.
[29] Lewis, 2002, p. 206.

(i.e., members of the Committee of Union and Progress [CUP]—the organization of the Young Turks movement) "were Ottoman patriots rather than Turkish nationalists."[30] They fought to restore the concept of "Ottomanism," uniting all persons within the empire, including minorities. The CUP was neither very Turkish nor very Muslim. Few of its leaders were "pure-blooded Turks," and most were secular in outlook.[31]

During this period, European powers exerted significant influence over the empire's affairs through financing its public debt, regulating import and export duties, and meddling in the treatment of minorities through the capitulations.[32] The capitulations were long-standing bilateral contracts between the Ottoman Empire and European countries, which expanded in the eighteenth century to include the right of Europeans to intercede on behalf of Christian minorities.[33] The European powers strategically used the capitulations to interfere in the domestic affairs of the Ottoman Empire. The Young Turks sought to break free from this foreign influence.[34] Yet, while they despised European meddling, the Young Turks were not anti-Western. They sought to become a peer of the powerful Western countries by preserving the territorial integrity of the Ottoman Empire and modernizing the state.[35]

In October 1912, the First Balkan War broke out over control of the Ottoman Empire's remaining European lands. Greece, Serbia, Montenegro, and Bulgaria formed a secret alliance and defeated the Ottomans in six weeks.[36] The subsequent peace treaty divided the spoils of the war, with Greece and Serbia the biggest winners. But disputes over the allocation of conquered lands left the situation unsettled. Bulgaria, unsatisfied with the allotment forced upon it, attacked Serbia and Greece, sparking the Second Balkan War, which lasted barely a month.[37] In this second war, the Ottomans managed to regain portions of their lost territory from Bulgaria in Eastern Thrace, but the overall results were still disastrous.[38] On August 10, 1913, the Treaty of Bucharest formally ended the Second Balkan War. The treaty granted Greece further territorial gains, including Crete, a portion of Epirus,

[30] Ahmad, 1982, p. 406.
[31] Lewis, 2002, p. 212.
[32] Ahmad, 1982, p. 403.
[33] Naimark, 2001, p. 20.
[34] Naimark 2001, pp. 20–21.
[35] Ahmad, 1966, pp. 305–306; Anderson, 2008.
[36] Ladas, 1932, p. 10; Macartney, 1934, p. 138; Mazower, 2004, p. 294; Psomiades, 1968, p. 21.
[37] Mazower, 2004, pp. 297–298; Psomiades, 1968, p. 22.
[38] Macartney, 1934, p. 139.

southern Macedonia, and the eastern Aegean Islands.[39] These acquired islands put Greece mere miles from the Ottoman coast. Over the course of a year, the Ottoman Empire lost more than 80 percent of its European lands and 70 percent of its European population.[40] Its European presence was essentially eliminated, ending over 500 years of territorial control.

6.3 Proximate Factors: Counter-Irredentist Motivations Emerge

During the two Balkan Wars, Greece and Bulgaria expelled hundreds of thousands of Muslims[41] to the Ottoman Empire.[42] These Muslim refugees and migrants, known as *muhacir*, dispersed throughout the empire along the coasts and into the Anatolian interior.[43] The territorial losses of the Balkan Wars were different than any previous Ottoman dismemberment. Most of the losses up until this point were on the periphery of the empire where there was minimal control and only nominal sovereignty. The Balkan territory, conversely, was "the life blood of the Ottoman Empire" and home to many of the Young Turk leaders.[44] This was personal.

After the Balkan Wars, the Young Turks had two main security concerns: preserving the territorial integrity of the remaining empire and ending foreign interference in their domestic affairs. Greece was the most serious threat. The country nearly doubled in size at the expense of Ottoman lands, and its occupation of the eastern Aegean Islands brought it closer than ever to the Ottoman coast.[45] Aware of the Megali Idea, CUP officials feared that Greek territorial ambitions would not cease with the new boundaries outlined in the Treaty of Bucharest and they would continue pressing east.[46] The loss of almost all of its European territory, and the corresponding influx of Muslim refugees, impacted the CUP's view of its subject populations. Loyalty

[39] Mylonas, 2012, p. 64.
[40] Akçam, 2012, p. xiv.
[41] A.A. Pallis notes that no records exist to precisely determine how many Muslims were killed or fled during the Balkan Wars. However, he estimates a minimum of 125,000 (1925, pp. 322–323); Ladas estimates 100,000 fled the Balkans in 1912 and another 48,570 in 1913 (1932, p. 15).
[42] Mourelos, 1985, p. 389; Naimark, 2001, p. 27.
[43] Kieser, 2018, p. 27.
[44] Unionist headquarters were in Salonika (Thessaloniki). After losing the city to Greece in the Balkan Wars of 1912, they moved to Istanbul (Ahmad, 1966, p. 320; Lewis, 2002, p. 222).
[45] Pentzopoulos, 1962, pp. 27–28.
[46] Bulutgil, 2016, p. 117.

was now equated with religion: Muslims were regarded as loyal citizens of the empire, while non-Muslims were perceived as disloyal.[47]

This shift in perceived loyalty was pivotal in the government's appraisal of the threat posed by the non-Muslim, "non-Turkifiable" populations within the shrunken empire.[48] The Greek Orthodox Christian population was regarded as a national minority, "a part of the population akin in race, language or religion to the neighboring state" (in this case, Greece).[49] Ottoman officials identified this group as an existential security threat to the survival of the state.[50] Though not all Greek Orthodox were complicit with the Greek government's foreign policy strategy, they were perceived to be contributing to the irredentist threat. This view was linked to the long history of the capitulations and persistent European interference in Ottoman domestic affairs on behalf of Christian minorities.[51] To counter the irredentist claims of Greece, and any further infringement on their territory, the Ottomans were motivated to remove the Greeks from the empire.

6.4 Preconditions for the Greek Orthodox Christian Expulsion

Although the winds of Turkish nationalism had been in the air before 1913, the Unionists held firm in their commitment to Ottomanism and the preservation of the multi-confessional empire. That ended in 1913. After devastating defeats in the Balkan Wars, the ruling elite adopted an exclusionary ethno-religious ideology, one of the key preconditions for mass expulsion. Influenced by sociologist Ziya Gökalp, the CUP sought to transform the shrunken Ottoman Empire into a Turkish nation-state and to create a Turkish national identity among Ottoman Muslims.[52] Asia Minor was deemed the Turkish homeland, *Türk Yurdu*, and the site of Turkification.[53] "Turkey for the Turks" became a popular nationalist slogan.[54] The trauma of the Balkan Wars fostered the perception that Christians were traitors, having supported anti-Muslim tactics during the wars.[55] They had to be eliminated.

[47] Üngör, 2008, p. 17.
[48] Üngör, 2008, p. 19.
[49] Ladas, 1932, p. 1.
[50] Ladas, 1932, p. 13; Morris & Ze'evi, 2019, p. 3; Pentzopoulos, 1962, p. 53.
[51] Alexandris, 1983, p. 25; Macartney, 1934, p. 433; Pentzopoulos, 1962, p. 53.
[52] Üngör, 2008, p. 22.
[53] Kieser, 2018, p. 9.
[54] Mazower, 2004, p. 264; Üngör, 2008, p. 36.
[55] Emin, 1930, p. 193; Naimark, 2001, p. 27; Üngör, 2008, p. 23.

While the Greek Orthodox were not the only Christians in the Ottoman Empire,[56] the nature of the threat they posed was distinct from that of other Christian groups, particularly the Armenians. Unlike other Christian populations, the Greek Orthodox did not revolt against the Ottoman state. There was no Ottoman Greek national movement, nor were there political demands for union with Greece (at least before 1919).[57] Most importantly, the existence of the Greek nation-state functioned as a protective umbrella over the Greek Orthodox population.[58] Ottoman officials believed the Kingdom of Greece might intervene on behalf of persecuted Greek Orthodox Christians or initiate reprisal attacks against Muslims living in Greece.[59] They were careful not to provoke Greece into abandoning its neutrality and entering World War I. Greece also had the support of European powers, so a significant attack on Greek Orthodox Christians may have provoked European intervention.[60] Although Greece eventually entered World War I in 1917, it was not because of Ottoman violence against the Greek Orthodox.[61] The Ottoman/Turkish authorities believed the nature of the Greek irredentist threat could be solved by removing the Greek Orthodox population from the territory, a second precondition for mass expulsion.

There was also a convenient alternative "homeland"—Greece—to send the expellees, satisfying a third precondition. The Ottomans viewed neighboring Greece as the place where the Greek Orthodox Christians "belonged." The fact that many Greek Orthodox had never set foot in the Kingdom of Greece, had lived in the Ottoman Empire for generations, and spoke only Turkish was immaterial to Ottoman authorities. The Ottomans also had the capability to physically remove the Greek population from their territory, which fulfilled the final precondition. Their military abilities were proven in battlefield victories against Allied troops in the Dardanelles during World War I, and against the Greek army during the Greco–Turkish War.[62] All four preconditions were in place for the Ottomans to expel the Greek Orthodox Christians.

[56] Other Christian communities included Armenians and Assyrians.
[57] Llewellyn-Smith, 1998, pp. 29–30; Morris & Ze'evi, 2019, p. 490.
[58] Morgenthau, 2017 [1918], pp. 38, 218.
[59] Morgenthau, 2017 [1918], p. 218; Morris & Ze'evi, 2019, p. 386.
[60] Naimark, 2001, p. 43.
[61] Morris & Ze'evi, 2019, p. 490.
[62] Kieser, 2018, p. 322.

6.5 Ottoman Expulsions of Greek Orthodox Christians Along the Aegean and Pontic Littorals (1913–1923)

The mass expulsion of Greek Orthodox Christians from the Aegean and Pontic littorals occurred in three phases in the decade from 1913–1923: 1) the post–Balkan Wars phase (1913–1914), culminating in the first (failed) attempt at a "population exchange" between the Ottoman Empire and Greece; 2) the Greco–Turkish War phase (1919–1922), in which the Greek population was expelled along with the retreating Greek military; and 3) the Lausanne Convention phase, part of the postwar Lausanne Peace Treaty, which authorized the first compulsory "population exchange," signed in January 1923. These phases were cumulative, each building on the next, but were also distinct chapters in a government strategy of population removal.

6.5.1 Phase 1: Post–Balkan Wars (1913–1914)

Greece's occupation of the eastern Aegean Islands after the Balkan Wars brought it perilously close to the prosperous Turkish coast. The Ottomans were concerned about securing the shoreline and preventing further Greek conquests of more than 1 million so-called "unredeemed Hellenes"[63]—a reference to Greeks that lived outside of the Greek nation-state. With the 1913 Protocol of Adrianople in mind, which authorized a "voluntary" population exchange along the new border between Bulgaria and the Ottoman Empire,[64] the Young Turks began expelling Greeks from coastal regions. The CUP believed that the Greek government would never willingly enter into a "population exchange" agreement like Bulgaria, so they forced the issue by violently removing Greek Orthodox Christians from their homes.[65] They hoped the expulsions would pressure Greece to return the annexed Aegean Islands, which the Allies had sanctioned.[66]

[63] Ladas, 1932, p. 20.

[64] As part of the 1913 peace treaty between the Ottoman Empire and Bulgaria at the end of the Second Balkan War, the Protocol of Adrianople authorized the expulsion of Bulgarians and Muslims within a 9.3 mile (15 kilometer) area on either side of the new border (Macartney, 1934).

[65] LNA, R84, 2/43317/31152: Article by A.A. Pallis, "The Exchange of Populations in the Balkans," in the journal *The Nineteenth Century* (p. 378), March 1925; UN Archives at Geneva; Psomiades, 1968, p. 61.

[66] Llewellyn-Smith, 1998, p. 32; Pallis, 1925, p. 318; Psomiades, 2011, p. 217.

In the months following the conclusion of the Balkan Wars, the Ottomans expelled an estimated 100,000–270,000[67] Greeks from the Aegean coast and Eastern Thrace.[68] These expulsions were carried out by irregular armed groups, comprised mostly of Balkan refugees (the *muhacir* who had recently been expelled from Greece), in collusion with Ottoman authorities.[69] Greek families were forced to flee through an official campaign of intimidation, threats, looting, and select killings.[70] Evidence of the government's involvement in and direction of these expulsions is found in a coded telegram from Interior Minister Talat Pasha to the district governor on April 14, 1914, in which Talat requested that it be "ensured" that the Greeks who had gathered on the coast should "emigrate by boarding steamships but without any indication being given that [the process] is the result of [a government] directive."[71] The Ottomans chartered the steamships, providing expellees free transport to Greece.[72] Simultaneously, Ottoman authorities organized an economic boycott of Greek products and businesses with the goal of forcing merchants to leave.[73]

In May 1914, the Ottoman minister in Athens, Ghalib Kemaly Bey, wrote to Greece's Prime Minister Eleftherios Venizelos to officially propose a "population exchange."[74] Kemaly emphasized that this was the only way to bring peace to the region. Greece was keen to end the violence and believed an exchange could both assist in populating its newly acquired Balkan territories and in overcoming economic losses from the emigration of 500,000 Greeks to the Americas between 1900 and 1914.[75] Venizelos also believed that through a formal exchange with an exchange commission, the expellees would be compensated for their losses.[76] He accepted the Ottoman proposal but insisted the agreement be voluntary and that the properties of the emigrants should be appraised and liquidated by a Mixed Commission.[77] The commission was established in Smyrna (now Izmir) and

[67] LNA, R84, 2/43317/31152: Article by A.A. Pallis, "The Exchange of Populations in the Balkans," in the journal *The Nineteenth Century* (p. 378), March 1925; UN Archives at Geneva.
[68] Ladas, 1932, p. 16; Macartney, 1934, p. 434; Pallis, 1925, p. 318; Psomiades, 1968, p. 62.
[69] Llewellyn-Smith, 1998, p. 31.
[70] Akçam, 2012, p. 55.
[71] Akçam, 2012, p. 71 (cites Prime Ministerial Ottoman Archive: BOA/DJ.ŞFR, no. 40/11).
[72] Akçam, 2012, p. 77.
[73] Akçam, 2012, p. 83.
[74] Akçam, 2012, p. 65; Macartney, 1934, p. 434; Mourelos, 1985, p. 393; Psomiades, 2011, p. 218.
[75] Psomiades, 2011, p. 219.
[76] Macartney, 1934, p. 435.
[77] Ladas, 1932, p. 21; Mourelos, 1985, p. 394; Psomiades, 2011, p. 218.

began its work in August 1914.[78] However, the outbreak of World War I suspended the commission's work, and the initial "population exchange" was not implemented.[79]

Aware of their isolated and weakened status after the Balkan Wars, and fearing Greek and Russian aggression, the Ottomans sought an alliance with a foreign power.[80] They first turned to the British and the French, but both refused, driving them into the arms of the Germans.[81] The alliance with Germany was a return to the days of Sultan Abdülhamid II, who had established strong ties with the Germans in the late nineteenth century. These relations had frayed when the Young Turks sought to overturn all elements of the previous era. But unable to secure any other external support, they accepted the Germans.

As early as January 1914, well before the outbreak of World War I, German officials held high-level positions in the Ottoman military.[82] In July, the Ottomans formally signed a defensive alliance with Germany "for the purpose of preserving peace."[83] The United States ambassador to the Ottoman Empire, Henry Morgenthau Sr., described the close German involvement in the Ottoman military in his memoirs. Morgenthau quoted the German Ambassador Baron Von Wangenheim saying in August 1914, "We now control both the Turkish army and the navy."[84]

Ottoman politicians debated entering World War I after its outbreak in Europe at the end of July. The Ottoman cabinet was divided between those who were strongly against war and others, particularly Talat and Enver Pasha, who were optimistic about the opportunities war might bring.[85] The anti-war cabinet members resigned after German officers, on Turkish vessels, attacked Russia from the Black Sea without cabinet approval.[86] On November 4, 1914, Russia declared war on Turkey, followed by Britain and France. The Ottomans joined Germany and Austria on the side of the

[78] Psomiades, 2011, p. 218.

[79] The negotiated convention was drafted but never signed (LNA, R1617, 41/19720/19720: Commission Mixte de Smyrne: Projet de Convention, undated; UN Archives at Geneva & LNA, R1617, 41/19720/19720: Letter from H. Alitcha to Helmer Rosting, 24 March 1922; UN Archives at Geneva).

[80] Ahmad, 1966, p. 325.

[81] Emin, 1930, p. 57.

[82] Morgenthau, 2017 [1918], pp. 32–33.

[83] Emin, 1930, p. 67.

[84] Morgenthau, 2017 [1918], p. 72.

[85] Mansel, 1996, p. 370; Morgenthau, 2017 [1918], pp. 87–88.

[86] Morgenthau, 2017 [1918], p. 87.

Central Powers.[87] The cabinet resignations left pro-war officials in charge of the Ottoman government under the full control of the CUP.

Intuitively, one might have thought that entry into World War I would expedite the ongoing Greek expulsions; however, it had the opposite effect. The Ottoman's new ally Germany wanted to court Greece, which had declared its neutrality in the war, to join the Central Powers. Germany's royal family also had familial ties with Greece. The wife of Greek King Constantine was Sophia of Prussia, the sister of German Emperor Wilhelm II.[88] Thus, the Germans directed the Ottomans to stop expelling Greek Orthodox Christians.[89] These orders were immediately implemented as documented in a cable from Talat Pasha to the provinces in November 1914, the same month the Ottomans entered the war: "In light of the state's current political situation, no attacks on or oppression of Greeks shall be allowed as such acts of oppression against them would not be appropriate."[90] The Greek expulsions of Phase 1 came to an immediate end.

6.5.2 The World War I Interlude (November 1914–1918)

During World War I, the Ottomans shifted their strategy from cross-border mass expulsions of the Greek population to internal deportations.[91] Their focus was on militarily securing the borders from external incursions by removing "suspicious populations" from the Aegean and Black Sea coasts.[92] Not all coastal Greeks were relocated internally, just those in strategic areas that were militarily vulnerable.[93] Events during this interlude critically shaped the context for Phase 2—the largest mass expulsion of Greeks—and merit a brief discussion.

The Allies heavily lobbied Greece to abandon its war-time neutrality and made significant territorial promises to persuade the country to join their side.[94] British ambassador to Athens, Sir Francis Elliott, offered Greek

[87] Emin, 1930, p. 77.
[88] Clogg, 2021, p. 291; Gilbert, 1994, pp. 105–106.
[89] Akçam, 2012, p. 99.
[90] Akçam, 2012, p. 75 (cites Prime Ministerial Ottoman Archive: BOA/DJ.ŞFR, no. 46/133).
[91] From late 1914 until Greece's entry into World War I in 1917, an estimated 500,000–550,000 Greek Orthodox were deported into the interior of the Ottoman Empire to protect the empire's flanks and quell fears of separatism (Kieser, 2018, p. 355; Morris & Ze'evi, 2019, p. 385; Psomiades, 2011, p. 223).
[92] Akçam, 2012, p. 97.
[93] Akçam, 2012, p. 106.
[94] Pentzopoulos, 1962, pp. 34–35; Psomiades, 1968, p. 23.

Prime Minister Venizelos the territories of Northern Epirus, the Dodecanese Islands (except Rhodes), and the western coast of Asia Minor.[95] The Greek government was divided on how to respond. Venizelos, a strong supporter of the Megali Idea, was eager to join the Allies and potentially reap significant territorial gains, whereas King Constantine, with family ties to the German emperor, wished to remain neutral. Unable to reconcile, Venizelos broke away and established his own government in Thessaloniki, where he joined the Allies and declared war on the Central Powers.[96] Internal deportations of the Greeks in the Ottoman Empire rapidly increased in late 1917 after Greece entered the war on the Allied side.[97]

On October 30, 1918, four years after the Ottomans entered the war, they unconditionally surrendered with the signing of the Armistice of Mudros.[98] The Ottomans were exhausted, and with no defenses left, resigned in defeat. The Ottoman government and the public generally viewed the armistice agreement as fair, if not favorable. The sultanate and caliphate remained intact, and although the empire was reduced in size, it still existed. The terms of the Treaty of Sèvres two years later would not be as generous.[99]

Ottoman officials, however, were concerned about two articles in the armistice agreement: Articles VII and XXIV. Article VII stated: "The Allies to have the right *to occupy* any strategic points in the event of any situation arising which threatens the security of the Allies," and Article XXIV said: "In case of disorder in the six Armenian vilayets, the Allies reserve to themselves the right *to occupy* any part of them" [emphasis added].[100] The Ottomans viewed these articles as mechanisms for continued foreign intervention and ripe for abuse by minority populations.[101] Their instincts were right.

6.5.3 Phase 2: Greco–Turkish War (1919–1922)

Empowered by the Allied victory in World War I, and their promised territorial gains, Greece invaded Turkey with 20,000 troops in the spring of 1919.[102] Greece sought to realize the Megali Idea, uniting "unredeemed

[95] Pentzopoulos, 1962, pp. 34–35.
[96] Pentzopoulos, 1962, p. 35.
[97] Morris & Ze'evi, 2019, p. 392.
[98] Üngör, 2008, p. 27.
[99] Zürcher, 1998, p. 273.
[100] Maurice, 1943, pp. 85–87.
[101] Zürcher, 1998, p. 271.
[102] Hirschon, 2003, p. 5.

Hellenes" within an expanded Greek nation-state. The British tacitly supported the Greek invasion, which blocked Italian advances north toward Smyrna from their occupation of Antalya.[103] On the heels of the Greek troops were an estimated 140,000–180,000 Greeks—previously expelled from Smyrna and Eastern Thrace—who sought to reinhabit their former homes.[104]

Shortly after Greece occupied western Anatolia, the Allied powers signed the Treaty of Versailles in June 1919, officially ending the war between the Allies and Germany. It was not until a year later in August 1920, during the Greco–Turkish War, that the Treaty of Sèvres was finalized. This treaty decapitated the Ottoman Empire and de facto proclaimed its final demise through multiple partitions.[105] The empire lost all its remaining European lands and some Aegean Islands (to Greece); Armenia (to independence); Syria, Mesopotamia, and Palestine (to Allied administrative mandates); Hedjaz and the holy sites of Mecca and Medina (to independence); Egypt and Cyprus (to Britain); Morocco and Tunis (to France); and a string of islands in the Aegean Sea (to Italy).[106] The treaty also reinstated the capitulations, granting the Allied powers large economic concessions.[107] Istanbul and the straits were deemed an "international zone" occupied by the British. Although the new Ottoman sultan remained de jure in control, he was effectively a stooge of the Allied powers.[108] Turkey never ratified the treaty.[109]

In 1922, Turkish envoys in London and Paris attempted to negotiate a peaceful end to the ongoing Greco–Turkish War, but the Allies refused.[110] The rejected peace was a fateful decision. That summer, nationalist leader Mustafa Kemal's forces defeated the Greek army, and the Greek troops quickly retreated to the Aegean coast.[111] Ottoman Greek civilians followed the retreating army, some on military orders,[112] and others in fear of Turkish reprisals.[113] Turkish forces entered the coastal city

[103] Lewis, 2002, pp. 240–241; Morris & Ze'evi, 2019, p. 429; Psomiades, 1968, pp. 27–28.
[104] Ladas, 1932, p. 16; Pallis, 1925, pp. 318–319.
[105] Kieser, 2018, p. 399.
[106] Treaty of Sèvres, 1920 (Articles 83–84; 88; 94; 98–99; 101; 116; 118; 120; 122, respectively).
[107] Treaty of Sèvres, 1920 (Article 261).
[108] Anderson, 2008; Mansel, 1996, pp. 381, 396.
[109] Psomiades, 1968, p. 30.
[110] Davison, 1965, p. 196.
[111] Hirschon, 2003, p. 5.
[112] ACICR Mis 15-5/524/1341; Proces-Verbal: Rapport de M. Burnier, délégué du C.I.C.R. à Constantinople, 27.11.1922.
[113] Morris & Ze'evi, 2019, p. 434.

of Smyrna on the morning of September 9, 1922, without resistance.[114] The scene was chaotic. Tens of thousands of Greeks crowded into public buildings and along the quay desperately seeking transport across the Aegean Sea to Greece. The Allied powers—Britain, France, Italy, and the US—watched events unfold from their ships in the harbor. They did not come to the aid of the Greeks.[115] Panicked, many people jumped into the water and attempted to swim to the Allied ships. Others crammed into small boats that capsized.[116] Four days later, Smyrna was burned to the ground.[117] Amid the disorder, and the risk of the fire to the masses of people, the Turkish authorities permitted the Allies to assist in transporting the Greeks to Greece.[118]

After the Greek withdrawal from Anatolia, the British reluctantly accepted the fait accompli of Turkish victory. They signed the Armistice of Mudanya on October 11, 1922, pledging to return Smyrna, Eastern Thrace, the Straits, and Istanbul to Turkey, and authorized a peace conference in Lausanne, Switzerland.[119] By the end of the month, another 250,000 Greeks were expelled with the departing Greek troops, this time overland from Eastern Thrace to Greece-controlled Western Thrace.[120] It is estimated that in the months leading up to the Lausanne Conference over 1 million Greek Orthodox Christians were expelled.[121]

6.5.4 Phase 3: Lausanne Convention (November 1922–January 1923)

On the banks of Lake Geneva at the Hôtel du Château, the Lausanne Conference began on November 20, 1922, in Lausanne, Switzerland. Delegates from the relevant Allied powers—Great Britain, France, Italy, and the US—attended along with representatives from Greece and Turkey. The aim of the conference was to secure peace in the Near East and relitigate

[114] Morris & Ze'evi, 2019, p. 435.
[115] Psomiades, 2011, p. 222.
[116] Naimark, 2001, pp. 47–48.
[117] Naimark, 2001, pp. 49–52; Pentzopoulous, 1962, pp. 46–47; Psomiades, 2011, p. 222. The origins of the fire are debated. The Turks blame an Armenian conspiracy and Greek historians blame the Turks (Naimark, 2001, pp. 51–52).
[118] Morris & Ze'evi, 2019, p. 450; Naimark, 2001, p. 50.
[119] Lewis, 2002, p. 254; Morris & Ze'evi, 2019, p. 455; Pentzopoulos, 1962, p. 47.
[120] Morris & Ze'evi, 2019, p. 453.
[121] Hirschon, 2003, p. 6; Morris & Ze'evi, 2019, p. 465.

the defunct Treaty of Sèvres, redrawing the boundaries of the soon-to-be Turkish Republic. Ismet Pasha, minister of foreign affairs, led the Turkish delegation; Eleftherios Venizelos was the lead for Greece.[122]

A wide range of issues were tackled at the conference by three different commissions—Territorial and Military Questions, the Régime of Foreigners, and Economic and Financial Questions—along with thirteen corresponding sub-commissions.[123] The third sub-commission of the first commission was the Sub-Commission for the Exchange of Populations, and it held twenty-four meetings between December 2, 1922 and January 24, 1923.[124] The output of this sub-commission was the Lausanne Convention, signed on January 30, 1923, distinct and separate from the peace treaty of the same name, and arguably the most transformative aspect of the peace. The convention authorized the first internationally sanctioned compulsory "population exchange" between two countries. Although the convention's title referred to an "exchange of populations," the criteria set out in Article 1 established a clear case of mass expulsion—a compulsory removal, of a religious group,[125] on the grounds of belonging to that group, without individual legal review, and denying the expellees the right to return.

Article 1 of the convention outlined who would be exchanged. Since many Greeks in the Ottoman Empire spoke only Turkish and were not part of a single race,[126] religion was the only criterion that united these diverse groups.[127] However, the goal of removing ethno-national minorities was clear in the convention's title—*Convention Concerning the Exchange of Greek and Turkish Populations*.[128] The first article stated:

> As from the 1st May, 1923, there shall take place a compulsory exchange of Turkish nationals of the Greek Orthodox religion established in Turkish territory, and of Greek nationals of the Moslem religion established in Greek territory. These persons shall not return to live in Turkey or Greece

[122] Davison, 1965, p. 199; Pentzopoulos, 1962, p. 52.

[123] Lausanne Conference on Near Eastern Affairs, 1923.

[124] LNA, C1112/8/N15: Sub-Commission for Exchange of Populations Meeting Minutes, December 1922; UN Archives at Geneva; Lausanne Conference on Near Eastern Affairs, 1923; Conférence de Lausanne sur les affairs du proche-orient, 1922–1923: Recueil des actes de la Conférence, 1923 (hereafter, Conférence de Lausanne sur les affairs du proche-orient).

[125] A.A. Pallis (1925) argued that "the test of religion was . . . well chosen as being the one least likely to give rise to difficulties of interpretation" in LNA, R84, 2/43317/31152: Article by A.A. Pallis, "The Exchange of Populations in the Balkans," in the journal *The Nineteenth Century* (p. 380), March 1925; UN Archives at Geneva.

[126] Religion was also the only criterion that united the Muslims in Greece as many Muslims in Greece spoke only Greek and were racially distinct from the Muslims of Anatolia.

[127] Ladas, 1932, p. 378.

[128] Ladas, 1932, p. 380.

> respectively without the authorisation of the Turkish Government or of the Greek Government respectively.[129]

An estimated 355,635 Muslims from Greece and 189,916 Greek Orthodox Christians from Turkey were affected by this article, implemented between 1923 and 1926.[130]

Article 3 denied the right to return to both Greek and Muslim refugees who fled Turkey and Greece, respectively, at any time in the previous decade: "Those Greeks and Moslems who have already, and since the 18th October, 1912,[131] left the territories the Greek and Turkish inhabitants of which are to be respectively exchanged, shall be considered as included in the exchange provided for in Article 1."[132] This article affected the largest number of persons and endorsed the fait accompli of their forced expulsion. It included 1 million refugees who fled to Greece following the defeat of the Greek army in 1922,[133] as well as hundreds of thousands of Muslims who fled from Greece to Turkey during or after the Balkan Wars.

Article 7 denationalized these refugee populations, who were denied the right to return, but immediately provided them the nationality of their new "home" country, preventing the creation of stateless populations:

> The emigrants will lose the nationality of the country which they are leaving, and will acquire the nationality of the country of their destination, upon their arrival in the territory of the latter country. Such emigrants as have already left one or other of the two countries and have not yet acquired their new nationality, shall acquire that nationality on the date of the signature of the present Convention.[134]

Throughout the convention, the word "emigrants" was used in reference to those being expelled, neither "expulsion" nor "expel" appeared in the text.

[129] LNA, S356, 21/Dossier 5: Convention Concerning the Exchange of Greek and Turkish Populations [Translation reprinted from the British Treaty Series—No.16/(1923).], 30 January 1923; UN Archives at Geneva.

[130] Ladas, 1932, pp. 438–439.

[131] October 18, 1912, was the day Greece declared war on the Ottoman Empire in the First Balkan War.

[132] LNA, S356, 21/Dossier 5: Convention Concerning the Exchange of Greek and Turkish Populations [Translation reprinted from the British Treaty Series—No.16/(1923).], 30 January 1923; UN Archives at Geneva.

[133] Oran, 2003, p. 100.

[134] LNA, S356, 21/Dossier 5: Convention Concerning the Exchange of Greek and Turkish Populations [Translation reprinted from the British Treaty Series—No.16/(1923).], 30 January 1923; UN Archives at Geneva.

While senior diplomats negotiated the terms of the convention—exchanging people like cattle—the public outrage was immense. Greek refugees angrily objected to not being allowed to return to Turkey, their country of birth and ancestral homeland for centuries. Refugees in Thessaloniki protested against the "disgraceful bartering of bodies to the detriment of modern civilization."[135] Many refugees saw themselves as Ottomans and Anatolian Christians, not Greeks, and felt like strangers in their new land.[136] Muslims in Greece also rejected the idea of leaving their homes in Greece and moving to a foreign land, forced to abandon their lives and livelihoods.[137] In addition to the outcry of the expellees themselves, international public opinion was against the idea of a mandatory, forcible exchange of populations.[138]

In response to the public outcry, the conference delegates fiercely denied paternity of the compulsory "population exchange."[139] Yet, in the end, they agreed and supported its implementation. A Mixed Commission was established to oversee the exchange of populations and compensation for properties, but by 1930, the Angora Convention abandoned all attempts at individual appraisals. The Greek and Turkish governments agreed to "wipe the slate clean," and most expellees were not properly compensated.[140] Throughout the three phases of mass expulsion—beginning after the Balkan Wars in 1913 and ending with the Lausanne Convention signed in 1923—over 1 million Greek Orthodox Christians were expelled.[141]

6.6 Istanbul as a Negative Case: Greek Orthodox Christians in the Imperial Capital (1913–1923)

Unlike the Greeks along the Aegean and Pontic littorals, the Greeks of Istanbul were not expelled during the decade from 1913 to 1923. The Lausanne Convention specifically exempted "Greek inhabitants of Istanbul" from the

[135] Mazower, 2004, p. 344.
[136] Mazower, 2004, p. 360.
[137] Ladas, 1932, p. 340.
[138] Ladas, 1932, p. 340.
[139] Pentzopoulos, 1962, p. 62; Psomiades, 2011, p. 213; Ladas, 1932, p. 340.
[140] Macartney, 1934, p. 447.
[141] Akçam, 2012, pp. 262–263 (cites Karpat, 1985); Emin, 1930, p. 210; Karpat, 1985, p. 45; Ladas, 1932, pp. 14, 438–439; Macartney, 1931, p. 81; Morris & Ze'evi, 2019, p. 24; Pentzopoulos, 1962, pp. 29–30 (cites Polybius, 1918, p. 44).

1923 "population exchange."[142] This is puzzling because the Greek population in Istanbul was more powerful, educated, and connected to foreigners than Greeks in any other part of the empire. The Ecumenical Patriarchate, the religious center of the Rum millet, was in the Phanar district of Istanbul and strongly influenced the ideological orientation of its flock. At the end of World War I, many Ottoman Greeks believed that the Allied occupation of the city would quickly fulfill the Megali Idea and restore the Christian glory of Byzantium.[143] Greeks cheered the Allied forces as they entered the city, and Greek flags hung from homes, businesses, and the Patriarchate itself.[144]

Because the Ottoman government's motivation in expelling the Greeks was to counter irredentism, those in Istanbul were arguably the greatest threat. In 1919, Greek Prime Minister Venizelos told King Alexander that the "city would be conquered from within," all but admitting that the Istanbul Greeks were the Trojan horse he hoped to use to win back the imperial city.[145] After the Greco–Turkish War, Ottoman Muslims strongly favored expelling the Greek Orthodox from Istanbul. They saw their continued presence as an enduring threat to the new republic.[146] Yet, in all three phases of mass expulsion, the Greeks of Istanbul were allowed to remain.

With its strategic location on the banks of the Bosphorus, Istanbul was the gateway from the Orient to the Occident. Straddling both Asia and Europe, it was a mosaic of languages, cultures, religion, and peoples. It was also a central hub of commerce, trade, and intellectual activity. French was as likely as Turkish to be heard on the streets, and most road signs were printed in both languages.[147] In addition to Ottoman Muslim elites, including the sultan and his advisors in the Sublime Porte,[148] the city was full of Christian intellectuals and prominent businessmen. For Greek Orthodox Christians, the capital was also their religious center, the seat of the Ecumenical Patriarchate.[149] Although reports vary, an estimated 205,375 Ottoman Greeks resided in

[142] Article 2 stated, "The following persons shall not be included in the exchange provided for in Article 1: (a) The Greek inhabitants of Constantinople. (b) The Moslem inhabitants of Western Thrace." This affected approximately 240,000 persons—130,000 Muslims in Western Thrace and 110,000 Greek Orthodox Christians in Istanbul, roughly equal populations on both sides (Alexandris, 2003, p. 118; Oran, 2003, p. 100).

[143] Mansel, 1996, p. 384.

[144] Alexandris, 1983, p. 59; Mansel, 1996, p. 385.

[145] Alexandris, 1982, p. 140; Alexandris, 1983, p. 53.

[146] Alexandris, 1983, p. 83.

[147] Morgenthau, 2017 [1918], p. 193.

[148] The Sublime Porte refers to the central government of the Ottoman Empire.

[149] Alexandris, 1982, p. 139.

Istanbul in 1914, 23 percent of the empire's total Greek population.[150] To this total were added an estimated 65,000 Greek citizens of Greece who lived in the capital as foreign nationals.[151]

The Greek Orthodox of Istanbul, like those along the Aegean and Pontic littorals, dominated commerce, banking, shipping, manufacturing, railways, and the professions.[152] Of the total capital investment in the Ottoman Empire in 1914, 50 percent was Ottoman Greek, highlighting their economic dominance.[153] The Greeks of Istanbul were politically divided into two main groups: those who supported the status quo under Ottoman rule and those committed to the Megali Idea. The former group was composed of religious and lay notables in the Ecumenical Patriarchate, government bureaucrats, and the commercial class; the latter group included medical, legal, and literary professionals.[154] The salience of these differences increased between 1913 and 1923, particularly in the aftermath of World War I and the Greek invasion of western Anatolia.

Despite their differences, both factions were committed to the spread of Greek culture through Hellenization efforts, which were achieved through educational, cultural, and literary societies. In the late nineteenth century, Greek cultural and educational institutions proliferated rapidly, financed by wealthy Greeks in Istanbul. There were 20 cultural societies, including the most prominent Greek Literary Society, and more than 113 Greek schools in the capital.[155] Except for an 1894 Ottoman law that mandated Turkish be taught in all schools, the Rum millet had complete autonomy over their educational curriculum.[156]

Politically, the Istanbul Greeks held prominent roles in the Ottoman bureaucracy, as ambassadors and attachés to European embassies, including Great Britain.[157] Greeks won twenty-four seats in the 1908 parliamentary elections.[158] However, after the disastrous First Balkan War, the Ottomans terminated Greek political participation, ending the presence of Greek bureaucrats, diplomats, and cabinet officials in the government.[159]

[150] Karpat, 1985, p. 170.
[151] Alexandris, 1983, p. 50.
[152] Clogg, 1982, p. 196.
[153] Alexandris, 1983, p. 32.
[154] Clogg, 1982, p. 197.
[155] Alexandris, 1983, pp. 45, 48; Clogg, 1982, p. 197.
[156] Alexandris, 1983, p. 45; Clogg, 1982, p. 198.
[157] Alexandris, 1983, pp. 29–30.
[158] Boura, 1999, p. 194; Clogg, 1982, p. 199.
[159] Alexandris, 1983, p. 43.

The Greek Orthodox religious leadership also played an important political role—the Ecumenical Patriarchate served as the spiritual and administrative center for Orthodox Christians, with the Ecumenical Patriarch as the leader of the Rum millet. The patriarch not only had religious, political, and administrative power over the Rum, but he was also a member of the sultan's bureaucracy.[160] The Patriarchate resisted the Young Turk idea of Ottomanism and equality for all citizens, because equality meant the dissolution of its political and administrative control. The Unionists introduced legislation to reduce the power of the millets, including in education—a core element of the Hellenization efforts.[161] These changes and the introduction of mandatory military service for non-Muslims were particularly offensive to the Patriarchate.[162]

After the World War I armistice and the election of a new patriarch in October 1918, the two factions of Greeks in Istanbul converged around the pursuit of the Megali Idea.[163] Both the Patriarchate and the Greek Orthodox commercial class sided with the Greek professionals in their support for irredentism.[164] Even the previously nonpolitical Greek Literary Society announced its desire for Istanbul to be incorporated into Greece.[165] Emboldened by the Allied occupation, the Patriarch formally ended the Rum millet in March 1919, issuing a resolution for the "Union with Greece," breaking off all relations with the Ottoman government, and assuming "unilateral and complete sovereignty over the community."[166] Greeks were discharged from their civic duties as Ottoman citizens, and the Patriarchate, with Allied permission, began issuing its own passports.[167] As directed, the Greek Orthodox did not participate in the 1919 elections.[168] In December 1921, the Patriarchate went a step further, appointing a Greek citizen as patriarch, breaking a centuries-old Ottoman tradition that the patriarch be an Ottoman citizen, further infuriating the Turkish nationalists.[169]

As this negative case shows, the Greeks of Istanbul were as much—if not more—of a security threat to the territorial integrity of the Ottoman Empire

[160] Alexandris, 1982, p. 22.
[161] Alexandris, 1983, p. 36.
[162] Alexandris, 1983, p. 33; Clogg, 1982, p. 199.
[163] Alexandris, 1982, p. 143; Mansel, 1996, p. 385.
[164] Alexandris, 1982, pp. 143–144.
[165] Alexandris, 1983, p. 61.
[166] Alexandris, 1982, p. 145; Alexandris, 1983, p. 57; Mansel, 1996, p. 385.
[167] Clogg, 1982, p. 200; Mansel, 1996, p. 385.
[168] Boura, 1999, p. 201.
[169] Alexandris 1983, pp. 75–76.

as Greeks elsewhere in the empire, particularly after World War I. Thus, the question remains: Why were the Istanbul Greeks not expelled alongside their co-ethnics from the Aegean and Pontic littorals?

6.7 Intervening Factors

Three pivotal intervening factors explain why the Ottomans expelled the Greek Orthodox Christians from the Aegean and Pontic littorals, as well as Anatolia, while sparing those in Istanbul: alliances, the "homeland" state, and pertinent international organizations (IOs). This section focuses on mass expulsion events in Phase 2 (1919–1922) and Phase 3 (November 1922–January 1923), with particular attention on the Lausanne Conference negotiations, where final decisions were made regarding the Greek Orthodox expulsion. Nevertheless, the intervening factors hold for all three phases.

6.7.1 Alliances

Domestic Alliances

After World War I, the Ottoman sultan collaborated with the Allied forces that occupied Istanbul. He was pleased that the empire had remained intact and his position secure. Outside of the capital, public opinion was not as sanguine. War hero Mustafa Kemal[170] arrived in Samsun on the Black Sea coast four days after the Greeks occupied Smyrna in the spring of 1919.[171] Kemal was tasked by the Ottoman government with demilitarizing Turkish troops as part of the postwar armistice. Disgusted by the sultan's cozy relations with the Allied forces, Kemal defied his orders and quickly began assembling soldiers and mobilizing a nationalist army.[172] To avoid any direct conflict with the Ottoman government, he resigned from his position as a military officer, and in the autumn of 1919, he chaired two unofficial congresses. The first was at Erzurum, with delegates from the eastern provinces, and the second at Sivas, with delegates from across the country.[173]

[170] Mustafa Kemal served in the Ottoman Army during the First World War, earning distinction for his role in the Battle of Gallipoli, the Ottomans' most significant victory in the war (Davison, 1965, p. 173; Kieser, 2018, p. 322).

[171] Davison, 1965, p. 176; Lewis, 2002, pp. 242–243.

[172] Lewis, 2002, pp. 242–243.

[173] Alexandris, 1982, p. 154; Davison, 1965, pp. 176–180; Lewis, 2002, pp. 248–251.

The Sivas congress drafted the first version of what became the Turkish "National Pact."[174] The core demands of the pact were independence and territorial integrity.[175] The dual aims of territorial integrity and sovereignty meant the preservation of the borders drawn in the postwar armistice and the end to foreign economic and political interference in Turkish affairs.[176] As summarized in Article 6 of the National Pact:

> It is a fundamental condition of our life and continued existence that we, like every country, should enjoy complete independence and liberty in the matter of assuring the means of our development; in order that our national and economic development should be rendered possible.[177]

The text went on to say, "For this reason we are opposed to restrictions inimical to our development in political, judicial, financial and other matters."[178] In January 1920, the nationalists released their National Pact, separated from the Sublime Porte in Istanbul, and proclaimed a new Turkish capital in Angora (now Ankara).[179] A few months later in April 1920, the first parliament, known as the Grand National Assembly, was inaugurated in the Anatolian heartland, officially abandoning the imperial capital.[180] When the Grand National Assembly met, a sovereignty crisis emerged. The sultan, with British backing, controlled Istanbul and the surrounding areas, while the nationalists controlled the rest of Asia Minor from their new capital, Angora.[181]

Mustafa Kemal, commander-in-chief of the Turkish Nationalist Forces, and his nationalist domestic allies believed that Greece's territorial aspirations would continue while there were still "unredeemed Hellenes" residing in the empire. They feared Greek advances in Smyrna and Eastern Thrace would turn the Aegean Sea into a "Greek lake."[182] Popular support grew behind Mustafa Kemal and the newly established nationalist government.

[174] LNA, S18/18/1/3: Copy of the Turkish National Pact, 28 January 1920; UN Archives at Geneva.
[175] Davison, 1965, p. 173; Lewis, 2002, p. 249.
[176] Davison, 1965, p. 173.
[177] LNA, S18/18/1/3: Copy of the Turkish National Pact, 28 January 1920; UN Archives at Geneva.
[178] LNA, S18/18/1/3: Copy of the Turkish National Pact, 28 January 1920; UN Archives at Geneva.
[179] Emin, 1930, p. 276; Pentzopoulos, 1962, p. 37.
[180] Emin, 1930, p. 278; Kieser, 2018, pp. 393, 396; Lewis, 2002, p. 251; Psomiades, 1968, p. 32.
[181] Llewellyn-Smith, 1998, p. 103.
[182] Pentzopoulos, 1962, p. 59.

His allies in the Grand National Assembly were in full agreement that the Greek Orthodox Christians had to be removed from the future Turkish sovereign state. The benefit to them was the realization of the National Pact's goals. Accordingly, at the end of the Greco–Turkish War, the Greeks along the Aegean and Pontic littorals, as well as throughout Anatolia, were summarily expelled and prohibited from returning under Article 3 of the Lausanne Convention.

The situation in Istanbul was different. Although the World War I Armistice of Mudros did not authorize the occupation of Istanbul, an Allied military administration was established in the imperial capital at the end of 1918, and 3,626 Allied troops de facto took control.[183] The occupying forces were composed of British, French, and Italian troops, most of whom were British, with a British commander at the head.[184] The British claimed the Ottoman sultan was still de jure head of state, but he simply provided legal cover for the occupation.[185] The Allies slowly took increasing power, establishing an International Police Commission with executive control of the city's police, creating military courts, and stationing their personnel at prisons, hospitals, banks, and embassies.[186] Over the next four years, a rotating group of Allied high commissioners were the de facto sovereigns of the city, and the Allied presence expanded to over 28,000 troops by 1920.[187] Despite the occupation, the sultan and his associates were pleased to have the façade of Allied endorsement of their sovereignty. Having lost all control to the CUP during World War I, the sultan was fiercely anti-nationalist and eager to cooperate with the Allies against them.[188] He went so far as to issue a fatwa against Mustafa Kemal.[189] Because the sultan wanted continued Allied support, and foreign troops controlled the city between 1918 and 1922, the Greeks in Istanbul were safe.

In the autumn of 1922, after the nationalists' decisive military victory at Smyrna, they had all but won the Greco–Turkish War and began marching toward Istanbul. To eliminate the need for the city to be taken by force, British General Charles Harrington, supreme commander of the Allied

[183] Lewis, 2002, p. 240; Mansel, 1996, p. 380.
[184] Mansel, 1996, p. 380.
[185] Mansel, 1996, p. 396.
[186] Mansel, 1996, p. 380.
[187] Mansel, 1996, pp. 381, 392.
[188] Lewis, 2002, p. 245; Mansel, 1996, p. 387.
[189] Mansel, 1996, p. 393.

occupation forces in the city, sagely agreed to an armistice.[190] Unlike the Greeks of the Aegean and Pontic littorals, the fate of the Istanbul Greeks would be decided at the Lausanne Conference. Two key considerations shaped the Turkish representatives' calculations regarding the expulsion of the Istanbul Greeks: domestic economic and political consequences.

At the outset of the conference, Turkish negotiators strongly refuted Greek and Allied arguments that the expulsion of the Greek Orthodox from Istanbul would be "complete commercial and financial suicide."[191] Shukri Bey, the Turkish delegation's expert on population exchanges, argued to the sub-commission that the Istanbul Greeks "were not an indispensable element" to the city; they were simply "intermediaries, not producers" and could easily be replaced.[192] Ismet Pasha similarly argued to the First Commission that "everyone knew that [the Greeks of Istanbul] formed a class of small traders (grocers, &c.), and that it would not be difficult to replace them."[193] Rather than economic and social ruin, Tewfik Bey, another Turkish representative to the conference, contended that "the disturbance to the commercial life of Constantinople would be of short duration."[194] Even if negative economic consequences would flow from the removal of the Greeks from the city, Shukri Bey said, "In any case, the anxiety of the Turks to secure their independence and immunity from disintegrating influences at home was a reason which exceeded in importance any economic consideration."[195]

Despite their initial vociferous statements to the contrary, domestic economic concerns proved to be an important internal restraint on the Turkish delegation's decision regarding the Istanbul Greeks. On January 19, 1923, in one of the last meetings of the Sub-Commission for the Exchange of Populations, Riza Nour Bey, second Turkish delegate, conceded:

> The Turkish delegation has accepted the obligatory exchange as a necessity and it is in order to mitigate the painful consequences that it admitted that the Greek inhabitants of Constantinople were not subject to it. *The*

[190] Davison, 1965, pp. 197–198.

[191] LNA, R1761/48/24318: Report by Dr. Nansen to the League of Nations Part 1: Reciprocal Exchange of Racial Minorities Between Greece and Turkey, 15 November 1922; UN Archives at Geneva.

[192] LNA, C1112/8/N15: Sub-Commission for Exchange of Populations Meeting Minutes, 05 December 1922; UN Archives at Geneva, p. 3.

[193] Lausanne Conference on Near Eastern Affairs, 1923, p. 326.

[194] LNA, C1112/8/N15: Sub-Commission for Exchange of Populations Meeting Minutes, 07 December 1922; UN Archives at Geneva, p. 3.

[195] LNA, C1112/8/N15: Sub-Commission for Exchange of Populations Meeting Minutes, 05 December 1922; UN Archives at Geneva, p. 3.

> *economic reasons for which this derogation was accepted* must also apply to the Strouma valley [emphasis added].[196]

Here Riza Nour Bey reluctantly acknowledges that "economic reasons" were a decisive factor in the decision to accept a derogation from the expulsion of the Greeks of Istanbul. Given the high level of economic interdependence between Istanbul and European commerce, banking, and manufacturing—much of which passed through the hands of prominent Greek Orthodox financiers and traders—concern about risking foreign financial investment in the country's largest city was an essential domestic consideration for the new nation-state. While it may have been difficult to accept, the removal of the Istanbul Greeks would have been a domestic economic catastrophe the nascent nationalist government could not afford.

Another key Turkish delegation demand, stemming from Article 3 of the Turkish National Pact, was for a plebiscite in Greece's Western Thrace.[197] The Turks believed that given the right to choose, the residents of Western Thrace, mostly Muslims, would vote to become part of the new Turkish Republic. Western Thrace was particularly meaningful to the Turkish nationalists dating back to the empire's European territorial losses in the Balkan Wars. At the outset of the peace conference, the Turkish delegation put forward its request for a plebiscite in Western Thrace and, in turn, argued for the Muslims living in this region to be exempted from the "population exchange."[198] They presented their case as a numerical argument, suggesting that the numbers to be exchanged on each side would be roughly equivalent if the Muslims of Western Thrace were *excluded* from the exchange and the Greek Orthodox of Istanbul *included*. But Greece and the Allied powers contested their figures.[199] Instead, the Great Powers proposed the Muslims of Western Thrace *and* the Greek Orthodox of Istanbul both be exempted from the "population exchange."[200]

[196] Conférence de Lausanne sur les affairs du proche-orient, 1923, p. 607 (translated from the French original).

[197] Article 3 stated, "The determination of the judicial status of Western Thrace also, which has been made dependent on the Turkish peace, must be effected in accordance with the votes which shall be given by the inhabitants in complete freedom" (LNA, S18/18/1/3: Copy of the Turkish National Pact, 28 January 1920; UN Archives at Geneva).

[198] LNA, C1112/8/N15: Sub-Commission for Exchange of Populations Meeting Minutes, 04 December 1922; UN Archives at Geneva, p. 5.

[199] LNA, C1112/8/N15: Sub-Commission for Exchange of Populations Meeting Minutes, 05 December 1922; UN Archives at Geneva, p. 2.

[200] LNA, C1112/8/N15: Sub-Commission for Exchange of Populations Meeting Minutes, 07 December 1922; UN Archives at Geneva, p. 27; Lausanne Conference on Near Eastern Affairs, 1923, p. 122.

Since the Allied powers refused to allow the Muslims of Western Thrace to remain without also allowing the Greeks in Istanbul to stay, the Turkish representatives reluctantly decided they were willing to accommodate a small population of Greeks in Istanbul in the hopes of a future plebiscite in Western Thrace. Insisting on the expulsion of the Istanbul Greeks would have meant forfeiting the possibility of reclaiming some of the empire's lost European territories. Although the plebiscite never came to pass, it was an important domestic political consideration at the conference. In this case, the interests of the Turkish authorities and their domestic nationalist allies would have been harmed by expelling the Istanbul Greeks. The negative economic and political consequences for the newly emerging Turkish Republic outweighed the desire to remove the Greek Orthodox from Istanbul, thereby restraining their decision to expel.

Transnational Alliances

After World War I, Ottoman finances and defenses were controlled by the Allied powers; in January 1921, the sultan handed over both the Ministry of Finance and the Ministry of War.[201] Mustafa Kemal had to identify alternative sources of financial and military support for his new government and nationalist forces. He first turned to the Soviets, a former nemesis of the Ottoman Empire, who had just experienced a revolution. From 1920–1921, the nationalist government established close ties with the Bolsheviks, who declared their support for the Turkish National Pact. With a shared enemy in the British, the Soviets and Turkish nationalists officially established diplomatic relations in August 1920 and signed a Treaty of Friendship in March 1921.[202] The treaty stated:

> The Government of the Russian Socialist Federal Soviet Republic and the Government of the Grand National Assembly of Turkey, sharing as they do the principles of the liberty of nations, and the right of each nation to determine its own fate, and taking into consideration, moreover, the common struggle undertaken against imperialism, foreseeing that the difficulties arising for the one would render worse the position of the other, and inspired by the desire to bring about lasting good relations and uninterrupted sincere friendship between themselves, based on

[201] Mansel, 1996, p. 395.
[202] Psomiades, 1968, p. 32.

> mutual interests, have decided to sign an agreement to assure amicable and fraternal relations between the two countries.[203]

The treaty expressed solidarity against imperialism and secured Turkey's eastern border.[204] This transnational alliance provided vital economic and military support to the nationalist government and its military forces.

Mustafa Kemal's impressive military victories in 1921 drew further attention and support. Western states began to recognize that he and his new nationalist government, not the sultan in Istanbul, were the true leaders of the country. Soon after solidifying support from the Soviets, Kemal secured additional military and financial backing from the Italians and French, who had begun to sour on the British. Both the Italians and French were concerned about Britain's increasing control of the Bosphorus and their support for Greece's expansionist aims.[205] A French newspaper jeeringly referred to Istanbul (Constantinople) as "Constantinobralter"—a reference to British control of Gibraltar along another key trading route at the southern tip of Spain.[206] The Italians also negotiated with Kemal, agreeing to withdraw from southern Anatolia if they could retain the Dodecanese Islands.[207] Then in October 1921, the French agreed to evacuate Cilicia and establish a new Syrian border that was more favorable to the Turks, allowing Turkish troops to turn their attention toward the Greek forces in the west.[208]

Trade deals with the Bolsheviks and the French provided resources the nationalist forces needed to advance against the Greek Army. The Turks used Russian money to purchase Italian weapons,[209] and following the January 1922 Turkish–Ukrainian treaty, additional military supplies arrived.[210] Kemal's skillful balancing of strange bedfellows—Soviet and Allied powers—enabled him to acquire sufficient military and financial resources to fuel his nationalist campaign. These arms and funds enabled the Turks to detach public support from the sultan and Istanbul through successive military victories, while simultaneously defeating Greece and its British backers. It is

[203] Hurewitz, 1956, p. 95.
[204] Davison, 1965, p. 191.
[205] Psomiades, 1968, p. 33.
[206] Mansel, 1996, p. 392.
[207] Davison, 1965, pp. 192–193; Lewis, 2002, p. 254.
[208] Davison, 1965, pp. 192–193; Hurewitz, 1956, p. 97; Kieser, 2018, p. 396; Lewis, 2002, pp. 253–254; Pentzopoulos, 1962, p. 45.
[209] Psomiades, 1968, p. 35.
[210] Davison, 1965, p. 194. This treaty was initiated by a Soviet mission from Ukraine, which in January 1922 was the Ukrainian Soviet Socialist Republic.

clear from their contributions that the nationalists' transnational allies were supportive of Kemal's war of independence and corresponding removal of the Greek Orthodox Christians, further enabling expulsion.

However, while Mustafa Kemal's transnational allies were supportive of the expulsion of the Greek Orthodox from the Aegean and Pontic littorals, they were not supportive of removing the Greeks from Istanbul. France and Italy had tremendous financial and strategic interests in maintaining a Greek presence in the city. While they supported the nationalists in the Greco–Turkish War, and approved of their reclaiming Istanbul, they did not want to lose their key financial liaisons within the city. Since European investments and transactions were largely processed through Greek intermediaries, French and Italian commercial interests would have been harmed by their expulsion.[211] At the Lausanne Conference, these transnational allies strongly opposed the expulsion of the Istanbul Greeks. While the Turkish nationalists' transnational allies helped them win the war and supported the expulsion of Greeks along the Aegean and Pontic littorals, those same allies also constrained their efforts to expel the Greeks from the imperial city.

6.7.2 "Homeland" State of the Target Group

In the first decades of the twentieth century, Greece was one of the Ottoman Empire's greatest enemies, gaining large chunks of its prized European territory during the Balkan Wars. When Greece invaded the Aegean coast in the spring of 1919, any possible détente after World War I evaporated. As the war waged on, the expulsion of the Greek Orthodox Christians was not at all restrained by the relationship between the two states—their ties were extremely weak. Furthermore, the nationalists' military victory over Greece in the autumn of 1922 made it difficult for Greece to resist Turkish expulsions and deny entry to the expellees. When the nationalist army reclaimed Smyrna, Turkish troops compelled the Greeks to depart, forcing them into the sea. Greek ships, with Allied support, acquiesced to their defeat and resettled the expellees. Overland, in Eastern Thrace, the situation was similar. The nationalists' triumph resulted in the expulsion of Greeks from Eastern Thrace, which the Greek government de facto accepted as the loser

[211] Alexandris, 1983, p. 31; Clogg, 1982, p. 196.

of the war. They had no capacity to resist and deny entry to the hundreds of thousands of Greek expellees.

The weak ties between Greece and Turkey were not mended at the start of the Lausanne Conference in November 1922. In fact, at this stage, relations may have been at the nadir of the ten-year period examined. While Greece had de facto accepted the expulsion of its co-ethnics from the Aegean and Pontic littorals, the Greek negotiators at the conference fiercely resisted the expulsion of the remaining Greeks in Istanbul. The Greek delegation tried to persuade the Allied powers, as the adjudicators of the peace, to sympathize with their appeals and join their resistance to Turkish demands to expel the Greeks from Istanbul. They put forward four main arguments.

First, Greece claimed that the expulsion of the Greek Orthodox from Istanbul would have international consequences. They argued that many of the Allied powers had political and economic interests in the city that would be harmed by the removal of this group. Nicolas Politis, former Greek foreign minister and Greek delegate to the peace conference, wrote to Fridtjof Nansen, League-appointed head of Near East refugee relief, before the peace conference began: "It is impossible that all the foreign nations which have interests in this city do not realize that the mass departure of Greeks would condemn Constantinople and would bring their interests to irremediable economic and social ruin."[212] Later at Lausanne, Venizelos, head of the Greek delegation, formally argued to the First Commission "Such an expulsion would amount to an unprecedented political, economic and social catastrophe."[213] In the Sub-Commission for the Exchange of Populations, Demetrius Caclamanos, Greece's second delegate to the conference, "besought the Turkish Delegates to reconsider their position. If they persisted, they would repent of the loss of an indispensable factor, a loss which would be disastrous to the economic life of their capital."[214]

Greece's second argument was that the Greek Orthodox in Istanbul had no irredentist tendencies and that they should not be considered a threat by the Turkish government. Caclamanos told the sub-commission, "Constantinople was not an irredentist centre" and that although some Greeks participated in demonstrations, "those who had taken part in

[212] LNA, R1761/48/24318: Letter from Le Gerant Ministre Plenipotentiaire, Ch. Sienopoulos, with message from Monsieur Politis to Nansen, 03 November 1922; UN Archives at Geneva (translated from the French original).

[213] Lausanne Conference on Near Eastern Affairs, 1923, p. 121.

[214] LNA, C1112/8/N15: Sub-Commission for Exchange of Populations Meeting Minutes, 07 December 1922; UN Archives at Geneva, p. 5.

them . . . had already left." Venizelos further argued to the First Commission, "The Greeks of Turkey hav[e never] revolted against the Turkish administration. Throughout the history of the Turkish Empire no Greeks had ever revolted against Ottoman rule at any place in Thrace or Asia Minor, or at Istanbul."[215] Caclamanos concurred:

> [The Greek Orthodox] had always lived on good terms with the Turks; they had continued to do so even after the outbreak of the general war and before Greece had joined in the war. Constantinople had been so little a centre of irredentism that the Constantinople Greeks were sometimes reproached by other Greeks with their failing in this respect.[216]

Third, the Greek delegation argued that it was not viable to resettle Istanbul's urban Greek community in the agricultural lands that would be vacated by Muslims during the proposed exchange.[217] Caclamanos insisted that this urban population "could not possibly be absorbed by Greece . . . [the] burden would be intolerable if she had to accommodate this large number of city-bred people in addition to the vast number of immigrants already on her hands."[218] Fourth, Greece pleaded that it simply could not absorb any more refugees.[219] Delegates insisted that an additional 300,000 people would overwhelm their already strained capacity.[220]

The Turkish delegation, naturally, refuted each of the Greek delegation's arguments. As previously discussed, they initially rejected the economic rationale, although in the end conceded that it was an important consideration. They also vehemently disagreed with Greece's claim that the Greeks of Istanbul were not irredentist. Shukri Bey acknowledged that previously the Greeks of Istanbul did live peacefully with their Turkish neighbors, however,

> a point had been reached at which the only thing to do was to separate them out from each other...Turkey could not agree to make an exception

[215] Lausanne Conference on Near Eastern Affairs, 1923, p. 226.

[216] LNA, C1112/8/N15: Sub-Commission for Exchange of Populations Meeting Minutes, 05 December 1922; UN Archives at Geneva, p. 5.

[217] LNA, C1112/8/N15: Sub-Commission for Exchange of Populations Meeting Minutes, 07 December 1922; UN Archives at Geneva, p. 5.

[218] LNA, C1112/8/N15: Sub-Commission for Exchange of Populations Meeting Minutes, 04 December 1922; UN Archives at Geneva, p. 5.

[219] By the time the Peace Conference started in November 1922, it was estimated that Greece had received one million refugees from Turkey (Hirschon, 2003, p. 6; Ladas, 1932, p. 392; Mazower, 2004, p. 345; Morris & Ze'evi, 2019, p. 465).

[220] Lausanne Conference on Near Eastern Affairs, 1923, p. 318.

> in favour of the Greek population of Constantinople which was the main centre of Turkish life and a political centre of Greek political activity if the Greeks remained.[221]

Tewfik Bey added, "So long as [the Greek Orthodox] remained Constantinople would be a centre of conflict which would provoke European intervention."[222] He suggested that removing the Greek Orthodox from Istanbul would increase European security by extracting "a hotbed of trouble" from the East.[223] Tewfik Bey further argued, "The Turks wanted to be friends after peace; but . . . their experience had shown that Turks and Greeks could no longer live together side by side and all the Greeks must leave."[224] Addressing the Greek delegation's argument that it was unfair to have an urban-for-rural population swap, the Turks maintained that the Muslim population in Greece also included "townspeople" and therefore the expulsion of the Greeks of Istanbul would be an even trade.[225] Finally, to the point of Greece being overwhelmed with refugees, the Turks argued that they too had absorbed hundreds of thousands of Muslim refugees after the Balkan Wars.[226] Greece could do the same.

Although the "homeland state" of Greece, represented by the Greek delegation at Lausanne, resisted the expulsion of the Greek Orthodox from Istanbul, their efforts would have come to naught without the backing of the Great Powers. It was up to the Allied representatives overseeing the peace conference to adjudicate these competing claims. In this case, two of the intervening factors—"homeland" state and IOs—worked in tandem to further constrain the expulsion of the Greek Orthodox from Istanbul.

6.7.3 International Organizations

During this period, the pertinent IOs included the League of Nations, founded in 1920, and the "Great Powers" or the "Big Four"—Britain, France, Italy, and the US—that served as the international body adjudicating the

[221] LNA, C1112/8/N15: Sub-Commission for Exchange of Populations Meeting Minutes, 04 December 1922; UN Archives at Geneva, p. 6.

[222] LNA, C1112/8/N15: Sub-Commission for Exchange of Populations Meeting Minutes, 07 December 1922; UN Archives at Geneva, p. 3.

[223] LNA, C1112/8/N15: Sub-Commission for Exchange of Populations Meeting Minutes, 05 December 1922; UN Archives at Geneva, p. 4.

[224] LNA, C1112/8/N15: Sub-Commission for Exchange of Populations Meeting Minutes, 07 December 1922; UN Archives at Geneva, p. 7.

[225] Lausanne Conference on Near Eastern Affairs, 1923, p. 326.

[226] Lausanne Conference on Near Eastern Affairs, 1923, p. 120.

postwar peace at the Lausanne Conference. There are two key elements of this intervening factor to assess: the relationship between the new Turkish nationalist government and the IOs, and the response of these organizations to the expulsion of the Greek Orthodox Christians.

As the Ottoman Empire crumbled, the Turkish nationalists believed that only through battlefield victories would they obtain political respect and legitimacy. Although the new government in Angora wanted to cultivate strong ties with IOs, they knew they first had to secure military control and reclaim territory to negotiate from a position of power. Thus, during the Greco–Turkish War, known by the Turks as the Turkish War of Independence, the nationalist forces were not restrained by how their actions would impact relations with IOs. They sought international acceptance, but believed that could only be achieved by first securing their territory, which involved eliminating the Greek Orthodox population and, in turn, Greece's irredentist claims to their land. During Phase 2, while the nationalists were at war with Greece, IOs did not restrain their actions; however, the dynamics changed in Phase 3 at the Lausanne Conference.

After the Greco–Turkish War, the Turkish nationalists sat at the negotiating table in Lausanne as military victors and de facto rulers of the Ottoman Empire, soon-to-be Turkish Republic. The Turkish delegation's diplomatic strategy at the conference was not to isolate itself from IOs and the Great Powers but to establish itself as an equal. Ismet Pasha announced that Turkey was willing to join the League of Nations at the end of the proceedings and become a member of the international community.[227] The desire to cultivate strong ties with IOs negated the possibility of completely ignoring Allied arguments on behalf of the Istanbul Greeks. This restrained the nationalists' decision to expel all Greek Orthodox Christians from the empire, leading to their concession to exempt those in Istanbul from the "population exchange." The Turks were not deterred, however, from driving a hard bargain, extending the duration of the conference much longer than the Allies wanted or anticipated.

Throughout the first two phases of mass expulsion, the Great Powers ignored the Ottoman's removal of Greek Orthodox Christians along the Aegean and Pontic littorals. In 1914, as Greece and the Ottomans attempted to negotiate the first "population exchange," there was no resistance from the Great Powers. Similarly, during the Greco–Turkish War, they ignored the Greek Orthodox expulsions and even facilitated their transportation

[227] Lausanne Conference on Near Eastern Affairs, 1923, p. 221.

from the Aegean coast to Greece. Then in the third phase, at the Lausanne Conference, the Great Powers, under the purview of the League of Nations, authorized the first compulsory "population exchange" agreement. The League then coordinated the subsequent expulsion and provided international relief to the expellees. In this case, IOs enabled mass expulsion during Phase 1 and Phase 2 by ignoring the policy, and in Phase 3, actively supported and facilitated the expulsion through the "population exchange."

Their position on the Greeks of Istanbul was markedly different. While there was strong backing from the Great Powers and the League at the peace conference for the "population exchange," there was no international support for the removal of the Istanbul Greeks. The Allied arguments against their expulsion largely mirrored those of the Greek delegation. They included economic anxieties, political concerns, refugee absorption, and making a "fair trade."

The Great Powers were concerned about their financial interests in Istanbul. Erik Colban, director of Administrative Commissions and the Minorities Questions Section for the League of Nations Secretariat, wrote in a letter to British politician Noel Buxton two days after the peace conference began, "The Great Powers with strong economic interests in Istanbul would never agree to the total evacuation of the Christians from that town . . . because all the European business in Istanbul is based upon the collaboration of the Greek element."[228] While the Allied powers were openly concerned about their own economic interests, they also believed the economic losses would be too great for Turkey to withstand. Nansen, head of Near East refugee relief for the League, wrote to the Greek delegate Politis on October 31 before the peace conference opened that he believed, "the Turkish government will find it cannot afford to expel the Constantinople Greeks if it has to pay for their possessions."[229] In an official report to the League on November 15, five days before the start of the conference, Nansen wrote, "It would be superfluous to stress what a complete commercial and financial suicide would result from the flight of the Greek and Armenian populations from Constantinople; in effect by such an event . . . Turkey will sacrifice her richest asset."[230]

[228] LNA, S18/18/1/3: Note from Mr. Colban to Major Buxton, 22 November 1922; UN Archives at Geneva.

[229] LNA, R1761/48/24318: Letter from Nansen to Monsieur Politis, 31 October 1922; UN Archives at Geneva.

[230] LNA, R1761/48/24318: Report by Dr. Nansen to the League of Nations Part 1: Reciprocal Exchange of Racial Minorities Between Greece and Turkey, 15 November 1922; UN Archives at Geneva.

Sentiment was similar within the Political Section of the League Secretariat. Thanassis Aghnides, a League official and an Ottoman Greek born and raised in Istanbul, wrote in an internal report, "The removal of the non-Turkish elements will mean financial ruin for Turkey including instant ruin for Constantinople and Smyrna. Turkey would be reduced to a country of no economic importance whatever."[231] Lord Curzon, British foreign secretary and president of the Conference's First Commission, believed that the removal of the Greek Orthodox from Istanbul "would entail a very serious economic and industrial loss to Turkey herself. He believed this population was vital to the existence of Constantinople as a great city of commerce and industry, and that without it Constantinople would be in danger of losing its authority, wealth and trade."[232]

Other League of Nations officials expressed political concerns, including the possibility of Russia benefiting from the expulsion of the Greeks from Istanbul. Internal correspondence from Aghnides stated:

> In my opinion, the real motive of the Turks...is the political motive....You have, perhaps, observed that the Russians back up the Turks in this respect, as in many others. Again I must point out, the reason for this is that to-day [sic], as in the past, Russia has an eye on Constantinople.[233]

He continued on to say that removing the Greeks from Istanbul would diminish the city's role as a center of international commerce and complex politics, making it easier for Russia to pursue its aims: "That explains both the Russian attitude and also why the Allies are against the expulsion of the non-Turks from Constantinople."[234] Importantly, British troops still occupied Istanbul during the peace conference.[235] Control and influence within the city was still an open question in early 1923. The Great Powers were keen to maintain their political advantage and not to cede it to rival powers.

[231] LNA, S18/18/1/3: Report on "The Expulsion of Non-Turkish Elements from Asia Minor" by T. Aghnides, 23 November 1922; UN Archives at Geneva.

[232] Lausanne Conference on Near Eastern Affairs, 1923, p. 122.

[233] LNA, S18/18/1/3: Letter from Mr. Aghnides to Major Buxton, 23 November 1922; UN Archives at Geneva.

[234] LNA, S18/18/1/3: Letter from Mr. Aghnides to Major Buxton, 23 November 1922; UN Archives at Geneva.

[235] British troops did not leave Istanbul until October 1923. At the same time, the nationalists deposed the sultan, allowing him to remain as caliph but not as sultan, and established themselves as the sole governing authority (Mansel, 1996, pp. 405, 407). They would later abolish the caliphate on March 3, 1924 (Kieser, 2018, p. 415; Lewis, 2002, p. 264; Mansel, 1996, p. 413).

Nansen, responsible for the League's refugee relief effort, was also concerned about the number of expellees in Greece and the consequences of adding more. He advocated that Greece could not accept any additional refugees, that it was fully saturated.[236] Lord Curzon agreed with Nansen, stating in a commission meeting on January 10, 1923, "it would enormously aggravate the difficulty experienced by Greece in finding homes for all these refugees" if the Greek Orthodox from Istanbul were included.[237] The Allies also echoed the Greek delegation's argument about the inability of Greece to accommodate an urban population: "Residents in towns [i.e., Istanbul Greeks] could not be exchanged for residents in country districts."[238] H. G. Dwight of the American delegation, an observer at the conference, stated that the Americans also could not approve of the Istanbul expulsion, "particularly under conditions which will send an urban people used to artizanship [sic] and commerce to a rural district."[239]

Giulio Cesare Montagna, second Italian delegate, and chair of the Sub-Commission for the Exchange of Populations, summarized the general sentiment of IOs, urging the Turkish delegation to reconsider its insistence on expelling the Greek Orthodox from Istanbul:

> [You] should not bring about catastrophe by expelling the Greek population of Constantinople... everyone including the American Representative [is] against [you] on this question. [You] were wrong from every point of view, including the political point of view. [You] were preparing [your] own ruin. If the Greeks in Constantinople had compromised themselves, those compromised Greeks had left.[240]

Although the Allied powers were united against the Turks proposed expulsion of the Greek Orthodox of Istanbul, Lord Curzon tried to appear unbiased by suggesting that if the Muslims of Western Thrace were exempted from the exchange, then the Greeks of Istanbul should be as well, a fair trade.[241] French delegate de Lacroix agreed and offered that the Muslims

[236] LNA, R1762/48/24888: Message from Nansen to Lord Curzon, M. Poincaré and Italian MFA, 06 November 1922; UN Archives at Geneva.

[237] Lausanne Conference on Near Eastern Affairs, 1923, p. 318.

[238] Lausanne Conference on Near Eastern Affairs, 1923, p. 326.

[239] LNA, C1112/8/N15: Statement made by Mr. Dwight at the Meeting of the Sub-Commission for Prisoners of War and the Exchange of Populations, 07 December 1922; UN Archives at Geneva.

[240] LNA, C1112/8/N15: Sub-Commission for Exchange of Populations Meeting Minutes, 07 December 1922; UN Archives at Geneva, pp. 6–7.

[241] Lausanne Conference on Near Eastern Affairs, 1923, p. 122.

of Western Thrace and the Greeks of Istanbul should be "left over for a future possible exchange."[242] In the end, there was significant international resistance to expelling the Greek Orthodox from Istanbul, constraining the nationalists' policy position.

6.8 Conclusion

The 1923 "population exchange" was the culmination of a decade of mass expulsions of the Greek Orthodox Christian population in the Ottoman Empire. Beginning with the Balkan Wars and continuing through Greece's 1919 invasion of the Aegean coast, the Ottoman/Turkish authorities viewed the Greek Orthodox population, with their co-ethnic ties to the Greek nation-state, as a security threat that had to be removed. The continued presence of "unredeemed Hellenes" in the country would only justify further territorial incursions into their lands.[243] The Turkish delegates to the Lausanne Conference stated those concerns directly. After eight weeks of negotiations with the Sub-Commission for the Exchange of Populations, Riza Nour Bey, second Turkish delegate, stated that "it [is] necessary to recall the true reason which motivated, on the part of the Turkish Government, the proposal to exchange the populations. *The Turkish Government wishes to eliminate Greek irredentism in Turkey*" [emphasis added].[244] Ismet Pasha, head of the Turkish delegation, concurred, articulating that the Turkish view toward expelling the Greek Orthodox was "based on their legitimate desire to prevent minorities in Turkey becoming *weapons in the hands of foreigners, capable of being utilised for subversive purposes*" [emphasis added].[245]

The negative case of Istanbul complicates this narrative. While the Ottoman/Turkish government expelled the Greek Orthodox minority along the Aegean and Pontic littorals between 1913 and 1923, the wealthy, politically active, irredentist Greeks of Istanbul were allowed to remain. Key restraints and constraints prevented the wholesale expulsion of all Greeks from the new Turkish nation-state. Domestic economic and political concerns regarding the loss of Greek financiers in Istanbul and the loss of a

[242] LNA, C1112/8/N15: Sub-Commission for Exchange of Populations Meeting Minutes, 07 December 1922; UN Archives at Geneva, p. 7.

[243] Macartney, 1934, p. 432.

[244] Conférence de Lausanne sur les affairs du proche-orient, 1923, p. 577 (translated from the French original).

[245] Lausanne Conference on Near Eastern Affairs, 1923, p. 207.

potential plebiscite in Western Thrace led to concessions by the Turkish delegates. The fierce resistance by their transnational allies—France and Italy, who supported the nationalists with funds and arms to defeat the Greek invasion—also pressured them to exempt the Greeks of Istanbul to secure their own financial interests in the city. While Greece, as the "homeland" state, was not a critical restraint on the Turkish delegation's decision to allow the Istanbul Greeks to remain, the Greek delegation persuaded Great Power delegates and League of Nations officials at Lausanne to pressure the Turks to exempt the Greeks of Istanbul for economic, political, and humanitarian reasons. Given that the Turkish nationalists sought to join the League and be recognized as an equal power to the Allies, they could not ignore their arguments and ultimately conceded, permitting the Greeks of Istanbul to remain.

6.9 Epilogue

The new Turkish Republic, officially declared in October 1923, accommodated the approximately 110,000 Greek Orthodox Christians remaining in Istanbul,[246] though they continued to face discrimination.[247] Three decades later, in the 1950s, ethnic tensions rose again as diplomatic crises emerged between Turkey and Greece over the issue of Cyprus.[248] In response to rumors of an impending massacre of Turkish Cypriots and a bombing in the garden of the Turkish Consulate in Thessaloniki, Greece, violent anti-Greek riots erupted across Istanbul in September 1955.[249] While statistics vary, thousands of Greek businesses were attacked and looted; Greek residences, churches, and schools were destroyed; and lives were lost.[250] Estimated damages exceeded $100 million, with some estimates even higher.[251] The Turkish police did not intervene, and in some cases supported the assailants.[252] While the government initially blamed the attacks on "communists," a military court later convicted senior Turkish government officials, including the

[246] Approximately two-thirds were Ottoman nationals who were granted Turkish citizenship, while the remaining third were Greek nationals permitted to remain in the country (Alexandris, 1983, p. 281; Alexandris, 2003, p. 118; Kaliber, 2019, p. 375).

[247] Alexandris, 2003, p. 118.

[248] Icduygu et al., 2008, p. 371.

[249] Alexandris, 2003, p. 119; Güven, 2021, pp. 283, 290; Human Rights Watch, 1992, pp. 8–10.

[250] Güven, 2021, pp. 283–285; Human Rights Watch, 1992, pp. 9–10.

[251] Human Rights Watch, 1992, p. 10.

[252] Güven, 2021, pp. 279–280; Human Rights Watch, 1992, pp. 9–10.

prime minister, of complicity in the anti-Greek violence[253]—a precursor to the final expulsion of the Istanbul Greeks.

Turkish-Greek relations were further strained in the 1960s, again over Cyprus, with the Greeks of Istanbul caught in the crossfire. In November 1963, President Makarios of Cyprus, a Greek Cypriot, proposed amendments to the Cyprus constitution designed to transform the existing governing structure. He suggested replacing the equitable Greek and Turkish Cypriot representation with a majoritarian system in which Turkish Cypriots would be the minority.[254] Turkish Cypriots condemned this move, and intercommunal violence subsequently erupted between Greek and Turkish Cypriots.[255] The Turkish government responded in March of 1964 by unilaterally annulling the 1930 treaty guaranteeing the right of Greek nationals to remain in Turkey and ordered their expulsion.[256] As articulated by the Turkish Ministry of Foreign Affairs, this reprisal expulsion was initiated from "the natural consequences of the fact that the Turkish government regarded the question of Cyprus and that of Greco–Turkish relations as forming a single whole, and therefore was unable to continue to grant Greek nationals favoured treatment."[257] The Turkish government openly acknowledged the expulsion was in retaliation for the Greek government's support to Makarios.[258]

While the cancellation of the treaty specifically targeted Greek nationals, many Turkish citizens were de facto expelled alongside their family members because of the prevalence of mixed marriages between Greek nationals and Turkish citizens of Greek origin.[259] Like the Greek Orthodox Christian expellees of 1923, many of these expellees had been born in Turkey and had never set foot in Greece.[260] They were permitted to leave with only the clothes on their backs, a small suitcase of not more than 44 pounds (20 kilograms), and 200 Turkish lira.[261] The Turkish government prevented expellees from selling their property, confiscated businesses before assets could be liquidated, and blocked bank transactions.[262] Before departing,

[253] Güven, 2021, pp. 286, 290.
[254] Kaliber, 2019, p. 374.
[255] Alexandris, 1983, p. 280; Kaliber, 2019, p. 374.
[256] Alexandris, 1983, pp. 280–281; Kaliber, 2019, pp. 365, 375.
[257] Alexandris, 1983, p. 282.
[258] Alexandris, 1983, p. 283.
[259] Alexandris, 1983, p. 286; Kaliber, 2019, p. 375.
[260] Alexandris, 1983, p. 281; Human Rights Watch, 1992; Walz, 1964.
[261] Kaliber, 2019, p. 376; Walz, 1964.
[262] Alexandris, 1983, p. 284; Kaliber, 2019, p. 376; Walz, 1964.

Turkish authorities forced expellees to sign a document admitting to false allegations, including violating laws, transferring money to "terrorists" in Cyprus, and consenting to leave the country willingly.[263] An estimated 36,000 to 47,000 Greeks were expelled between 1964 and 1965.[264]

Some scholars suggest that the Greek population in Istanbul was used as a pawn by Ankara to pressure Athens to reign in the Cypriot government;[265] others argue that the violence in Cyprus was a convenient justification for the premeditated mass expulsion.[266] Regardless, the 1964 expulsion achieved what the 1923 Lausanne Convention did not: the elimination of the Greeks from Istanbul.

*

The Ottoman expulsion of Greek Orthodox Christians from 1913 to 1923 was driven by security concerns related to territorial control and countering irredentist claims. Next, we turn to a different security concern: Burma's expulsion of its Rohingya population to secure and maintain internal political control.

[263] Alexandris, 1983, p. 284; Kaliber, 2019, p. 376.
[264] Alexandris, 1983, p. 286; Alexandris, 2003, p. 119; Human Rights Watch, 1992, p. 11; Icduygu et al., 2008, p. 372.
[265] Icduygu et al., 2008, p. 372; Walz, 1964.
[266] Kaliber, 2019, pp. 366, 381.

7

Counter-Subversive Expulsion: Rohingya in Burma

Burma[1] has been, and remains, at war with its ethnic minorities in the world's longest-running civil conflict.[2] The Rohingya have been a unique target group in this complex ethnic landscape. From March 1991 through July 1992, the Burmese military, paramilitary, border guards, military intelligence, and police systematically expelled over 250,000 Rohingya Muslims from Arakan State in Western Burma.[3] Burmese forces burned their homes, destroyed mosques and Muslim cemeteries, confiscated identity documents, and forced the Rohingya across the border into Bangladesh.[4] They shouted at the fleeing refugees: "You are not Burmese" and that they would "shoot them if they returned."[5] However, the next year, Burma halted the expulsions and signed a bilateral agreement with neighboring Bangladesh to "repatriate" the Rohingya, with the support and sanction of international organizations. Between September 1992 and the end of 1995, nearly the entire expelled population returned to Burma.[6] This final case study uses a within-case design, like that in Chapter 6, but instead of examining geographic variation—differing treatment of Greek Orthodox Christians along the Aegean and Pontic littorals compared to Istanbul—this case examines

[1] I use the country name Burma as well as the pre-1989 state and capital names (i.e., Arakan instead of Rakhine State, Rangoon instead of Yangon) for the sake of consistency in discussing the colonial and postcolonial periods and because of the politicized nature of the 1989 English-language name changes (see discussion on pp. 183–184).

[2] Myint-U, 2021, p. 3.

[3] Amnesty International, 1992 (Apr), pp. 13–14; Amnesty International, 1992 (Sept), p. 24; Human Rights Watch, 2000; Piper, 1994, p. 14; Smith, 1994, pp. 29, 56; UN Commission on Human Rights, 1993, p. 6; Van Hear, 1998, p. 94.

[4] Amnesty International, 1992 (Apr), p. 14; Amnesty International, 1992 (Sept), p. 24; Asia Watch, 1992, pp. 1, 5; Lambrecht, 1995, pp. 4, 14; Piper, 1994, pp. 15–16; Van Hear, 1998, p. 98; Yegar, 2002, p. 63.

[5] Amnesty International, 1992 (Sept), p. 24; Asia Watch, 1992; 18; Piper, 1994, p. 24; Smith, 1994, p. 82.

[6] Loescher, 2001, p. 286.

Mass Expulsion. Meghan M. Garrity, Oxford University Press. © Oxford University Press (2026).
DOI: 10.1093/9780197829097.003.0007

temporal variation. The theory of expulsion decision-making explains why Burma expelled its Rohingya minority in the early 1990s and why, under new leadership, it shifted course and agreed to take them back just over a year later, despite no change in the environment in Arakan State.

7.1 Background Context: The Rohingya in Burma

The Muslim presence in the boundaries of contemporary Burma dates to the arrival of Moorish, Arab, and Persian traders who settled in the area between the ninth and tenth centuries and intermarried with the local population.[7] European travelogues from as early as the fifteenth century document bustling Muslim settlements conducting commercial trade from ports that were conveniently located at the halfway point along shipping routes from the Red Sea to the Spice Islands and China.[8] Over the following centuries, Muslim migration continued across the Bay of Bengal. Many settled in Arakan, which is topographically separated from the rest of Burma by a coastal mountain range, making contact with—and migration from—the west much easier than from the east.[9] In 1785, the Kingdom of Burma annexed Arakan, putting the Burmese on a collision course with British imperial hegemony in South Asia.[10]

Beginning in 1824, the British fought multiple wars against Burmese monarchs to expand their colonial possessions.[11] In the first war, the British annexed Arakan (1824–1826); in the second, they conquered "Lower Burma," including the Irrawaddy Delta and Rangoon (1852–1853); and in the third, they captured the Burmese heartland of "Upper Burma" (1885).[12] From 1885, the British ruled Burma as a province of their larger Indian Empire with the administrative capital in Calcutta.[13] The territory served as a convenient buffer between French Indochina and British India.[14] By ruling Burma as an Indian appendage, the British stifled the political development

[7] Ibrahim, 2018, p. 21; Piper, 1994, p. 12; Van Hear, 1998, p. 94; Yegar, 1972, p. 72; Yegar, 2002, p. 19.

[8] Yegar, 2002, pp. 19–20.

[9] Ibrahim, 2018, p. 18; Yegar, 2002, p. 23.

[10] Christie, 1996, p. 163; Cockett, 2015, p. 6; Ibrahim, 2018, p. 18; Yegar, 2002, p. 24.

[11] Callahan, 2003, pp. 22–23; Human Rights Watch, 2000; Myint-U, 2021, p. 14; Yegar, 2002, p. 27.

[12] Christie, 1996, p. 164; Cockett, 2015, p. 7; Ibrahim, 2018, pp. 18, 26; Myint-U, 2021, p. 15.

[13] Callahan, 2003, p. 23; Cockett, 2015, pp. 9–10; Ibrahim, 2018, p. 26.

[14] Callahan, 2003, p. 21.

of Burmese society. They used the Indian Army to maintain "internal security" and repress any resistance to their rule.[15]

During the colonial period, the British governed Burma in two distinct parts: "Ministerial Burma," including the capital, Rangoon, and the Irrawaddy Delta, and the "Frontier [or Excluded] Areas," composed of the territory in the border regions.[16] The British invested most of their resources in central Ministerial Burma, where the Burmese majority was concentrated. Rangoon became a major commercial hub, and the British exploited the territory's vast natural resources, including oil, rubber, jade, tungsten, teakwood, and rice.[17] The Frontier Areas, by contrast, were much less developed, with limited penetration by the colonial state.[18] These areas were more mountainous and physically separated from the Burmese core, which contributed to the dual governance structure. This division of center and periphery, Burmese and non-Burmese, would have important implications for the postcolonial state.

Given freedom of movement within the British Empire, many Hindus, Muslims, Sikhs, and others traveled by ship to Rangoon to work as laborers, administrators, and professionals.[19] A similar pattern of migration occurred in Arakan State, which was a hub for the rice export trade from Burma's Irrawaddy Delta, a global center of rice cultivation.[20] Arakan's main port town, Akyab (Sittwe), became the fourth-largest city in colonial Burma.[21] During this period, Muslim Chittagonians from Bengal migrated to Arakan to work as agricultural laborers.[22] Some returned to the homes their ancestors had fled after the Kingdom of Burma's annexation in the late eighteenth century.[23] Colonial figures estimated that 58,000 Muslims lived in Arakan in 1872.[24] Nearly forty years later, in 1911, there were three times as many, with the Arakanese Buddhist population only slightly outnumbering the Muslims.[25] Large-scale Muslim migration, and rising Burmese (Buddhist) nationalism, contributed to growing resentment toward "unwanted outsiders" in Arakan.[26]

[15] Callahan, 2003, pp. 22, 43.
[16] Ibrahim, 2018, p. 26; Walton, M. J., 2013, p. 7.
[17] Callahan, 2003, p. 23; Cockett, 2015, pp. 12–13.
[18] Callahan, 2003, p. 27.
[19] Cockett, 2015, p. 16; Myint-U, 2021, p. 18; Yegar, 2002, p. 27.
[20] Cockett, 2015, pp. 13, 37.
[21] Cockett, 2015, pp. 36–38; Myint-U, 2021, p. 26.
[22] Cockett, 2015, p. 37; Myint-U, 2021, p. 18; Van Hear, 1998, p. 94; Yegar, 2002, p. 28.
[23] Myint-U, 2021, p. 26.
[24] Cockett, 2015, p. 37.
[25] Cockett, 2015, p. 37.
[26] Yegar, 2002, pp. 28, 30.

The British did not use the term "Rohingya" to describe the Muslim population in Arakan.[27] Some Muslims in the northern part of the state used the label Rohingya, which translates into English as "of Rohang" or "of Arakan."[28] Others referred to themselves as Arakanese Mohammedans, descendants of the ancient Mrauk-U Kingdom, terms the British also used.[29] And some were Chittagonian immigrants who intermarried with "Rohang" or "Arakanese Mohammedans" who had lived in the region for generations.[30] Regardless of the label, they spoke an Indo-Aryan language that combined elements of Arakanese, Bengali, and Urdu.[31] Many Rohingya, therefore, had roots in Arakan before British colonization, but many more arrived with British colonial expansion into Burma.[32] Intermarriage between these various groups created a complex picture of descent and origin.

In 1922, the British granted Burma a semi-elected parliament, like its other Indian provinces, with a governor and a legislative council, but with limited power.[33] Then in 1937, in the first partition of the Indian subcontinent, the British created Burma as a separate colony.[34] A few years later, in 1942, during World War II, the Japanese invaded Burma, destroying the British colonial and administrative structure that had been in place for more than five decades.[35] Burmese nationalists seeking independence supported the Japanese to defeat their British colonizers.[36]

After the initial Japanese victory, the British recruited and trained ethnic minorities in clandestine intelligence operations and formed paramilitary organizations to fight back.[37] Their psychological warfare officers used propaganda to attract recruits to their side, praising "loyal" ethnic minorities against "treacherous" Burmans supporting the Japanese.[38] The Rohingya and other ethnic minorities supported the British, fearing Buddhist-majority rule. They were also optimistic about British promises of postwar self-determination—in the case of the Rohingya, an autonomous

[27] Myint-U, 2021, p. 27.
[28] Myint-U, 2021, p. 27.
[29] Myint-U, 2021, p. 36.
[30] Myint-U, 2021, p. 30.
[31] This language is distinct but mutually intelligible with the Bengali dialect spoken by the Chittagonians across the contemporary border of Bangladesh (Ibrahim, 2018, p. 21; Myint-U, 2021, p. 27; Yegar, 2002, p. 51).
[32] Cockett, 2015, p. 38.
[33] Callahan, 2003, p. 32; Myint-U, 2021, p. 27.
[34] Callahan, 2003, p. 32; Ibrahim, 2018, p. 26; Myint-U, 2021, p. 29.
[35] Callahan, 2003, p. 45.
[36] Cockett, 2015, p. 47; Ibrahim, 2018, p. 27; Piper, 1994, p. 12.
[37] Callahan, 2003, p. 71; Christie, 1996, p. 165; Yegar, 1972, p. 96.
[38] Callahan, 2003, pp. 72, 85.

Muslim National Area.[39] Yet, as with promises to other minority groups in their vast empire, the British failed to deliver. In late 1944, British forces united with Burmese nationalists, who had become disillusioned with Japanese rule, and in August 1945, they jointly defeated the occupying forces.[40] The British briefly retook control of war-ravaged Burma before granting the country independence on January 4, 1948.[41]

The independent government of Prime Minister U Nu attempted to govern Burma as a unitary state, something the British had never tried. The 1947 constitution established three ethnic minority states, granting them some local autonomy and allowing for the possibility of secession via a plebiscite after a ten-year period.[42] The autonomy concessions, however, did not prevent the outbreak of civil war.[43] Various insurgencies sprouted with different political and ethnic factions fighting for civil, economic, and territorial control. The central government tried to contain them, but the fighting raged on, leading to an "equilibrium of instability."[44] Although Burma was perpetually in crisis in its early independence period, it did manage to hold elections in 1951–1952, 1956, and 1960.[45] But in 1962, its short life as a parliamentary democracy ended when General Ne Win took power in a military coup d'état.[46] One of the driving forces behind Ne Win's coup was the military's fear that Prime Minister U Nu was granting too many concessions to the ethnic minority states, risking Burma's territorial sovereignty.[47] On the morning of the coup, Ne Win was quoted as saying, "Federalism is impossible; it will destroy the Union."[48]

After taking power, Ne Win suspended the constitution, dissolved parliament, outlawed political parties, and ruled through a "Revolutionary Council."[49] The Revolutionary Council introduced a Marxist–Leninist state ideology with one-party rule by the Burma Socialist Programme Party (BSPP) and the "Burmese Way to Socialism" as the guiding strategy to create

[39] Callahan, 2003, p. 85; Christie, 1996, p. 166; Ibrahim, 2018, pp. 7, 27; Walton, M. J., 2013, p. 9; Yegar, 1972, p. 96; Yegar, 2002, p. 34.
[40] Callahan, 2003, pp. 78–85, 96; Walton, M. J., 2013, p. 9.
[41] Myint-U, 2021, p. 30; Rau, 1948; Smith, 1991, p. 27.
[42] Constitution of the Union of Burma, 1947.
[43] Myint-U, 2021, pp. 3, 30.
[44] Christie, 1996, p. 78.
[45] Callahan, 2003, pp. 142, 144, 208.
[46] Smith, 1991, p. 28.
[47] Smith, 1999, p. 196; Walton, M. J., 2013, p. 14.
[48] Smith 1999, p. 196.
[49] Callahan, 2003, p. 208; Cockett, 2015, pp. 53–54; Steinberg, 1980, pp. 180–181.

a centralized command economy without foreign influence or control.[50] Economically, Ne Win's Burmese Way to Socialism had devastating consequences. The government nationalized businesses in the 1960s and expelled over 300,000 Indian Tamils (a nativist expulsion) to create a "Burman run economy solely for the Burmans."[51] International travel was banned, except for privileged military elites, with the intention of eliminating any foreign engagement or influence.[52] The country became further economically and politically isolated, and the people suffered as a result. Ne Win pursued a dual-track strategy of centralizing control in Rangoon while conducting ruthless counterinsurgency operations in peripheral regions to crush ethnic insurgent opposition.[53] Though he successfully pushed some insurgent groups into remote areas of the border regions, he could not fully suppress them.[54]

7.2 Structural Factors: End of the "Burmese Way to Socialism" and Rise of the SLORC

By the late 1980s, the military junta known as the Tatmadaw had ruled Burma for over a quarter century.[55] The junta's Burmese Way to Socialism was an abysmal failure, and the economy was in tatters.[56] In September 1987, Ne Win decided to demonetize major currency notes, resulting in approximately 70 percent of all currency being rendered valueless, wiping out people's limited savings.[57] The currency devaluation occurred in tandem with shortages of goods and the collapse of the rice market, Burma's main connection with international trade.[58]

In response to the economic collapse and years of restricted civil and political rights, in March 1988, student-led protests erupted across the country. The students called for the end of one-party military rule, the introduction of democratic reforms, including free and fair multiparty elections, and the end of human rights abuses.[59] The government responded with repression

[50] Callahan, 2003, p. 209; Cockett, 2015, p. 54.
[51] Chakravarti, 1971, p. 181; Cockett, 2015, p. 54; Tinker, 1990, p. 45; Yegar, 2002, p. 52.
[52] Smith, 1999, p. 200.
[53] Smith, 1999, p. 199.
[54] Smith, 1991, p. 28.
[55] Amnesty International, (Apr) 1992, p. 4.
[56] Ibrahim, 2018, p. 38.
[57] Ibrahim, 2018, p. 39; UN Commission on Human Rights, 1993, p. 5.
[58] UN Commission on Human Rights, 1993, p. 5.
[59] Amnesty International, 1992 (Sept), pp. 3–4; Holliday, 2005, p. 330; Yegar, 2002, p. 62.

and introduced new restrictions, including a ban on all public gatherings.[60] Hundreds of nonviolent protestors were arrested and killed. In response to public pressure and internal demands within the Tatmadaw, General Ne Win resigned as head of the ruling BSPP in July 1988.[61] Nonetheless, protests continued, with protestors unsatisfied with the new leaders.

On August 8, demonstrators called for a nationwide general strike and slowly gained the support of workers, Buddhist monks, government ministries, state media, and even some police.[62] The strike resulted in some of the bloodiest days of the year. The UN Commission on Human Rights estimated 3,000 people were killed between August 8 and 12.[63] The army reasserted control on September 18 and replaced the BSPP with the State Law and Order Restoration Council (SLORC) under the chairmanship of Chief of Staff Senior General Saw Maung. These moves were more of a rebranding than a break with the past.[64]

The SLORC imposed martial law, suspended the constitution, banned opposition parties, arrested party leaders, and detained protestors. Simultaneously, they announced democratic elections and opened the country's economy.[65] Relatively free elections were held in May 1990. To the military's surprise, the opposition National League for Democracy (NLD) won a landslide victory, capturing 80.8 percent of parliamentary seats, compared to 2.1 percent for the military's National Unity Party.[66] Dismayed, the SLORC ignored the results and refused to transfer power to the NLD. Instead, they announced the SLORC would remain in power until a new constitution was drafted.[67] The Tatmadaw arrested some of the newly elected NLD politicians and continued its repression. In the post-election period, Amnesty International documented human rights abuses throughout the country, including the arrest of over 1,500 political prisoners—charges the SLORC vehemently denied.[68]

While the Tatmadaw espoused its preference to move toward democracy, repression continued, and the military dramatically expanded from

[60] UN Commission on Human Rights, 1993, p. 5.

[61] Amnesty International, 1992 (Sept), pp. 3–4; Charney, 2009, p. 151; Ibrahim, 2018, pp. 38–39; Yegar, 2002, p. 62.

[62] Myint-U, 2021, p. 38; Van Hear, 1998, p. 97; Yegar, 2002, p. 62.

[63] UN Commission on Human Rights, 1993, p. 5.

[64] Amnesty International, 1992 (Sept), p. 4; Callahan, 2003, p. 210; Charney, 2009, pp. 159–160; Myint-U, 2021, p. 43; Smith, 1994, p. 27; UN Commission on Human Rights, 1993, p. 5; Yegar, 2002, p. 62.

[65] Amnesty International, 1992 (Apr), p. 4; Callahan, 2003, p. 210; Smith, 1994, p. 27.

[66] Charney, 2009, p. 168; Ibrahim, 2018, p. 41.

[67] Ibrahim, 2018, p. 41.

[68] Amnesty International, 1992 (Apr), p. 4; Amnesty International, 1992 (Sept), p. 6.

an estimated 180,000 troops in 1988 to between 250,000 and 300,000 by mid-1992.[69] Thousands of student protestors fled to the eastern border areas to build an armed resistance against the new government. Ethnic insurgent groups offered them weapons and training.[70] The military government viewed the demonstrators, like the ethnic insurgencies, as an existential threat to the state and mounted a fierce counterinsurgency campaign across the country to snuff out any protestor–insurgent partnerships as well as insurgent secessionist or autonomy revivals.[71] Yet, the SLORC also negotiated with some insurgent groups, offering economic and territorial autonomy compromises.[72] Between 1989 and 1992, the government negotiated ceasefires with nine armed ethnic opposition groups and another five between 1994 and 1995.[73] The two Rohingya groups—the Rohingya Solidarity Organization (RSO) and the Arakan Rohingya Islamic Front (ARIF)—were not among them.[74]

7.3 Proximate Factors: Counter-Subversive Motivations Emerge

The Rohingya had long been viewed as a subversive ethnic minority. After World War II, Arakanese Buddhists saw the Rohingya as national traitors for supporting the British and fighting against the Japanese and their Arakanese-Buddhist backers.[75] This resentment, and competition over land and resources, led to localized intercommunal violence and segregation in Arakan State. Previously mixed Rohingya-Arakanese communities separated into a largely Muslim north and Buddhist south.[76] During the postwar period, a new wave of Muslim immigrants from Chittagong, Bangladesh, moved into northern Arakan along with Rohingya who had fled during the war.[77]

In the postwar but pre-independence period, the Muslim community in northern Arakan was politically divided. In May 1946, some Muslim leaders

[69] Amnesty International, 1992 (Sept), p. 4; Smith, 1994, p. 28.
[70] Charney, 2009, p. 163; Smith, 1994, pp. 45, 79.
[71] Charney, 2009, p. 169.
[72] Callahan, 2003, p. 220; Charney, 2009, p. 188; Ferguson, 2015, p. 16.
[73] Callahan, 2003, pp. 215, 220; Myint-U, 2021, p. 51; Smith, 1999, pp. 16–17.
[74] Smith, 1999, p. 17.
[75] Piper, 1994, p. 12; Smith, 1994, p. 55; Van Hear, 1998, p. 95.
[76] Christie, 1996, p. 165; Ibrahim, 2018, p. 27; Yegar, 1972, p. 95.
[77] Christie, 1996, p. 166; Yegar, 1972, p. 96.

called for the secession of Muslim-majority areas to join what was soon to be East Pakistan.[78] Later in July, the North Arakan Muslim League called for self-determination and the creation of an independent Muslim state.[79] Both movements were largely supported by Chittagonian Muslims rather than the Rohingya.[80] These ideas were quickly squashed by Muhammad Ali Jinnah, head of India's Muslim League, who did not want to arouse Burmese hostility.[81] Jinnah told General Aung San, the lead Burmese negotiator with the British, that he did not support the irredentist Muslim groups.[82] In April 1947, at a meeting in Maungdaw, a third Muslim group called for a special Muslim region, or "Frontier State," that would be separate from Buddhist Arakan but within the state of Burma.[83] Many Muslims of Arakan, including the Rohingya, supported this proposal.

After Burma's independence in January 1948, violence in Arakan continued.[84] Arakanese Buddhists replaced Muslims in political positions such as civil servants, police, and headmen, and were allowed to claim Muslim land and homes abandoned during the Japanese invasion.[85] In April 1948, four months after independence, Muslim religious leaders called for a jihad, and many Rohingya took up arms with the Mujahideen rebels.[86] When the government failed to recognize the Mujahideen's demands for autonomy, language and education rights, and legal status for their movement, they continued their guerilla warfare.[87] From 1948 to 1951, the Mujahideen, sometimes called the Mujahid movement, fought for control of northern Arakan. While the Burmese government was focused on battling a communist insurgency in the north of the country, and larger ethnic minority insurgencies in the east, the Mujahideen successfully reclaimed large portions of northern Arakan.[88] During this period, competing ideas of secession versus autonomy persisted within the rebel movement.

Without the capacity to suppress all the insurgencies simultaneously, the Burmese government embarked on scattered short-term scorched-earth

[78] Christie, 1996, pp. 167–168; Human Rights Watch, 2000; Ibrahim, 2018, p. 27; Myint-U, 2021, p. 36; Smith, 1999, p. 64; Yegar, 1972, pp. 96–97; Yegar, 2002, pp. 34–35.
[79] Yegar, 2002, p. 35.
[80] Christie, 1996, p. 168; Yegar, 1972, pp. 96–97; Yegar, 2002, p. 35.
[81] Christie, 1996, p. 168.
[82] Yegar, 2002, p. 35.
[83] Christie, 1996, p. 168; Yegar, 2002, p. 38.
[84] Myint-U, 2021, p. 30; Smith, 1994, p. 55.
[85] Christie, 1996, p. 168; Yegar, 1972, p. 98; Yegar, 2002, p. 37.
[86] Christie, 1996, p. 168; Yegar, 2002, p. 37.
[87] Yegar, 1972, p. 96; Yegar, 2002, p. 40.
[88] Christie, 1996, p. 168; Yegar, 2002, pp. 38, 40.

policies before departing to fight a different insurgency in another part of the country.[89] This only further galvanized support for the Mujahideen. However, from 1951 to 1954, the government allocated more resources to repressing the Muslim rebel groups. In November 1954, they launched a major offensive called Operation Monsoon, killing many Mujahideen leaders and breaking the strength of the group.[90] Small-scale skirmishes continued in the late 1950s, but eventually, in 1961, the remaining Mujahideen fighters surrendered to the Burmese army.[91]

Although the Muslim insurgency was suppressed in 1961, underground organizations emerged throughout the 1960s and 1970s. In 1963, the Rohingya Independence Front (RIF) and the Muslim/Arakan National Liberation Party were created, seeking separation from Burma rather than autonomy.[92] A little over a decade later, in 1974, the Rohingya Patriotic Front (RPF) broke away from the RIF, aspiring to obtain territorial autonomy for two areas in northern Arakan: Maungdaw and Buthidaung.[93] The RPF quickly fractured, in 1982, into the Islamic-oriented Rohingya Solidarity Organization (RSO) and the Arakan Rohingya Islamic Front (ARIF), the latter known for being more moderate.[94]

In 1991–1992, the SLORC increased its military presence in Arakan, which it claimed was in direct response to "insurgent activity in the area."[95] They accused Muslim armed opposition groups, specifically the RSO and the ARIF, of causing the crisis and precipitating their response.[96] In fact, the SLORC blamed Muslim insurgents for a December 1991 incident along the Bangladesh–Burma border in which the Lone Htein, a paramilitary border force, killed four Bangladeshi nationals whom the Burmese border guards were pursuing across the border.[97] The leaders of the RSO and ARIF fed into this narrative. An RSO leader told the media that "50,000 Rohingyas inside Burma were trained and ready to fight Burmese troops deployed in Arakan."[98] Nurul Islam, chairman of the ARIF, told Agence France-Presse

[89] Yegar, 2002, p. 42.
[90] Christie, 1996, p. 169; Yegar, 2002, p. 44.
[91] Smith, 1999, p. 194; Yegar, 1972, p. 101; Yegar, 2002, p. 46.
[92] MacLean, 2019, p. 86; Smith, 1999, p. 219; Yegar, 2002, p. 53.
[93] MacLean, 2019, p. 86; Yegar, 2002, pp. 54, 59.
[94] MacLean, 2019, pp. 86–87; Piper, 1994, p. 12.
[95] Amnesty International, 1992 (Sept), p. 25; Piper, 1994, p. 17; Van Hear, 1998, p. 99.
[96] Smith, 1994, p. 56.
[97] Amnesty International, (Sept) 1992, p. 25; Paper calls for ASEAN change on Burma. *The Nation* (Bangkok) (January 26, 1992). FBIS-EAS-92-018.
[98] Dissident Muslims: Rangoon wants Bangladesh war. *Hong Kong AFP* (February 24, 1992). FBIS-EAS-92-038.

(AFP): "We are determined to fight to free our homeland from the tyranny of the Burmese military junta."[99]

Despite claims of sizable armed forces, evidence on the ground indicated that the RSO and ARIF exaggerated their tactical military capabilities.[100] When compared with other subversive groups in Burma such as the Karen or the Kachin guerrillas, the Rohingya groups were small, unorganized, and poorly armed.[101] In the early 1990s, it was estimated that the ARIF had 200 fighters and the RSO 600; neither group was organized into regular fighting units, and they were armed with outdated weaponry.[102] The RSO and ARIF also had limited support within the broader Rohingya civilian community. Unlike other ethnic armed groups in Burma, they lacked strong political leadership and organization.[103] Nevertheless, the Tatmadaw believed that any sign of weakness would cause the country to break apart.[104] It saw itself as embodying the "true spirit of the nation," the sole institution capable of defending the country from threats to the state.[105] Though the Burmese military distrusted all ethnic minority groups, viewing many as subversive threats to the internal control of the state, the Rohingya were different.

7.4 Preconditions for the Rohingya Expulsion (1991–mid-1992)

The Ne Win regime's first attempt to eliminate the Rohingya was in the late 1970s in "Operation Nag-min" (Dragon King). In advance of a national census, the regime alleged they needed to conduct a routine check of "illegal immigrants" in Arakan State.[106] The administrative process quickly turned violent, and the military expelled over 200,000 Rohingya between April and July 1978.[107] However, to Ne Win's chagrin, the expulsion was quickly reversed. Bangladesh refused to host the influx of refugees, and by the end

[99] Burmese guerilla chief asks for military aid. *Hong Kong AFP* (March 13, 1992). FBIS-NES-92-051.

[100] Yegar, 2002, p. 66.

[101] Amnesty International, 1992 (Sept), p. 20; Asia Watch, 1992, p. 2; Piper, 1994, pp. 12–13; Walton, M. J., 2013, p. 8.

[102] Piper, 1994, pp. 12–13.

[103] MacLean, 2019, p. 86; Parnini, 2013, p. 282.

[104] Smith, 1999, p. 424.

[105] Ibrahim, 2018, p. 46; MacLean, 2019, p. 93; Smith, 1999, p. 423.

[106] MacLean, 2019, p. 87; Piper, 1994, p. 13; Van Hear, 1998, p. 96.

[107] Loescher, 2001, p. 224; Myint-U, 2021, p. 37; Piper, 1994, p. 13; Smith, 1991, p. 37; Smith, 1994, p. 56; Van Hear, 1998, p. 93; Weiner, 1993, p. 157.

of 1979, most of the Rohingya were back in Burma.[108] Not discouraged by the failure of Operation Dragon King, the Ne Win regime passed a new citizenship law in 1982 to further marginalize the Rohingya. In a speech to the Central Committee members, General Ne Win explained the rationale for the new law:

> During the period between 1824 and the time we regained independence in January 1948, foreigners, or aliens, entered our country un-hindered under various pretexts.... We then find that our country comprised true nationals, guests, issues from unions between nationals and guests or mixed bloods, and issues from unions between guests and guests.... This became a problem after independence. The problem was how to clarify the position of guests and mixed bloods.[109]

To resolve this issue, the 1982 law created three categories of citizens—full, associate, and naturalized—all of which were limited to members of Burma's "national ethnic races"[110] (see Table 7.1). Ne Win declared that "racially, only pure-blooded nationals will be called citizens."[111]

The regime used 1823 as the critical date for determining citizenship.[112] Those whose ancestors lived in Burma before 1823—the year before Britain first invaded Burma and annexed parts of Arakan—were considered natives, whereas those whose ancestors arrived after 1823 were classified as foreigners.[113] This decision particularly affected the Rohingya, whom the Burmese government, and large segments of the Burman majority, as well

Table 7.1 Categories of Citizens in the 1982 Citizenship Law[a]

Full citizens	Descendants of ethnic groups residing in Burma before 1823
Associate citizens	People who obtained citizenship under the 1948 Union Citizenship Law
Naturalized citizens	Residents of Burma before 1948 but who failed to obtain citizenship under the Union Citizenship Law

[a]Center for Diversity & National Harmony, 2018, pp. 205, 249; MacLean, 2019, p. 88.

108 Cheesman, 2017, p. 472; Loescher, 2001, p. 225.
109 Ne Win, 1982.
110 Cheesman, 2017, p. 471; Kyaw, 2015, p. 55; MacLean, 2019, p. 88.
111 Ne Win, 1982.
112 Ibrahim, 2018, p. 50; Myint-U, 2021, p. 15; Smith, 1991, p. 37.
113 Myint-U, 2021, p. 15; Yegar, 2002, p. 61.

as the Arakanese Buddhists, saw as *kala*[114] or Bengalis.[115] The claim that the Rohingya were not indigenous to Burma but rather "illegal Bengali" migrants from Bangladesh was used to justify their discrimination and persecution.

The 1982 law also stated that the Council of State would "decide whether any ethnic group is national or not."[116] It provided a specific body to which one could appeal citizenship disputes, but the law did not set forth how the Council of State would determine who qualified as an ethnic group, nor did it provide an authoritative list of the "national ethnic races."[117] These determinations were left up to the council—a political, not a judicial, body. The Rohingya were therefore not denied citizenship because of the 1982 law, but rather through the application of the law and the absence of any safeguards against discrimination.[118]

Ne Win's focus on citizenship and the deliberate exclusion of the Rohingya from the allegedly indigenous "national ethnic races" made their situation distinct from other ethnic minorities in the country. During the 1970s and 1980s, in the face of ethnic heterogeneity, the military shifted to viewing Buddhism as the litmus test for national belonging.[119] The largest ethnic minorities—Shan, Karen, Mon—were all majority Buddhist. They had cross-cutting religious ties with the majority Burmese that were absent with the Muslim Rohingya. From the perspective of the government, the Rohingya were ethnic, national, and religious outsiders. Therefore, their policy was not just to suppress and control the "subversive" Rohingya, like their policy toward other "subversive" ethnic minorities, but to remove them. Ne Win failed in his efforts to do this; the new SLORC regime would try again.

The exclusionary ideology of the Ne Win regime created a hierarchy of "pure-blooded" Burmans and loyal non-Burmans, and "non-pure-blooded" outsiders, like the Rohingya. This precondition for expulsion escalated

[114] In this context, *kala* is a term used to describe a foreigner. In precolonial times, *kala* was used to describe people to the west (e.g., India). Later, it took on a derogatory connotation to describe outsiders—either Bengali or Muslim—often regarded as one and the same in the Rohingya case. *Kala* also has a racial dimension, used as a slur against anyone with dark skin. Currently, it is reserved for Muslims, including the Rohingya (Kyaw, 2015, pp. 55–56; Myint-U, 2021, pp. 11, 35).

[115] Human Rights Watch, 2000; Myint-U, 2021, p. 36.

[116] This is stated in Chapter II (4) of the law (Center for Diversity & National Harmony, 2018, p. 50).

[117] Center for Diversity & National Harmony, 2018, pp. 203–204; Cheesman, 2017, p. 471.

[118] Center for Diversity & National Harmony, 2018, p. 207.

[119] Ibrahim, 2018, p. 37.

under the SLORC. In 1989, the government changed the country's official English-language name from Burma to Myanmar,[120] while the name in Burmese remained unchanged: *Myanma pyi*.[121] They also changed the names of lower administrative units such as Arakan to Rakhine, and the capital city of Rangoon to Yangon.[122] The government explained these changes as efforts to distance itself from the British colonial era, revising names in line with their ancient roots, which was more inclusive to the country's indigenous peoples.[123] However, during the colonial period, the British recorded the English-language names of locations in the country based on transliterations of the local names in the respective local languages.[124] Thus, the SLORC's English-language name revisions were actually an effort by the authorities to reflect the Burmese language pronunciation of names in locales throughout the country rather than the local indigenous languages.[125]

Many ethnic minorities rejected these changes. They protested that "*Myanma*" only referred to the Burmese majority, accusing the government of a larger campaign of Burmanization.[126] Aung San Suu Kyi, opposition leader at the time, and a member of the Burmese majority, criticized the country's name change while under house arrest:

> No one should be allowed to change the name of the country without referring to the will of the people. They [the government] say that "Myanmar" refers to all the Burmese ethnic groups, whereas "Burma" only refers to the Burmese ethnic group, but that is not true. "Myanmar" is a literary word for "Burma" and it refers only to the Burmese ethnic group. Of course I prefer the word "Burma."[127]

These changes were the first of several actions toward the "Burmanization" of the country.[128] The SLORC also rewrote textbooks emphasizing

[120] Myint-U, 2021, p. 43; Walton, M. J., 2013, p. 12.
[121] Myint-U, 2021, p. xvii; Permanent Committee on Geographical Names, 2007, p. 7.
[122] Charney, 2009, p. 172; Myint-U, 2021, p. 43; Permanent Committee on Geographical Names, 2007, p. 6; Walton, M. J., 2013, p. 12.
[123] Ferguson, 2015, p. 16; Myint-U, 2021, p. xviii; Permanent Committee on Geographical Names, 2007, p. 7; Walton, M. J., 2013, p. 12.
[124] Permanent Committee on Geographical Names, 2007, p. 7.
[125] Charney, 2009, p. 171.
[126] Amnesty International, 1992 (Sept), p. 43; Ferguson, 2015, p. 16; Myint-U, 2021, p. 44; Smith, 1994, p. 18; Walton, M. J., 2013, pp. 11–12, 21.
[127] Cockett, 2015, p. 82.
[128] Cheesman, 2017, pp. 467–468; MacLean, 2019, p. 89; Smith, 1991, p. 30.

the unifying Burmese identity over generations.[129] It launched initiatives to rehabilitate the Mandalay Palace, where the last Burmese monarch resided, and to restore Buddhist stupas, emphasizing the centrality of Buddhism to the Burmese nation.[130] These efforts aimed to consolidate the state's national identity around the dominant Buddhist, Burman ethno-religious majority.[131]

The SLORC's exclusionary ideology was also demonstrated in its release of a list of 135 "national ethnic races," identifying the "true" people of Burma—the "pure-blooded nationals" Ne Win had described in 1982.[132] These national/ethnic races became the central determinant of membership in the political community of the new Burma, rebranded as Myanmar.[133] The government did not explain how the 135 races were selected, nor release any data to support the classification.[134] Some of the national/ethnic races were categorized based on their language, others based on their location or home area, and one group—the Mro/Wakim—was listed twice.[135] While the naming of the 135 national/ethnic races may have seemed like the Tatmadaw's recognition of the diversity of Burma's 40 million people, of which at least one-third were ethnic minorities, in reality it was part of a strategy to divide and rule the ethnic minority groups.[136] For example, the Shan minority was separated into thirty-three subgroups and the Kachin into twelve subgroups, though no new administrative units were created.[137]

The Rohingya were not included in the list of 135 national/ethnic races.[138] Because citizenship in Burma was predicated on membership in a national/ethnic race, this solidified the Rohingya's exclusion from the state. Burma's Minister of Foreign Affairs U Ohn Gyaw stated in a press release:

> In fact, although there are 135 national races residing in Myanmar today, *the so-called Rohingya people are not among them.* Historically, *there has never been a Rohingya race in Myanmar*.... Since the First Anglo-Myanmar War in 1824, people of the Muslim faith from the adjacent country have

[129] Walton, M. J., 2013, pp. 12, 15.
[130] Hein, 2018, pp. 362–363; MacLean, 2019, p. 89; Myint-U, 2021, p. 44.
[131] Buddhism is the dominant religion of over 80 percent of the population (Smith, 1994, p. 18).
[132] Center for Diversity & National Harmony, 2018, p. 202; Cheesman, 2017, p. 468; MacLean, 2019, p. 88.
[133] Cheesman, 2017, pp. 462–463.
[134] Cheesman, 2017, pp. 468–470; Ferguson, 2015, p. 15; Smith, 1994, p. 18.
[135] Ferguson, 2015, p. 15.
[136] Callahan, 2003, p. 225; Charney, 2009, p. 189; Smith, 1994, p. 17; Walton, M. J., 2013, p. 6.
[137] Aung, 2007, p. 267.
[138] Cheesman, 2017, p. 462; Ferguson, 2015, p. 16; MacLean, 2019, p. 88.

> *entered Myanmar illegally*, particularly Rakhine State. . . . It should be categorically stated that *there is no persecution based on religious grounds* [emphasis added].[139]

The SLORC rejected the use of the term "Rohingya" and denied that they were part of the Myanmar nation.[140] Importantly, the exclusion of the Rohingya from the list of 135 national/ethnic races was not simply an attempt to eliminate Muslims from majority-Buddhist Burma. The Kaman (also known as Kamein), another Muslim group living in Arakan State, were included in the list of 135 national/ethnic races. This intra-Muslim delineation indicated the SLORC viewed the Kaman as assimilable, at the time, while the Rohingya were not.[141] The fact that the Kaman were not expelled in 1991–1992 is evidence that the junta was not just targeting Muslims, nor Muslims specifically in Arakan State, but rather a specific subpopulation of Muslims: the Rohingya.

The last component of the SLORC's exclusionary Burmanization ideology was a change in identity documentation with the introduction of citizenship scrutiny cards (CSCs) to replace the national registration cards (NRCs).[142] The SLORC required all citizens to obtain a CSC, which documented the nationality and religion of the cardholder as well as residence, occupation, father's name, and blood type.[143] These identification cards further cemented the bond between race/ethnicity and citizenship in Burma, and in turn, further marginalized the Rohingya. To obtain a CSC one had to surrender his NRC. The Rohingya who did so were not issued CSCs[144] and were left undocumented.[145]

The Tatmadaw viewed all ethnic minorities in Burma as a security threat that needed to be suppressed, but they approached these "subversive" groups differently. While historically Muslim groups in northern Arakan had made territorial claims, the Rohingya consistently preferred autonomy within Burma, and those demands largely died out in the early 1960s. In the 1990s,

139 Foreign Ministry statement on Rohingya Muslims. Radio Burma (Rangoon) (February 21, 1992). FBIS-EAS-92-036.

140 Smith, 1994, pp. 56–57.

141 Aung, 2007, p. 267; Cheesman, 2017, p. 479, footnote 17; Kyaw, 2017, pp. 279, 283–284.

142 Center for Diversity & National Harmony, 2018, p. 209; Charney, 2009, pp. 167–168.

143 Aung, 2007, pp. 278–279; Center for Diversity & National Harmony, 2018, p. 203; Hein, 2018, p. 371.

144 Some Rohingya were issued temporary registration cards, but many others remained undocumented (Center for Diversity & National Harmony, 2018, p. 209).

145 Center for Diversity & National Harmony, 2018, p. 209; Hein, 2018, p. 371.

the RSO and the ARIF were seeking protection of their civil and political rights within Arakan.[146] The nature of the alleged security threat posed by the Rohingya was nonpersistent, meaning that the Tatmadaw was not concerned that the Rohingya would continue to pose a security threat if they were removed from the country—a second important precondition for expulsion. While "pure-blooded" non-Burmans had to "prove" their loyalty by overcoming their ethnic identity and becoming "modern" Burmese-speaking people,[147] the "non-pure bloods," such as the Rohingya, could never be incorporated into the Burmese nation. Thus, the Rohingya were targeted with expulsion with the intent to remove, while ethnic minorities included in the list of 135 national/ethnic races were targeted with control policies to suppress their subversive activities but to manage them within the state.

Another important precondition for expulsion is the presence or construction of an alternative "homeland" to which the government believes the target group "belongs." Burmese authorities repeatedly claimed the Rohingya were "not Burmese," that they were "illegal Bengalis," and that they should "go home" to Bangladesh. Given northern Arakan's shared border with the Chittagong Division of Bangladesh, the alternative "homeland" was both present and nearby. The Tatmadaw also had robust military capabilities to force the Rohingya from the territory of Burma. They demonstrated this in 1978 and were prepared to do so again in the early 1990s.

7.5 Burma's Expulsion of the Rohingya (1991–mid-1992)

While many ethnic minority groups, as well as Burman protestors, faced repression in the early 1990s, the treatment of the Rohingya was unique.[148] Systematic abuses against the Rohingya forced many to flee to Bangladesh in March 1991, with numbers increasing throughout the early part of the following year.[149] In August 1991, the conflict intensified with a dramatic increase in the military presence in Arakan State. An estimated 10,000–20,000 troops arrived in Mawdaung and Buthidaung townships—double the total from the previous year.[150] The military personnel deployed

[146] Smith, 1999, p. 422; Yegar, 2002, p. 67.
[147] Callahan, 2003, p. 222; Walton, M. J., 2013, p. 13.
[148] Piper, 1994, p. 15.
[149] Asia Watch, 1992, p. 21.
[150] Charney, 2009, pp. 184–185; Piper, 1994, p. 17.

included various army contingents, local riot police, and the Lone Htein, a paramilitary border force known for its brutality.[151] The Lone Htein destroyed mosques and Muslim cemeteries, burned Muslim villages, and evicted Rohingya from their homes, replacing them with Arakanese Buddhists.[152] They confiscated the Rohingya's NRCs, in addition to money and other goods, and in some cases destroyed their documents.[153] The army also forced the Rohingya to construct new villages for Arakanese Buddhists.[154]

In September 1991, the Tatmadaw launched a "border development programme" in which Rohingya were systematically expelled from the area. Muslim lands and property were forcibly transferred to Arakanese (Buddhist) or Burmese settlers.[155] The first settlers were seventy families of former military personnel who moved north from Akyab to Maungdaw.[156] It was alleged that the resettlement of Buddhists into former Muslim areas and homes was to create a "religious and ethnic buffer" along the Burma–Bangladesh border.[157]

By October, the Bangladeshi government was increasingly concerned about the rising number of refugees, no doubt with memories of the 1978 Operation Dragon King in mind. Officials in Bangladesh's capital, Dhaka, raised the issue of the forced removal of the Rohingya with their Burmese counterparts.[158] Their diplomatic efforts went unheeded. According to one Bangladeshi official, "The Burmese military government has not responded positively to our letter on the exodus of the refugees and we will seek international help if diplomatic initiatives bear no fruit."[159]

During this period, the RSO and ARIF tried to revitalize their armed struggle, shifting their demands away from independence, or local autonomy, and toward support for the opposition coalition NLD. They hoped that the NLD would offer the Rohingya improved civil and political rights.[160] In November 1991, the RSO clashed with Burmese armed forces.[161]

[151] Piper, 1994, p. 17; Smith, 1994, p. 56.
[152] Amnesty International, 1992 (Sept), p. 24; Asia Watch, 1992, p. 1; Lambrecht, 1995, p. 4; Piper, 1994, pp. 15–16; Van Hear, 1998, p. 98; Yegar, 2002, p. 63.
[153] Amnesty International, 1992 (Apr), p. 14; Asia Watch, 1992, p. 5; Lambrecht, 1995, p. 14.
[154] Amnesty International, 1992 (Apr), p. 2.
[155] Amnesty International, 1992 (Sept), p. 24; Charney, 2009, p. 184; Smith, 1994, pp. 56, 82; Van Hear, 1998, p. 98.
[156] Smith, 1994, p. 82.
[157] Smith, 1994, p. 82.
[158] Burmese refugee "problem" continues. *Hong Kong AFP* (October 20, 1991). FBIS-NES-91-204.
[159] Burmese refugee "problem" continues. *Hong Kong AFP* (October 20, 1991). FBIS-NES-91-204.
[160] Smith, 1999, p. 422; Yegar, 2002, p. 67.
[161] Paper calls for ASEAN change on Burma. *The Nation* (Bangkok) (January, 26 1992). FBIS-EAS-92-018; Smith, 1999, p. 422.

The same month, Bangladesh sent its foreign minister, Mustafizur Rahman, to Rangoon to discuss the ongoing expulsion and the necessity of returning the Rohingya.[162] Radio Bangladesh broadcast that the foreign minister "received firm assurance from his Myanmar counterpart that Yangon [Rangoon] will take expeditious steps in this regard."[163] Yet in early December, a Rohingya refugee from Buthidaung told Asia Watch that "soldiers announced that all Muslims must leave."[164]

Tension between Burma and Bangladesh increased in December when the Lone Htein attacked the Rejupara border outpost in Bangladesh—allegedly in pursuit of Rohingya rebels.[165] The Burmese paramilitary unit killed four Bangladeshis, including one soldier, wounded twenty-two others, and stole weapons and ammunition from the border post.[166] The Burmese junta accused Bangladesh of harboring insurgents and allowing them to use their territory as a base from which to launch attacks against the army, a charge Dhaka fiercely denied.[167] The *Working People's Daily*, a state-controlled Burmese newspaper, reported on January 27, 1992, that "fighting along the border will continue as long as there are insurgents who cross and re-cross the border carrying out their operations."[168] Atrocities against the Rohingya intensified at the end of January with an increase in killings of forced laborers as well as death by starvation and inhumane conditions.[169] By the end of January and early February, between 40,000 and 45,000 Rohingya had fled to Bangladesh, with hundreds crossing the border daily.[170]

Throughout the first two months of 1992, Bangladesh and Burma held four rounds of talks to deescalate border tensions and avoid interstate war.[171] By mid-February, the SLORC retracted its explanation that the

[162] Commentary: Restoration of Burma ties "Imperative." Radio Bangladesh External Service (Dhaka) (January 8, 1992). FBIS-NES-92-008; Yegar, 2002, p. 64.

[163] Commentary: Restoration of Burma Ties "Imperative." Radio Bangladesh External Service (Dhaka) (January 8, 1992). FBIS-NES-92-008.

[164] Asia Watch, 1992, p. 11.

[165] Asia Watch, 1992, p. 6.

[166] Amnesty International, (Sept) 1992, p. 25; Asia Watch 1992, p. 6; Parliament begins debate on Burma border tension. Radio Bangladesh Network (Dhaka) (February 3, 1992). FBIS-NES-92-023.

[167] Fears of war with Bangladesh allayed. *Hong Kong AFP* (January 27, 1992). FBIS-EAS-92-018; Karens, Nagas report army atrocities; aid urged. *The Nation* (Bangkok) (January 28, 1992). FBIS-EAS-92-019.

[168] Fears of war with Bangladesh allayed. *Hong Kong AFP* (January 27, 1992). FBIS-EAS-92-018.

[169] Asia Watch, 1992, p. 10.

[170] Commentary: Restoration of Burma ties "imperative." Radio Bangladesh External Service (Dhaka) (January 8, 1992). FBIS-NES-92-008; Ministry says Burmese border under control. Radio Bangladesh External Service (Dhaka) (February 4, 1992). FBIS-NES-92-024.

[171] Sources say Burma returns "looted" weapons. *Hong Kong AFP* (February 11, 1992). FBIS-NES-92-029.

border raid was in pursuit of Rohingya rebels and returned the stolen weapons, but refused to apologize for the Bengali soldier's death.[172] The junta blamed external forces for "trying to drive a wedge between Myanmar and Bangladesh."[173] By the end of February, the number of Rohingya in Bangladesh had doubled to 80,000.[174]

The expulsion outflows reached their apex in March 1992, one year after the first expellees arrived in Bangladesh, with 5,000 Rohingya crossing the border daily.[175] Bangladeshi Prime Minister Khaleda Zia announced that the total number of refugees had risen to more than 200,000.[176] The Bangladeshi authorities established twelve camps to shelter Rohingya refugees with support from the United Nations (UN).[177] The Burmese military revealed the intended permanence of the expulsion by increasing security along its border with Bangladesh to prevent the Rohingya from returning to their homes.[178]

Once in Bangladesh, Rohingya described a consistent pattern of abuse by the Burmese armed forces. They reported that they were told to "leave and . . . weren't wanted in Burma," that they were "Bangladeshi tourists," and that "this is not your land, it is ours."[179] They were warned that they "would be killed if [they] tried to go back."[180] When one Rohingya refugee tried to report the rape of several women to the local police, he was arrested and told, "You are not Burmese. We are torturing you so you will leave this country. We will continue until you are gone."[181] Another said, "When we were beaten at different times we were often told that we should leave and that we weren't wanted in Burma."[182] Refugees recounted that their documents were

[172] Asia Watch, 1992, p. 6.

[173] Amnesty International, (Apr) 1992, p. 3; Foreign Ministry statement on Rohingya Muslims. Radio Burma (Rangoon) (February 21, 1992). FBIS-EAS-92-036.

[174] "Dialogue" with Burma on refugees. Radio Bangladesh External Service (Dhaka) (February 25, 1992). FBIS-NES-92-038.

[175] Burmese Muslim exodus termed great "tragedy." Voice of Malaysia (Kuala Lumpur) (March 10, 1992). FBIS-EAS-92-048; Dhaka denies claim on refugees' immigrant status. *Hong Kong AFP* (March 12, 1992). FBIS-NES-92-051.

[176] Zia Apprises UN of Burmese refugee problem. Radio Bangladesh Network (Dhaka) (March 21, 1992). FBIS-NES-92-060.

[177] Minister discusses refugees, list given to Burma. Radio Bangladesh Network (Dhaka) (March 29, 1992). FBIS-NES-92-061; Muslim rebels to increase anti-Rangoon offensive. *Bangkok Post* (April 15, 1992). FBIS-EAS-92-073.

[178] Envoy summoned over "oppression." Radio Malaysia Network (Kuala Lumpur) (March 10, 1992). FBIS-EAS-92-048.

[179] Amnesty International, 1992 (Apr), p. 3; Asia Watch, 1992, p. 14.

[180] Amnesty International, 1992 (Apr), p. 3; Asia Watch, 1992, p. 14.

[181] Asia Watch, 1992, p. 18; Smith, 1994, p. 82.

[182] Amnesty International, 1992 (Apr), p. 3; Piper, 1994, p. 24.

confiscated by the Lone Htein border guards, who told them that they would "shoot them if they returned."[183] The common refrain was "go back to your own country" and "get out of Burma and go to Bangladesh."[184]

Rohingya refugees in Bangladesh recounted the military's alleged accusations about insurgent activity in Arakan. A farmer from Buthidaung township told Amnesty International, "One day the MI 18 [military intelligence] came and dragged me from my house and beat me with a stick stuck through with two nails. They accused me of having contact with the insurgents and of going to Bangladesh to meet them."[185] Two students reported a similar experience of being arrested and interrogated by the military and police who accused them of "having contacts with the insurgent group the Rohingya Solidarity Organisation."[186] Others were not so lucky. Refugees described a thirty-year-old man who was shot outside his home: "They said he was an RSO [Rohingya Solidarity Organization] insurgent, but he was just an ordinary farmer."[187]

The ethnic targeting, the pattern of language used by the military units, and the public announcements from senior government officials indicate a clear intention to remove the Rohingya from Burma through a policy of mass expulsion. By July 1992, more than 250,000 Rohingya had been expelled, an estimated 18–36 percent of the total Rohingya population.[188]

7.6 Burma as a Negative Case (mid-1992–1995): Halted Expulsion & Repatriation of Rohingya

The negative case presented here differs from those in the previous chapters. Similar to the Ottoman Empire case study in Chapter 6, this chapter examines variation within a single country. However, rather than geographic variation, this negative case explores variation over time. Between April 1991 and July 1992, Burma's military government expelled over 250,000

[183] Amnesty International, 1992 (Sept), p. 24; Piper, 1994, p. 24.

[184] Amnesty International, 1992 (Apr), p. 15; Asia Watch, 1992, pp. 10, 19.

[185] Amnesty International, 1992 (Apr), p. 14.

[186] Amnesty International, 1992 (Apr), p. 14.

[187] Amnesty International, 1992 (Sept), p. 25.

[188] Piper, 1994, p. 14; Van Hear, 1998, p. 99. In the 1990s, the SLORC estimated that the total Muslim population in Arakan was 690,000, whereas Muslims claimed the figure was 1.4 million, out of a total state population of 2.4 million (Smith, 1994, p. 57). Thus, between 18 and 36 percent of the Rohingya were expelled. In both absolute and relative terms, this was a large-scale expulsion targeting a significant portion of the group.

Rohingya from Arakan State. Yet, in a surprising turn of events, following five days of talks between the foreign ministers of Burma and Bangladesh in the spring of 1992, the Burmese authorities agreed "to take all necessary measures that would halt the outflow of Myanmar (Burmese) residents to Bangladesh, and encourage those who left Burma to return voluntarily and safely to their homes."[189] Over the course of the next three years, from September 1992 through 1995, the expulsions stopped and the expellees returned to Burma.[190]

These two time periods can be conceptualized as distinct cases, each under different SLORC leaders: T_1 (1991–mid-1992) and T_2 (mid-1992–1995). During the first period examined, General Saw Maung headed the SLORC; in the second, General Than Shwe assumed the position after Saw Maung was removed by the military government.[191] This leadership change corresponded with crucial shifts in the governing regime, which is why the periods are treated as separate cases.

7.7 Intervening Factors

Many governments use violence to suppress subversive groups within their territory, yet this does not always, nor often, involve mass expulsion. Once a government carries out such an operation, it is unlikely to abruptly reverse course and allow the alleged subversives to return. This section examines the shifting SLORC policies from expelling Rohingya "terrorists" from 1991 to mid-1992 to halting the expulsion and accepting the Rohingya's return from mid-1992 to 1995, albeit with continued discrimination. The SLORC's "Burmanization" policies remained constant throughout the full period examined (1991–1995), and their view of the Rohingya as outside of the ethnonational vision of the state did not change, despite the change in military leadership. The security threat that the Tatmadaw accused the Rohingya of posing did not materially change across the two periods examined. The SLORC's volte-face is explained by unpacking the key intervening factors: alliances, the target group "homeland" state, and international organizations.

[189] Burmese pact unacceptable to refugee leaders. *Hong Kong AFP* (April 28, 1992). FBIS-NES-92-083.

[190] Loescher, 2001, p. 286.

[191] Burma duplicity, foreign pressure viewed. *The Nation* (Bangkok) (May 2, 1992). FBIS-EAS-92-087; Charney, 2009, p. 177; Hein, 2018, p. 374; Myint-U, 2021, p. 45; Smith, 1999, p. 425.

These factors explain what enabled the Tatmadaw to expel in T_1 and constrained them in T_2, leading to a reversal of their mass expulsion policy.

7.7.1 Alliances

Domestic Alliances

The Burmese military junta had ruled Burma since 1962. Although Ne Win resigned in July 1988, and his BSPP was ousted by the new SLORC government under the leadership of General Saw Maung, the Tatmadaw continued to control the state. The Tatmadaw was not simply a group of military officers but an entire social class made up of active military personnel, veterans, and their families. They dominated the political, social, and economic institutions of the country.[192] Throughout the 1970s and 1980s, the Tatmadaw further isolated itself from the rest of the country and focused on its own enrichment.[193] In 1988, when the SLORC decided to abandon socialism and pursue a capitalist, market-oriented economy, the junta and its families became "Burma's nouveau riche," while the rest of the country remained in poverty.[194]

The military's central concern was maintaining power at all costs, believing that it was the only organization capable of protecting the unity of the country.[195] The name of the military party—National Unity Party—indicated as much. But the Tatmadaw was not a homogenous block. There were factional disputes about the best way to preserve control and the best tactics to achieve its objectives.[196] Internal divisions emerged in 1988 over both the level of repression used against student protestors, which some believed was too harsh, and the decision for Ne Win to resign, or be forced out.[197] Nonetheless, these internal disputes were always over how to protect the power of the military, including its political and economic privileges, not about offering concessions to civilians.[198] Accordingly, the SLORC's key domestic allies were Burmese soldiers, military veterans, and their dependents—satisfying these groups was vital.

192 Smith, 1994, p. 29.
193 Charney, 2009, p. 171; Ibrahim, 2018, p. 38.
194 Charney, 2009, pp. 150, 171.
195 Callahan 2003, p. 207; Smith, 1994, p. 423.
196 Charney, 2009, pp. 159–160; Ibrahim, 2018, p. 38.
197 Charney, 2009, p. 151; Ibrahim, 2018, pp. 38–39.
198 Charney, 2009, p. 159; Ibrahim, 2018, pp. 38–39.

In the late 1980s and early 1990s, the Tatmadaw faced concurrent economic and political crises. Ne Win's failed fiscal policies led the country into economic free fall, and a united Burmese public challenged the junta's hold on power for the first time.[199] The Tatmadaw's control of the state was in danger. At the same time, the Communist Party of Burma (CPB), the oldest and largest of Burma's domestic insurgencies, collapsed among internal mutinies.[200] A fortuitous political-cum-economic opportunity arose to combat the junta's dual threats.

In 1989, the Tatmadaw saw an opening to end the conflict with the ex-communist armies to their mutual advantage. They engaged Lo Hsing-han, a Kokang Chinese drug kingpin, to broker a deal with the communist insurgents.[201] The two sides agreed to a ceasefire, and the Tatmadaw granted each of the four CPB ex-communist armies a dedicated area of operation in which they could conduct business "as they pleased."[202] The Tatmadaw, in turn, redirected its forces in the northeast toward other insurgencies in the country and reaped the financial windfall of the booming illicit narcotics trade.[203] This filled its coffers while eliminating a key opposition force to the benefit of its domestic allies.

When it came to combating insurgencies in northern Arakan, the SLORC aimed to succeed where General Ne Win had failed. While the military struggled to repress ethnic minorities in frontier areas that were better armed and trained, the Rohingya were more easily removed, and their expulsion furthered the junta's ethnonationalist "Burmanization" agenda. In addition to the benefit of achieving something the previous regime had failed to do, anti-Rohingya policies united odd bedfellows.[204] After the 1990 election, NLD politicians colluded with the military in accusing the newly elected Rohingya members of parliament of falsifying their identity documents to run for office and stripped them of their seats.[205] Though the SLORC did not seek NLD approval or support for the Rohingya expulsion, these shared objectives bolstered broader domestic support for the policy.

[199] Myint-U, 2021, p. 49.

[200] Amnesty International, 1992 (Sept), p. 31; Callahan, 2003, p. 13; Charney, 2009, pp. 164, 188; Myint-U, 2021, pp. 48–50.

[201] Amnesty International, 1992 (Sept), p. 31; Callahan, 2003, p. 13; Myint-U, 2021, p. 50.

[202] Amnesty International, 1992 (Sept), p. 31; Myint-U, 2021, pp. 50–51.

[203] Myint-U, 2021, p. 51.

[204] Ibrahim, 2018, p. 42.

[205] Ibrahim, 2018, p. 42.

The expulsion of the Rohingya benefited the SLORC and its domestic military allies on three fronts: It completed the failed 1978 Operation Dragon King, furthered its ethnonationalist objectives, and removed a group that the Burman majority rejected—all of which further cemented its hold on power and secured the position and benefits for its domestic allies.

However, in the spring of 1992, internal divisions within the SLORC emerged over the issue of the Rohingya expulsion. International pressure on the new regime had initially focused on the government's actions suppressing democratic reforms and nullifying the 1990 election results. But throughout the spring of 1992, this pressure, including economic sanctions and the withdrawal of foreign businesses, expanded beyond pushing for democracy promotion to a growing outcry over the treatment of the Rohingya. As this pressure increased, so too did internal dissension within the SLORC. Moderate factions within the Tatmadaw pushed senior SLORC leaders to temper their policies against the Rohingya in order to increase their legitimacy.[206] They believed the hardline positions of General Saw Maung were harming the interests of the Tatmadaw.

The seeds of this growing moderate faction appeared at the end of March 1992. Burma's foreign minister, Ohn Gyaw, led an international delegation to northern Arakan, followed by a visit from the UN under-secretary-general for humanitarian affairs, Jan Eliasson, hoping to shift the narrative about the situation of the Rohingya.[207] In the absence of major policy changes, dissent within the Tatmadaw reached a boiling point in April, and the SLORC reshuffled its top leadership. General Saw Maung was removed and replaced with the more pragmatic General Than Shwe.[208]

Following the leadership changes, the SLORC instituted policy changes. In the last week of April, they rescinded most of the martial law restrictions, released political prisoners, and agreed to halt the expulsion of the Rohingya and repatriate the refugees.[209] The SLORC had consistently ignored invitations from Bangladesh for talks on the Rohingya issue, but at the end of

[206] Charney, 2009, p. 177; Hein, 2018, p. 374; Smith, 1999, p. 425.

[207] Muslims deny rape, prosecution. Radio Burma (Rangoon) (April 4, 1992). FBIS-EAS-92-066; Thai paper cites diplomatic source on Arakan tour. *The Nation* (Bangkok) (April 2, 1992). FBIS-EAS-92-064.

[208] Burma duplicity, foreign pressure viewed. *The Nation* (Bangkok) (May 2, 1992). FBIS-EAS-92-087; Charney, 2009, p. 177; Hein, 2018, p. 374; Myint-U, 2021, p. 45; Smith, 1999, p. 425.

[209] Burma duplicity, foreign pressure viewed. *The Nation* (Bangkok) (May 2, 1992). FBIS-EAS-92-087; Charney, 2009, p. 178; Smith, 1999, p. 425.

April, Foreign Minister Gyaw met with President Abdur Rahman Biswas in Bangladesh and assured him of Burma's "sincerity to resolve the Rohingya refugee problem."[210] Speaking about the meeting afterward, Gyaw said, "Myanmar and Bangladesh . . . are two close neighbors who have trust and complete understanding and good neighborliness."[211] A hasty reversal from flouting Bangladesh's previous requests to meet and discuss the issue. Thai newspaper *The Nation* noted that "the recent concessions may indicate that there are elements pushing for reform within military circles in Rangoon . . . their tolerance within SLORC has its limits."[212] Under the leadership of General Shwe, the SLORC was captured by the moderates within the Tatmadaw.

Importantly, these shifts within the military junta did not overturn the previous approach or ideology of the SLORC. In May, Foreign Minister Gyaw again denied the Rohingya were being persecuted by the government, and told the BBC in an interview that "the Rohingyas had left Myanmar for their own reasons, possibly being incited to do so by rebel insurgents."[213] The halting of the expulsion and the agreement for the Rohingya's return did not negate the Tatmadaw's motivation to counter subversive security threats. However, in this second period (beginning in mid-1992), the negative impact of the Rohingya expulsion on the SLORC's domestic allies outweighed the benefit of maintaining the hardline policy.

Transnational Alliances

In the late 1980s and early 1990s, Burma's junta was isolated from the rest of the world through economic and political sanctions over its authoritarian rule and human rights abuses.[214] Its engagement in illicit industries and domination of the domestic economy enabled its financial survival. This limited Burma's transnational alliances, but key partnerships with China and Thailand were critical.

Since Burma's independence, the country had a tenuous relationship with China. They shared a long border in the northeast, and there was a

[210] Burmese foreign minister vows to end disputes. Radio Bangladesh Network (Dhaka) (April 26, 1992). FBIS-NES-92-083; Zia apprises UN of Burmese refugee problem. Radio Bangladesh Network (Dhaka) (March 21, 1992). FBIS-NES-92-060.

[211] Burmese foreign minister vows to end disputes. Radio Bangladesh Network (Dhaka) (April 26,1992). FBIS-NES-92-083.

[212] Burma duplicity, foreign pressure viewed. *The Nation* (Bangkok) (May 2, 1992). FBIS-EAS-92-087.

[213] Amnesty International, 1992 (Sept), p. 25.

[214] Holliday, 2005, pp. 329, 332; Steinberg & Fan, 2012, pp. 263, 331.

sizable ethnic Chinese minority in Burma, approximately 400,000 in the early 1990s.[215] In 1967, violent anti-Chinese riots erupted throughout the country, allegedly incited by the government. Hundreds of Chinese were killed or injured, property was looted and destroyed, and many fled the country.[216] The Chinese government responded by financially and militarily supporting the CPB insurgents.[217]

In the 1980s, as part of Chinese leader Deng Xiaoping's reformist shift, China cut off military aid to the communist insurgents.[218] Not long after, the CPB collapsed leading to a thaw in relations with the Tatmadaw and the opening of the Burma–China border to trade and movement.[219] These events occurred in the spring of 1989, while the Chinese Communist Party (CCP) faced its own student uprisings. Like the Burmese junta, the CCP ruthlessly suppressed the protestors, notably in the Tiananmen Square massacre.[220] After the massacre, SLORC Secretary Khin Nyunt called China's ambassador to Burma and "expressed sympathy and understanding on the Chinese government['s] use of force against the demonstration at Tiananmen Square in Beijing."[221] As the CCP partially opened to the forces of globalization and launched its communist market economy, it created tremendous economic growth.[222] Large numbers of Chinese businessmen returned to Burma. With the passage of new laws in the late 1980s, most of Burma's foreign investment had come from the Chinese.[223] The end of the CPB insurgency and the events of Tiananmen Square drew Burma and China closer together.[224]

In 1989, trade relations between China and Burma rapidly increased. They agreed to a $1.2 billion arms deal, including aircraft, patrol boats, tanks, armored personnel carriers, and military training—critical to the dramatic expansion of the Tatmadaw in the early 1990s.[225] China also

[215] Smith, 1994, p. 64.
[216] Myint-U, 2021, p. 35; Smith, 1994, pp. 63–64.
[217] Myint-U, 2021, p. 49; Smith, 1994, p. 64.
[218] Myint-U, 2021, p. 49.
[219] Myint-U, 2021, p. 59; Steinberg & Fan, 2012, pp. 210, 316.
[220] Holliday, 2005, p. 331.
[221] Steinberg & Fan, 2012, p. 401.
[222] Myint-U, 2021, p. 50.
[223] Steinberg & Fan, 2012, p. 253.
[224] Smith, 1994, p. 64; Smith, 1999, p. 426; Steinberg & Fan, 2012, p. 315.
[225] ASEAN called to act on Burmese situation. *The Nation* (Bangkok) (March 5, 1992). FBIS-EAS-92-044; Asia Watch, 1992, p. 23; Burma's policy, Muslim Rohingyas' plight viewed. *New Strait Times* (Kuala Lumpur) (March 11, 1992). FBIS-EAS-92-051; Charney, 2009, p. 187; Crossette, 1991; Holliday, 2005, p. 331; Rohingya leader demands citizenship guarantees. *Hong Kong AFP* (April 5, 1992). FBIS-EAS-92-068; Smith, 1994, p. 90; Smith, 1999, p. 426; Steinberg & Fan, 2012, pp. 163, 317.

invested in large-scale development projects throughout Burma, including the construction of roads and hydroelectric dams, and provided cheap consumer goods.[226] In addition to its official trade relations, the Chinese were involved in illicit trading and smuggling in the timber, gems, and narcotics sectors.[227] Lo Hsing-han, who had helped to broker the historic ceasefire with the ex-communist armies on behalf of the Tatmadaw, was a prominent Kokang Chinese drug smuggler.[228] Between 1988 and 1995, trade between the two countries grew at an average annual rate of 25 percent.[229] Burma was also a strategic security partner for China. Establishing strong relations with Burma—including access to its transportation network and ports—gave Beijing a route to the Bay of Bengal, a strategic waterway to bolster its naval presence and influence over the Straits of Malacca, while also providing closer proximity from which to monitor India.[230]

Although China was not the behemoth in 1989 that it is today, Burmese government officials prioritized the relationship as one of mutual interest and economic gain. Therefore, in 1991, at the outset of Burma's expulsion of the Rohingya, China was the country's preeminent transnational ally—its largest trading partner and arms dealer. If there was a country with leverage over the military junta, it was China.[231] However, China did not interfere in the domestic politics of Burma; instead, it pursued a "no strings attached" investment approach.[232] The Chinese government ignored the expulsion of the Rohingya and did not pressure the Tatmadaw to change course.[233] This lack of opposition to the expulsion decision further enabled the removal to proceed.

Burma's second key transnational ally at the time was Thailand. The two countries historically had close economic ties, and the Thai and Burmese militaries had an especially close relationship.[234] After the SLORC asserted control in September 1988, Thailand's commander of the army, General Chavalit Yongchaiyudh, was the new regime's first high-level foreign visitor.[235] The two countries signed lucrative cross-border logging contracts

[226] Crossette, 1991; Smith, 1994, p. 90; Steinberg & Fan, 2012, pp. 187, 210, 317.
[227] Crossette, 1991; Steinberg & Fan, 2012, p. 208.
[228] Myint-U, 2021, p. 50.
[229] Steinberg & Fan, 2012, pp. 208–209.
[230] Steinberg & Fan, 2012, pp. 312–313, 318, 340.
[231] Asia Watch, 1992, p. 22.
[232] Steinberg & Fan, 2012, p. 187.
[233] Burma duplicity, foreign pressure viewed. *The Nation* (Bangkok) (May 2, 1992). FBIS-EAS-92-087.
[234] Asia Watch, 1992, p. 22; Crossette, 1991.
[235] Steinberg & Fan, 2012, p. 326.

during his visit, allowing Thai companies connected to the ruling junta to engage in the clear-cutting of forests along the southeastern border.[236] Like China, trade relations included official and unofficial trade—the latter largely timber smuggling.[237]

Given these close economic and military ties, Thailand could have influenced the actions of the SLORC. But Thailand was facing its own domestic turmoil in the early 1990s, with a military coup toppling the democratically elected prime minister in February 1991.[238] General Suchinda Kraprayoon, Commander-in-Chief of the Royal Thai Army and leader of the coup, had very close ties with the Tatmadaw.[239] Despite growing international pressure, Thailand also ignored the Rohingya expulsion policy and refused to condemn the Tatmadaw. In March 1992, Thailand's foreign minister stated, "Everybody shares concern, but there is no need for us to take part in any official declaration to condemn Burma."[240] Thailand had battled its own Muslim insurgency in the south of the country, and although relations with its Muslim insurgents had thawed in the 1980s, the military's fresh takeover in 1991 was laden with memories of battling Islamic challenges to the dominant Buddhist state.[241] In sum, both influential transnational allies—China and Thailand—were indifferent to the Rohingya expulsion, further enabling the policy.

Because this is a within-case comparison, Burma's two key transnational allies remained the same in the second period examined (mid-1992–1995). Intuitively, one might conclude that China and Thailand would have continued to prioritize their strong economic relations with Burma and not interfere in the expulsion decision. China, however, was a vital ally of Burma and Bangladesh. The Bangladeshi government strongly lobbied China to help resolve the Rohingya issue. Although China had no concerns with the SLORC's repressive policies—in fact, it shared a common experience violently suppressing student dissent—it was anxious about maintaining regional stability for its own economic and strategic benefit.[242] In January 1992, shortly after the border clashes between Burma and Bangladesh, Chinese authorities assured Bangladesh they would use their influence with

[236] Myint-U, 2021, p. 49; Smith, 1994, p. 90; Steinberg & Fan, 2012, p. 326.
[237] Crossette, 1991; Steinberg & Fan, 2012, pp. 263–264.
[238] Croissant, 2007, p. 2.
[239] Asia Watch, 1992, p. 22.
[240] Bangkok not to condemn Burma over Muslims. *Bangkok Post* (March 13, 1992). FBIS-EAS-92-050.
[241] Croissant, 2007, p. 2; Parnini, 2013, p. 289.
[242] Steinberg & Fan, 2012, pp. 309–310.

Burma to "diffuse the tension" between the two countries, but did not pledge to stop the human rights abuses.[243] A senior Bangladeshi government official told the AFP that "China, which has close ties with both Bangladesh and Burma [noting that Beijing was a major source of weapons for both countries], has extended its helping hand to ensure that the two neighbouring countries can settle their problems amicably."[244]

Throughout 1992, Bangladeshi authorities held conversations with senior Chinese officials about repatriating Rohingya refugees to Burma. In November, Bangladesh's foreign secretary held talks with Chinese Vice Minister of Foreign Affairs Xu Dunxin.[245] Dunxin stated during the talks that the Chinese government "would utilize its close relationship with Myanmar . . . to persuade the Myanmar authorities toward speedy repatriation of Rohingya refugees."[246] Human rights protections were of no concern to the Chinese, "except insofar as their absence, or perceived absence . . . contributes to instability."[247] Bangladesh asserted that the massive refugee influx was destabilizing.

Since documented conversations between Chinese and Burmese authorities are not available, public statements by Bangladeshi and Chinese officials serve as a useful proxy for China's intentions. Although Chinese recommendations to senior Burmese authorities were conveyed in private, given the crucial economic support that China provided to the SLORC, their views would have been taken seriously.[248] The Tatmadaw likely calculated that repatriating the Rohingya was useful to protect both its domestic and transnational alliances, contributing to stopping and reversing the expulsion policy.

7.7.2 "Homeland" State of the Target Group

Bangladesh is the relevant "homeland" state in this case—the country to which the SLORC alleged the Rohingya "belonged." Ties between

[243] Asia Watch, 1992, p. 22.

[244] PRC helping to restore ties with Burma. *Hong Kong AFP* (January 27, 1992). FBIS-NES-92-018.

[245] Talks held with PRC vice foreign minister. Radio Bangladesh Network (Dhaka) (November 4, 1992). FBIS-NES-92-215.

[246] Talks held with PRC vice foreign minister. Radio Bangladesh Network (Dhaka) (November 4, 1992). FBIS-NES-92-215.

[247] Steinberg & Fan, 2012, p. 330.

[248] Steinberg & Fan, 2012, pp. 311, 333–334.

Burma and Bangladesh were moderate. The 104 mile (167 kilometer) border between the two countries is short and geographically isolated from lower Burma by a coastal mountain range.[249] After the partition of India, and Bangladesh's subsequent secession from Pakistan, the poor Muslim-majority country was not a priority partner for the Burmese Buddhist military regime. The two countries had limited trade relations, and since Bangladesh's independence, there had been an ongoing dispute regarding the maritime boundaries in the Bay of Bengal related to oil exploration.[250] Still, the two countries had maintained cordial ties. Injuring relations with Bangladesh was not a significant restraint on the SLORC's decision to expel.

Bangladesh was no stranger to the Tatmadaw's efforts to remove the Rohingya from its territory and force them into Chittagong Division. The Bangladeshi government had witnessed this in 1978, and was aware of the SLORC's renewed rhetoric in this regard after it came to power in 1988. Nevertheless, in 1991 and early 1992, by *force majeure*, Bangladesh acquiesced and resettled Rohingya refugees in camps along the border, overwhelmed by the influx.[251] The Bangladeshi government's initial response was welcoming and the public was sympathetic to the Rohingya refugees' plight.[252] The area of concern was a peripheral region in the southeast of the country, far from the center of power in the capital Dhaka, and not of immediate political concern.[253]

Bangladesh was also a very poor country, with a GDP per capita in 1991 of less than $300[254] and limited resources to patrol and prevent refugees crossing the border. In April 1991, just as the Rohingya expulsion began, a violent cyclone struck south and southeastern Bangladesh, affecting 15 million people, killing over 135,000, and causing more than $1.5 billion in damages.[255] The country was focused on responding to the natural disaster. Bangladesh had neither the capability nor the resources to deny entry to the Rohingya expellees, and the lukewarm ties between the two countries did not restrain Burma from moving forward with the expulsion.

[249] Hein, 2018, p. 365; Ibrahim, 2018, p. 18; Myint-U, 2021, p. 9.
[250] Parnini, 2013, pp. 288, 294; Yegar, 2002, p. 54.
[251] Minister discusses refugees, list given to Burma. Radio Bangladesh Network (Dhaka) (March 29, 1992). FBIS-NES-92-061.
[252] Barnett & Finnemore, 2004, p. 107; Lambrecht, 1995, p. 5.
[253] Parnini, 2013, p. 287.
[254] World Bank, 2025b.
[255] Asia Watch, 1992, p. 21; Khalil, 1993, pp. 263–265.

The strength of ties between Bangladesh and Burma did not change dramatically in the two periods examined. While their relations were strained in December 1991 when Lone Htein forces crossed into Bangladesh and killed four people, the Bangladeshi government was upset but remained committed to communication and amicable relations with its neighbor. Bangladeshi Information Minister Nazmul Huda described the country's approach to dealing with the situation as "pursuing quiet diplomacy to resolve the crisis."[256] The moderate relations between the two countries remained constant. What changed was Bangladesh's reception and response to the Rohingya refugees.

In early 1992, Bangladeshi Prime Minister Zia and Foreign Minister A. S. M. Mostafizur Rahman mounted an international lobbying campaign for relief funds to temporarily accommodate the Rohingya and for commitments to return the Rohingya to Burma as soon as possible. In February, Rahman traveled to eight European and Middle Eastern countries to brief leaders on the refugee situation and to plead for their support.[257] The next month, Prime Minister Zia traveled to Washington, DC, to meet with President George H. W. Bush, securing his support for refugee assistance.[258] This was followed by a trip to New York to brief UN Secretary-General Boutros Boutros-Ghali on the Rohingya situation.[259] Prime Minister Zia "urged the secretary general to take urgent measures to create pressure on [the] Myanmar Government to settle [the issue] so that the refugees can go back to their country with safety and dignity."[260] While Bangladesh was unable to prevent the influx of Rohingya expellees, it fiercely resisted the idea that they would remain in the country. The worldwide campaign by the Bangladeshi government to force Burma to take back the Rohingya—from the UN in New York to powerful governments around the world—was essential to the change in Burma's policy.

[256] Parliament begins debate on Burma border tension. Radio Bangladesh Network (Dhaka) (February 3, 1992). FBIS-NES-92-023.

[257] Rahman leaves for Europe, Middle East visit. Radio Bangladesh Network (Dhaka) (February 14, 1992). FBIS-NES-92-031.

[258] Asia Watch, 1992, p. 21; Zia apprises UN of Burmese refugee problem. Radio Bangladesh Network (Dhaka) (March 21, 1992). FBIS-NES-92-060.

[259] Asia Watch, 1992, p. 21; Zia Apprises UN of Burmese refugee problem. Radio Bangladesh Network (Dhaka) (March 21, 1992). FBIS-NES-92-060.

[260] Zia apprises UN of Burmese refugee problem. Radio Bangladesh Network (Dhaka) (March 21, 1992). FBIS-NES-92-060.

One bargaining chip that allowed Bangladesh to wield outsized influence in convincing the UN to repatriate the Rohingya was its dramatic increase in contributions to the UN Department of Peacekeeping Operations. Although Bangladesh began contributing personnel to UN peacekeeping in 1988, it was not until four years later, in 1992, that it provided substantial personnel. While there is no direct evidence of a quid pro quo, Bangladesh increased its peacekeeping troops from 5 in January 1992 to 1,128 by December 1992, rising further to 3,451 by the end of 1993.[261] In December of 1991, Bangladesh was the forty-ninth largest contributor of forces to UN peacekeeping, tied with Romania, Thailand, and Turkey—a year later it rose to thirteenth largest, and by December 1993, it was the fourth-largest contributor in the world.[262]

Senior Bangladeshi officials noted their increased contributions to and prioritization of UN peacekeeping in public statements. On September 29, 1992, in Bangladesh's UN General Assembly speech, Foreign Minister Rahman stated:

> We have *purposefully* contributed to United Nations peace-keeping efforts through the dispatch of military and civilian contingents. . . . We strongly support the strengthening of the financial and institutional base of peace-keeping and its growth in new and imaginative directions" [emphasis added].[263]

Separately, after a week-long visit to the UN in January 1993, Rahman told reporters that

> his talks with [UNSG] Dr. Butrus Ghali [sic] went on very well. The secretary general has assured all possible help of the world body for an early repatriation of all refugees from Bangladesh . . . Mr. Ghali . . . also commended Dhaka for its participation in the peacekeeping operations in the trouble spots in the world.[264]

261 United Nations Peacekeeping, 2021.
262 United Nations Peacekeeping, 2021.
263 UN General Assembly, 47th Sess., 17th mtg., UN Doc A/47/PV.17 (October 8, 1992), p. 36.
264 Rahman on UN, US talks, Burmese refugees. Radio Bangladesh Network (Dhaka) (January 28, 1993). FBIS-NES-93-018.

While the UN and its affiliated agencies were supportive of repatriation as a policy, the small, impoverished country marshaled support at the UN far above its fighting weight. It may have used contributions to UN peacekeeping as a bargaining chip—the correlation is certainly conspicuous.

7.7.3 International Organizations

Despite its membership in the UN since 1948, and Burmese diplomat U Thant's leadership of the organization as UN secretary-general (1961–1971), Burma's relationships with pertinent international organizations in the early 1990s were weak. The Tatmadaw had long been an international pariah. Its international isolation increased after its aggressive, militarized response to the 1988 student protests, the arrest of NLD opposition leader Aung San Suu Kyi, and the annulment of the 1990 elections. Many Western countries, including the United States and European countries, cut off aid and imposed arms embargoes, while the few UN agencies that remained reduced their budgets.[265] In the face of these external pressures, the Tatmadaw was unfazed. It had survived since 1962 without much international engagement, and it perceived international actors as suspicious, intrusive, and seeking regime change.[266] The key regional organization was the Association of Southeast Asian Nations (ASEAN).[267] Though the treatment of the Rohingya was a significant topic of conversation within ASEAN, Burma's lack of membership limited the internal restraining aspect of this factor. When the SLORC began implementing its expulsion policy, its weak ties, or not-yet-formalized ties, with IOs was not a viable restraint.

The response of IOs to the expulsion was mixed. The UN condemned the expulsion, while ASEAN took the position of "constructive engagement," which manifested in noninterference. At first, IOs were more vociferous in their response to Burma's suppression of the democracy movement than they were to the Rohingya expulsion. But by March 1992, the UN Commission on Human Rights passed a resolution calling for a special rapporteur to Burma to investigate human rights abuses and for an end to "the exodus of Myanmar refugees to neighboring countries as well as to facilitate their early

[265] Asia Watch, 1992, p. 23; Myint-U, 2021, p. 46; Smith, 1994, p. 90.

[266] Steinberg & Fan, 2012, p. 308; Ibrahim, 2018, pp. 44, 46.

[267] In the early 1990s, ASEAN had six member states: Brunei, Indonesia, Malaysia, the Philippines, Singapore, and Thailand. Burma joined in 1997.

repatriation."[268] The US, Australia, the European Union, Japan, Kuwait, and others responded with pledges to the UN and Bangladesh for refugee support.[269] However, the UN had minimal leverage with the Tatmadaw since its presence in the country was small and Burma had not signed on to the 1954 Convention Related to the Status of Stateless Persons. Their condemnation of and resistance to the expulsion went unheeded.

Although Burma was not a member of ASEAN, the organization could have exerted influence on the country. But throughout early 1992, as the expulsion reached its apogee, ASEAN members collectively agreed not to condemn Burma over the Rohingya removal. Thailand's foreign minister, Arsa Sarasin, stated on March 13, "ASEAN will not take a collective position on Burma's repression of its Muslim minority."[270] The organization's official policy was "constructive engagement," resisting Western pressure to apply sanctions or to be more critical of the ruling junta.[271] Brunei and Singapore voiced "concern" and called for a "peaceful solution" but took no actions to convince the Tatmadaw to stop the Rohingya expulsion.[272] Sarasin stated that "despite its 'concern' over the influx of Rohingya refugees to Bangladesh, Thailand will not join the chorus of condemnation of the Rangoon military regime's operations."[273]

Muslim-majority Indonesia and Malaysia, by contrast, were more outspoken in their criticism than the other ASEAN states. In a statement to the Indonesia House of Representatives, Minister of Foreign Affairs Ali Alatas said, "Indonesia appeals to the Myanmarese [Burmese] Government to take the necessary steps to solve the problem regarding the Rohingya ethnic group and to deal with the fundamental questions that have led to the flow of refugees into neighboring countries."[274] Yet he also noted that the "problems inside Myanmar [are] essentially its internal affairs," but nevertheless "recent developments show that the situation inside Myanmar has carried

[268] ASEAN called to act on Burmese situation." *The Nation* (Bangkok) (March 5, 1992). FBIS-EAS-92-044; Asia Watch, 1992, p. 23.

[269] Asia Watch, 1992, p. 21; Islamic envoys briefed. Radio Bangladesh Network (Dhaka) (February 27, 1992). FBIS-NES-92-040.

[270] Bangkok not to condemn Burma over Muslims. *Bangkok Post* (March 13, 1992). FBIS-EAS-92-050.

[271] ASEAN ministers discuss Cambodia, Burma, Spratlys. *Bangkok Post* (July 25, 1992). FBIS-EAS-92-144; Asia Watch, 1992, p. 22; Charney, 2009, p. 184; Crossette, 1991; Yegar, 2002, p. 65.

[272] Asia Watch, 1992, p. 22.

[273] Bangkok not to condemn Burma over Muslims. *Bangkok* Post (March 13, 1992). FBIS-EAS-92-050.

[274] Jakarta wants Burma to solve Rohingya problem. *The Jakarta Post* (March 12, 1992). FBIS-EAS-92-055.

over into some international dimensions and tends to have an adverse effect on the peace and stability in Southeast Asia."[275]

Malaysia similarly spoke out against the Tatmadaw's human rights violations, specifically its treatment of the Rohingya.[276] In early March, the Malaysian government demanded that the Tatmadaw "immediately cease acts of alleged oppression and expulsion of about 135,000 Rohingyas from the country's Arakan Province."[277] Deputy Prime Minister Ghafar Baba stated a few days later that he hoped Burma would take its criticism over the Rohingya issue "as that from a friend."[278] The Malay Ministry of Foreign Affairs summoned the Burmese ambassador over the Rohingya issue to "immediately cease the oppression of Rohingya Muslims and be prepared to accept them back."[279] Later in the month, the Malaysian Foreign Minister Abdullah Badawi announced in a television broadcast that the "government was deeply concerned over the attacks on Moslems in Myanmar."[280]

Though the Malaysian government spoke out against Rohingya abuses, and summoned the Burmese ambassador to outline its concerns, it did not directly engage with the SLORC. Instead, Malaysia preferred to go through the UN. Foreign Minister Badawi stated that "it would only be proper for Malaysia to openly declare its firm stand on the matter and any of the necessary action by the UN."[281] Malaysia was very careful to ensure its concerns about the Rohingya did not violate Burma's sovereignty or constitute any form of domestic interference.[282] Deputy Prime Minister Ghafar affirmed his confidence that the Rohingya issue would "not affect Malaysia-Myanmar relations."[283]

Despite differences among individual ASEAN members, the regional organization resisted interfering in Burma's domestic politics and refused

[275] Jakarta wants Burma to solve Rohingya problem. *The Jakarta Post* (March 12, 1992). FBIS-EAS-92-055.

[276] ASEAN–Burma links may strain Western ties. *The Nation* (Bangkok) (July 28, 1992). FBIS-EAS-92-145.

[277] Ghafar appeals to Burma. *Bernama* (Kuala Lumpur) (March 12, 1992). FBIS-EAS-92-049.

[278] Ghafar appeals to Burma. *Bernama* (Kuala Lumpur) (March 12, 1992). FBIS-EAS-92-049.

[279] Envoy summoned over "oppression." Radio Malaysia Network (Kuala Lumpur) (March 10, 1992). FBIS-EAS-92-048.

[280] Burma's impact on regional stability criticized. *The Jakarta Post* (March 14, 1992). FBIS-EAS-92-062.

[281] Minister to go through UN on Rohingya issue. Radio Malaysia Network (Kuala Lumpur) (March 12, 1992). FBIS-EAS-92-055.

[282] Burmese Muslim exodus termed great "tragedy." Voice of Malaysia (Kuala Lumpur) (March 10, 1992). FBIS-EAS-92-048; Ghafar urges caution. Radio Malaysia Network (Kuala Lumpur) (March 15, 1992). FBIS-EAS-92-051; Yegar, 2002, p. 65.

[283] Ghafar urges caution. Radio Malaysia Network (Kuala Lumpur) (March 15, 1992). FBIS-EAS-92-051.

to pressure the SLORC to improve its human rights record.[284] In this case, two key IOs were pulling in different directions. The UN resisted the Rohingya expulsion, condemning the SLORC policy, while ASEAN remained committed to "constructive engagement" and refused to intervene. These divisions diluted the impact of IOs to constrain Burma's expulsion. This, combined with the Tatmadaw's international isolation and generally weak ties with IOs, enabled expulsion in the first period examined.

By the spring of 1992, moderate elements within the Tatmadaw had concerns about growing international condemnation. After taking leadership of the SLORC in April 1992, General Than Shwe promised a "new direction," including rehabilitating its international reputation.[285] The desire to cultivate relations with IOs meant that the opinions of the UN, and its agency affiliates, were of greater concern to the SLORC than in the previous period. A dramatic shift. This is not to say that the military government improved its human rights record, but under Than Shwe it was more strategic about how it engaged with IOs. The SLORC facilitated international delegations to Arakan State, with access to civilians, however scripted. Than Shwe's aim to cultivate stronger ties with the UN influenced the decision to halt and reverse the expulsion.

Critically linked to Bangladesh's efforts to gain international support for returning the Rohingya to Burma was the backing of the UNHCR. International refugee law prohibits sending refugees back to a country where they will face a well-founded fear of persecution.[286] As the institution charged with refugee protection, the UNHCR's clearance of a country as "safe" for refugee return is critical for repatriation. Thus, when the UNHCR sanctioned the [forced] return of the Rohingya, despite the lack of improvement in the conditions in Arakan State, and the absence of Burmese guarantees of their safety upon return, the organization further enabled the reversal of the expulsion.[287]

Bangladesh's priority of removing the refugees from its territory coincided with the UNHCR's shifting emphasis on repatriation as the most durable

[284] ASEAN called to act on Burmese situation. *The Nation* (Bangkok) (March 5, 1992). FBIS-EAS-92-044.

[285] Hein, 2018, p. 374; Myint-U, 2021, p. 45.

[286] Article 33 of the 1951 Refugee Convention states, "No Contracting State shall expel or return ('refouler') a refugee in any manner whatsoever to the frontiers of territories where his life or freedom would be threatened on account of his race, religion, nationality, membership of a particular social group or political opinion."

[287] Barnett & Finnemore, 2004, pp. 75–76, 106; Loescher, 2001, p. 225.

solution for refugees.[288] UNHCR High Commissioner Sadako Ogata stated in a 1991 address that repatriation was "a prime objective of the organization" and later deemed the 1990s as "the decade of repatriation."[289] Previously, the UNHCR's position, and that of the 1951 Refugee Convention, had been that repatriation was a *voluntary* choice made by refugees themselves.[290] The agency's new policies in the 1990s, and new terminology such as "safe return," meant that the UNHCR, not the refugees, would determine whether conditions in their home country had improved to allow for return.[291] The UNHCR also shifted its determination of "safe countries" to when conditions improved "appreciably" rather than "substantially."[292] Gil Loescher, a political scientist, refugee expert, and historian of the UNHCR, described the organization's internal policy shift: "There was a growing view that refugee safety did not necessarily always outweigh the security interests of states or broader peace-building and conflict resolution goals."[293]

As part of Than Shwe's new direction as SLORC chairman, he stopped the expulsions and acceded to the repatriation of the Rohingya according to the bilateral agreement with Bangladesh.[294] The new Burmese leadership's shift in policy to strengthen ties with IOs, combined with the stance of the UNHCR in favor of refugee repatriation as the preferred solution, contributed to constraining further expulsion and reversing the policy. By the end of 1995, nearly all 250,000 expelled Rohingya had returned to Burma.[295]

7.8 Conclusion

In March 1991, under the leadership of General Saw Maung, the SLORC aimed to achieve something that the Ne Win regime had failed to do: permanently remove the Rohingya. The counter-subversive mass expulsion eliminated the alleged security threat and strengthened the Tatmadaw's internal

[288] Barnett & Finnemore, 2004, pp. 74–75, 93–98; Human Rights Watch, 1996; Loescher, 2001, p. 284.

[289] Barnett & Finnemore, 2004, pp. 94, 98.

[290] Loescher, 2001, p. 284.

[291] Barnett & Finnemore, 2004, pp. 75, 100; Loescher, 2001, p. 284.

[292] Barnett & Finnemore, 2004, p. 99; Loescher, 2001, p. 284.

[293] Loescher, 2001, p. 284.

[294] Memorandum of Understanding between the Government of the Union of Myanmar and the Office of the United Nations High Commissioner for Refugees, 05 November 1993; 10a/1-1993/10; Series 1, Box 9; Fonds 10a; UNHCR; Myint-U, 2021, p. 45.

[295] Human Rights Watch, 1996; Loescher, 2001, p. 286.

control over the revitalized ethnonational state. A Ministry of Foreign Affairs press release in January 1992 stated:

> The very name Rohingya was a creation of a *group of insurgents in the Rakhine State*... Like all other countries of the world, Myanmar exercises its inherent *right of self-defense in suppressing insurgents* in the country, but it needs to emphasize that the action has no connection with race or religion, but was undertaken to *suppress armed terrorists* [emphasis added].[296]

The expulsion capitalized on anti-Rohingya public sentiment and strengthened the position of the SLORC's domestic allies. China and Thailand—Burma's two key transnational allies—refused to intervene in the internal affairs of their neighbor and partner, and increased their political and economic ties with the SLORC as the expulsion unfolded. Bangladesh, the alleged "homeland" of the Rohingya, was overwhelmed by the influx and acquiesced and resettled the expellees. After decades of international isolation, Burma was immune to condemnation by the UN, and ASEAN opted for "constructive engagement" rather than pressuring the government to reverse course. Together, domestic and transnational alliances, the "homeland" state, and IOs enabled expulsion in Burma during the first period examined (1991–mid-1992).

Less than a year later, the situation changed. Beginning in mid-1992, the Tatmadaw changed its policy and reversed the expulsion. The "new direction" of the SLORC, under the leadership of General Than Shwe, moderated the Tatmadaw's position toward the Rohingya, and they agreed to a bilateral agreement with Bangladesh to repatriate the refugees. Shwe's moderate faction pushed out General Saw Maung over concerns of eroding domestic and international legitimacy. China, allied with both Bangladesh and Burma, and concerned about regional instability, quietly urged Burma to reverse its policy, while not publicly commenting on its human rights abuses. This occurred in parallel with Bangladesh's fierce lobbying campaign at the UN and with countries around the world to support the immediate repatriation of the Rohingya. The UN, particularly the UNHCR, supported repatriation as its preferred refugee solution and sanctioned the "conducive and

[296] Amnesty International, 1992 (Apr), p. 3; Foreign Ministry statement on Rohingya Muslims. Radio Burma (Rangoon) (February 21, 1992). FBIS-EAS-92-036.

congenial"[297] environment in Arakan State for the Rohingya's return. Interested in shedding its international pariah status, the SLORC worked with the UNHCR to resettle the Rohingya while continuing its human rights violations against them.

7.9 Epilogue

The Rohingya faced further persecution once back in Burma. In 2012–2013, the government, under the administration of Thein Sein, expelled 20,000 Rohingya.[298] Then three years later, between 2016 and 2018, the Burmese military expelled over 800,000 Rohingya from Arakan in the largest expulsion of the group to date.[299] As of today, these Rohingya refugees continue to reside in camps in Cox's Bazar, Bangladesh. Initially, it seemed that Bangladesh would pursue a similar strategy of forced repatriation in response to the largest Rohingya influx; in fact, it signed a bilateral agreement with Burma to return the refugees in November 2017.[300] However, no significant action has been taken to implement the agreement. Unlike in 1992, neither the UN nor the UNHCR supports repatriation of the Rohingya; the Burmese government is not seeking international legitimacy; and the Bangladeshi government has received significant financial support to host the refugees.[301] To date, no moderate wing has emerged within the Tatmadaw to push the military junta in a "new direction"; rather, the junta has further intensified its repressive hold since its 2021 coup d'etat.[302] The Tatmadaw responded to student protests against the most recent coup with mass repression, reminiscent of events in 1988–1990. Fighting between an alliance of rebel groups and the military junta has since engulfed the country.[303] The Rohingya remaining in Arakan State have been caught up in the conflict once again, most recently between the ethnic Rakhine Arakan Army and the Burmese junta forces.[304] Abuses against Rohingya

[297] Stefano Severe, UNHCR head of Cox's Bazar Sub-Office in Bangladesh, described the situation in Burma as "conducive and congenial for the refugees to return." (Lambrecht, 1995, p. 12).

[298] Human Rights Watch, 2013.

[299] UN Human Rights Council, 2018.

[300] Refworld, 2018.

[301] Huang & Ginn, 2022; World Bank, 2025c

[302] Paddock, 2022.

[303] Human Rights Watch, 2024b.

[304] Human Rights Watch, 2024a; Human Rights Watch, 2024b.

civilians have led Rohingya armed groups to perversely ally with their former persecutors to fight against the Arakan Army.[305] In early 2024, this renewed conflict displaced 70,000 Rohingya from their homes.[306] Significant concern remains about future expulsions of the Rohingya from Burma as well as the possibility of *en masse* refugee expulsion of Rohingya from Bangladesh.

[305] Beech, 2024; Human Rights Watch, 2024a; Human Rights Watch, 2024b.
[306] OCHA, 2024.

8
Conclusion

This book explains the understudied eliminationist policy of mass expulsion. Governments around the world, from empires to nation-states, from authoritarian regimes to democracies, from Europe to Latin America, have used and continue to use this policy to remove "unwanted" groups they contend "belong" elsewhere. The recurring nature of mass expulsion throughout the twentieth and twenty-first centuries makes it an urgent and essential area of research alongside more well-documented atrocities such as genocide and mass killing. The concluding chapter summarizes the main findings, presents policy implications and recommendations, and proposes additional research questions to further investigate this abhorrent phenomenon.

This is the first systematic, cross-regional examination of why and how governments expel ethnic groups *en masse* over the *longue durée*. Three main findings emerge out of this macro-historical, theory-building analysis. First, mass expulsion is a distinct phenomenon of intentional group-based population removal with a different intention than related phenomena such as genocide, ethnic cleansing, or coercive assimilation. Conceptually, extracting mass expulsion from the ambiguous concept of ethnic cleansing allows for a more precise examination of government policies that seek *to remove* target groups from a territory. The distinct phenomenon of mass expulsion is documented in the novel Government-Sponsored Mass Expulsion (GSME) dataset, which records 139 cross-border expulsion events, affecting over 30 million people, in the 120-year period from 1900 to 2020. The data show when and where expulsion occurs, who is targeted, and what regimes are most likely to carry it out. Although mass expulsion is a relatively rare event, its persistent occurrence in the modern era merits more careful scrutiny.

The second main finding identifies two overarching categories of mass expulsion—security and economic—along with four corresponding types: counter-irredentist, counter-subversive, reprisal, and nativist. The four

Mass Expulsion. Meghan M. Garrity, Oxford University Press. © Oxford University Press (2026).
DOI: 10.1093/9780197829097.003.0008

expulsion types constitute the mass expulsion typology, which identifies patterns in government motivations to expel and highlights different governmental aims that produce the same policy outcome. Governments that identify a target group as a security threat to the state may employ counter-irredentist, counter-subversive, or reprisal expulsions. Counter-irredentist expulsions aim to secure territorial control by eliminating groups with real or alleged ties to an external state. Counter-subversive expulsions look inward and aim to remove target groups supporting, or perceived to be supporting, efforts to challenge the existing state or regime. Reprisal expulsions seek to retaliate against an external state in response to an unfavorable foreign policy position or decision by removing a group with ties to that state. While many mass expulsions are driven by security concerns, a significant portion of expulsion episodes are motivated by economic concerns, an aspect that has been largely overlooked in the existing literature. This dynamic gives rise to a fourth expulsion type, nativism, which accounts for a plurality of expulsion episodes. Nativist expulsions aim to protect the economic interests of the "indigenous" population by removing "foreign" groups that control or dominate key sectors, industries, or jobs desired by natives.

The third main finding is a theoretical framework of mass expulsion decision making that explains the process of mass expulsion. It presents the structural, proximate, precipitating, and intervening factors that shape the context and circumstances in which expulsion does or does not occur. The theory details important preconditions for expulsion, including a governing elite with an exclusionary ideology, a target group whose threat would be neutralized if removed, the presence or construction of an alternative "homeland" to send the target group, and a state with adequate capabilities to push out the unwanted population. The theoretical framework then expounds on key intervening factors that enable or restrain/constrain expulsion: the alliances of the ruling elite, the "homeland" state of the target group, and pertinent international organizations (IOs).

These central findings advance our understanding of the phenomenon of mass expulsion. They explain the conditions and factors that give rise to this policy option and the key restraints that induce some governments to refrain. This research contributes to the fields of international peace and security, political violence, and forced migration, and fills critical gaps in the conceptual, theoretical, and empirical literature.

Conceptually, mass expulsion is presented as a neovalent: an existing term assigned a new meaning through expanded defining attributes.[1] Mass expulsion is defined as a systematic government-sponsored policy to remove an ethnic, racial, religious, or national group as such, with no individual legal review and no recognition of the right to return.[2] Defining the term and describing its six core attributes help to more precisely identify and explicate this distinct form of population elimination. The detailed conceptual work contributes to the long political science tradition of conceptual clarification regarding contested concepts.[3]

Theoretically, the findings highlight an entire class of mass expulsions targeting alleged economic threats that expands existing explanations of eliminationist policies beyond war and security concerns and contestation over territory that currently dominate the literature. This underscores that most of what we know about expulsion and ethnic cleansing comes from studies of Europe, where explanations have focused on security threats emanating from "fifth column" populations.[4] The typology of mass expulsion introduced here, along with cross-regional case comparisons, illuminates a broader swath of causes, including economic drivers, that have been neglected by scholars and policymakers. In addition, this is the first study to systematically examine mass expulsion as the dependent variable, inclusive of the targeting of citizens and noncitizens, the latter of which has been conspicuously absent from existing analyses outside of sub-Saharan Africa. The analysis shows that most economically driven nativist expulsions target noncitizens, but that noncitizen-only expulsions also occur across all three types within the security category (i.e., counter-irredentist, counter-subversive, and reprisal expulsions). This challenges the notion that expulsions motivated by security threats are only concerned with citizens. The framework of mass expulsion decision making also expands our theoretical understanding of mass atrocity restraints/constraints. It explains the importance of alliances, both domestic and transnational, the "homeland" state of the target group, and pertinent IOs in both deterring and facilitating expulsion policies.

Empirically, this research contributes to our understanding of mass expulsion through the introduction of the GSME dataset. This dataset augments

[1] Sartori, 1984, p. 40.
[2] Garrity, 2022.
[3] Baldwin, 1997; Chandra, 2006; Collier & Levitsky, 1997; Sartori, 1984; Straus, 2001.
[4] Bulutgil, 2016; Mylonas & Radnitz, 2022, p. 3.

the work of other scholars of mass expulsion and ethnic cleansing[5] by expanding the temporal, geographic, and target group scope of the data collection. Additionally, the three case studies provide in-depth, empirical analyses of crucial mass expulsion episodes and key negative cases of non-expulsion. These chapters provide freshly researched accounts of how mass expulsion unfolded in each context, with new primary sources that enhance our existing understanding. The use of negative cases to tease out key restraints on expulsion decisions is a research design used by Scott Straus to explain why perpetrators escalate from large-scale killing to mass categorical violence or genocide,[6] but this is the first time the approach has been used to explain mass expulsion. The detailed analyses of Istanbul (1913–1923), Kenya (1967–1969), and Burma (mid-1992–1995) examine the factors that restrained/constrained decisions to expel. The research design illustrates the methodological utility of negative case studies in identifying key explanations as well as the value of cross-regional comparisons.[7]

This research also introduces new primary sources to the study of eliminationist policies. The expulsion typology and case studies are informed by the archives of IOs and humanitarian agencies, including the United Nations High Commissioner for Refugees (UNHCR) and the International Committee of the Red Cross (ICRC). These archives contain rich insights into how mass expulsion unfolded on the ground and the role of the United Nations (UN) and other international agencies in liaising with expelling governments and host states. While some historians have used these archives,[8] they are underutilized by political scientists. The research also leverages material from the League of Nations Archives, another source widely used by historians[9] but only minimally used by political scientists. Evidence from the Lausanne Conference Records of Proceedings as well as the meeting minutes of the Sub-Commission for the Exchange of Populations helped to explain the exemption of the Greek Orthodox Christians in Istanbul from the 1923 "population exchange" agreement. These contributions aim to improve our understanding of the specific policy of mass expulsion but also to enrich the growing field of research on eliminationist politics more broadly.[10]

5 E.g., Adida, 2014; Bulutgil, 2016; Henckaerts, 1995.
6 Straus, 2015.
7 Ahram et al., 2018.
8 Cosemans, 2021; Elie, 2010; Lipman, 2020; Loescher, 2001.
9 E.g., Frank, 2017; Pedersen, 2015; Robson, 2017.
10 Garrity & Mylonas, 2025; Garrity & Mylonas, 2026.

8.1 Policy Implications and Recommendations

The main arguments and findings presented here have important policy implications for deterring the use of mass expulsion. As a starting point, the GSME dataset could be used to complement existing early-warning and prevention systems. Integrating the expulsion data into the annual Early Warning Project report—created by the US Holocaust Memorial Museum's Simon-Skjodt Center and Dartmouth College's Dickey Center for International Understanding—would identify countries at high risk of mass expulsion to supplement those at risk of genocide and mass killing. This would augment the set of atrocities of concern and potentially highlight different groups at risk.

The data also shed light on the types of expulsion that are the most common in recent decades, which can inform trend analyses (see Figure 8.1). In the last four decades, nativist expulsions were the most common of the four expulsion types, with twenty-three total episodes. Their occurrence has remained fairly constant during this period, with at least five expulsions in each decade between 1981 and 2020. Counter-subversive and reprisal expulsions were the next most common, with an average of three per decade, but half as many as those motivated by nativism (thirteen and twelve episodes, respectively). The most recent spike in counter-subversive expulsions

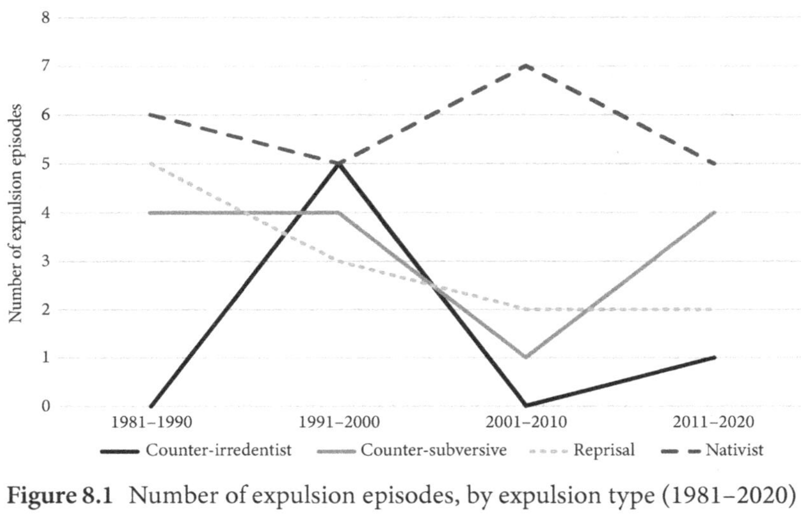

Figure 8.1 Number of expulsion episodes, by expulsion type (1981–2020)

between 2011 and 2020 was driven by two rounds of Rohingya expulsions from Arakan (Rakhine) State, Burma (2012–2013 and 2016–2018). Of the four types, counter-irredentist expulsions have declined most significantly, with two of the four most recent decades recording zero such events (1981–1990 and 2001–2010), and only one in the most recent decade (2011–2020). Apart from the 1990s Yugoslav wars of secession, counter-irredentist expulsions look to be in sharp decline. However, if territorial conquest returns to prominence in international politics, this type of expulsion may increase.

In addition to assessing recent trends in the frequency of expulsion types, data on the magnitude of persons expelled, by type, during the same period, is also instructive for those forecasting and monitoring atrocities (see Figure 8.2). In the most recent decade (2011–2020), counter-subversive expulsions affected over 1 million people, more than any other type, largely driven by the expulsion of the Rohingya from Burma (2016–2018). However, between 1981–1990 and 2001–2010, nativist expulsions had the largest magnitude, with 1.5 million and over 400,000 people expelled, respectively. In the 1990s, counter-irredentist expulsions affected the highest number of people, driven by over 2.5 million individuals expelled from countries of the former Yugoslavia. The swings in magnitude across expulsion types indicate that no single variant is driving the large numbers of persons expelled across the world—an average of 2.7 million people expelled in each decade since 1981. Prevention strategies must address all types of expulsion.

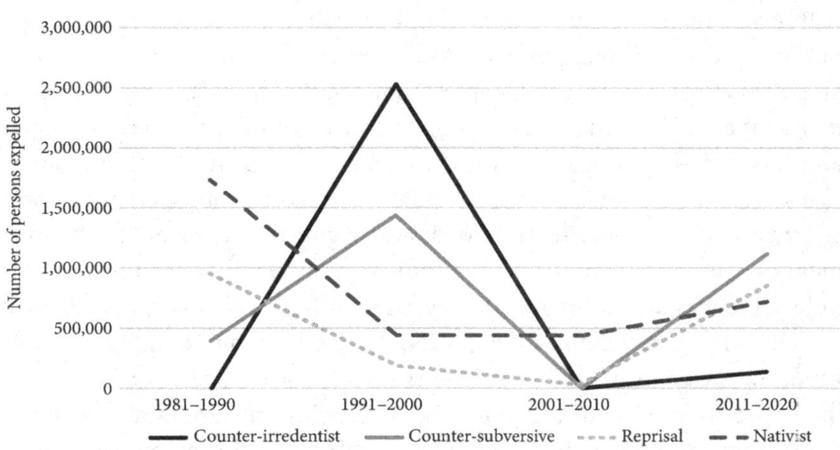

Figure 8.2 Number of persons expelled, by expulsion type (1981–2020)

Analyzing recent trends in the GSME data offers policymakers some key takeaways. Nativist expulsions are the most frequent, and likely to remain so, with counter-subversive expulsions on the rise. Potential warning signs of nativist expulsions include political leaders blaming "foreign" groups for economic crises or suggesting that "non-indigenous" groups are a burden on the state's social safety net, particularly in societies with ethnic/national divisions of labor. Warning signs for counter-subversive expulsions may include nondominant groups supporting opposition or rebel parties, engaging in armed or unarmed government resistance, siding with a belligerent during an interstate conflict, or residing in border areas during periods of unrest and instability. As protracted intrastate conflicts continue, and as the size and duration of refugee flows increase, the likelihood of counter-subversive expulsions remain. Furthermore, while counter-irredentist expulsions have significantly declined, they have historically affected the largest number of people; thus, policymakers should be on alert for governments seeking territorial annexation, as newly acquired populations may be expelled from conquered lands. More positively, expulsion trends are not linear, and in the first decade of the twenty-first century (2001–2010), there was a four-decade low in the number of expellees, with less than 500,000 total persons expelled. Unfortunately, numbers rose dramatically during the following decade, across all expulsion types, with over 2.8 million total persons expelled between 2011 and 2020. More attention must be paid to this strategy of population elimination and more resources allocated to its prevention.

While the magnitude of expulsion ebbs and flows, the data demonstrate that governments consistently turn to this policy option, with an average rate of 1.56 expulsions per year over the last fifty years. The restraints and constraints outlined in Chapter 4 inform the following policy recommendations organized under three main prevention strategies: 1) target and monitor the domestic and transnational allies of high-risk countries, 2) engage "homeland" state(s) of potential target groups in prevention efforts, and 3) increase international and regional organizations' involvement to deter expulsion. These recommendations are directed toward multiple audiences, including the US government (e.g., US State Department), the UN and agency affiliates (e.g., UNHCR and the International Organization for Migration), and regional organizations (e.g., African Union and the Association of Southeast Asian Nations). Not only are they relevant at the institutional level, but also at the practitioner level for positions such as UN secretary-general–appointed special envoys or special advisors (e.g., the special envoy for Myanmar or the special advisor on the responsibility to protect), and government-appointed special envoys (e.g., US special envoy for the Horn of Africa or EU special envoy for Bosnia and Herzegovina), who have direct connections to and influence on government decision making. The recommendations would also be useful to human rights organizations and nongovernmental organizations that are focused on atrocity prevention.

8.1.1 Target and Monitor Domestic and Transnational Allies of High-Risk Countries

Governments considering expulsion are cognizant of its effect on their core domestic allies. These domestic allies often directly benefit from removing the target group, making expulsion more likely. However, in some cases, the expulsion of a particular group would harm the economic or political interests of the ruling elite's internal allies. In these instances, leveraging relationships with the governing elite's core domestic allies can be a useful entry point to deter countries at high risk of mass expulsion.

- Recommendation 1: Policymakers and practitioners should directly engage the core domestic allies of governments at high risk of expulsion to raise awareness of its negative economic and political consequences. Presenting evidence from previous expulsion episodes in other contexts, or within the same country at an earlier period, may be persuasive in restraining expulsion from within.

In addition to attempting to influence and lobby a government's domestic allies, transnational allies are another important constituency. Governments with core transnational allies that support or ignore expulsion rhetoric, or initial actions, increase the likelihood a motivated ruling elite will move forward with expulsion. In circumstances in which governments are concerned that those same transnational partners would oppose the decision to expel, because of economic, security, or reputational costs, they may be less likely to choose this policy option. Governments concerned about losing or alienating transnational support (i.e., financial, military, or development aid) critically restrain expulsion decisions. Transnational allies may be a more effective and accessible conduit for transmitting information about the negative effects of expulsion on both the local economy and the government's external partners.

- Recommendation 2: Transnational allies of high-risk countries should be systematically included in dialogues and consultations on prevention strategies, both before expulsions occur and after any initial actions are taken.

While the transnational allies of high-risk countries may initially constrain expulsion out of their own self-interest, some governments will overcome this constraint by identifying new external partners willing to support their expulsionist objectives. In these cases, alternative allies may fill the financial or military void left by the former ally, increasing the likelihood of expulsion. Alternative sources of financing from new transnational allies can lead to a *carte blanche* for human rights violations, paving the way for a potential expulsion.

- Recommendation 3: Shifting transnational alliances of high-risk countries should be closely tracked and monitored as a potential warning sign for mass expulsion.

8.1.2 Engage "Homeland" State(s) in Prevention Efforts

In mass expulsion episodes, governments not only seek to remove a target group from their territory but also contend that there is another state—a "homeland"—to which the target group "belongs" that must take responsibility for the group. The potential physical ramifications of expulsion on the "homeland" state make it a critical actor in expulsion prevention. Governments contemplating expulsion that have strong ties to the "homeland" state, typically a neighboring country, are less likely to expel because of concerns about damaging the relationship. Strengthening ties between neighboring states with fraught relations over the treatment of potentially targeted minority groups is a useful preventive tactic that may help to restrain expulsion.

- Recommendation 4: External mediation and facilitation of constructive dialogue between governments likely to expel and the target group's "homeland" state should be pursued as a point of leverage to deter expulsion. Over the longer term, encouraging cultural exchange and interdependence (in trade, development, border management, etc.) are strategies to strengthen bilateral relationships, which may reduce the likelihood of expulsion.

There are risks associated with Recommendation 4. Countries considering mass expulsion may view such mediation efforts as external meddling, which may exacerbate tensions between the "homeland" state and the government motivated to expel. This recommendation must be implemented carefully and deployed only where it is not anticipated to worsen interstate relations. The choice of external mediator is critical. Regional actors may be most useful in bringing the parties together, which connects to the next set of recommendations.

8.1.3 Increase International and Regional Organizations' Involvement to Deter Expulsion

The relationship with pertinent international and regional organizations, and their actual or anticipated response to an expulsion, influences a government's expulsion calculus. Governments with strong ties to these organizations, or seeking to cultivate them, are more likely to be restrained in expulsion decisions than those with weak ties. Strong ties with the UN and respective regional bodies restrain governments from carrying out expulsion because of concerns about damaging relations with, or their status within, these organizations. This form of social deterrence has proven effective in achieving compliance with other international human rights norms, including the Rome Statute of the International Criminal Court,[11] and is a productive avenue to pursue in relation to mass expulsion.

- Recommendation 5: IOs, particularly regional organizations, should develop and foster deeper relationships with countries at high risk of mass expulsion. Relevant IOs should take any opportunity to engage segments of the government, even peripheral ministries, to build relationships and promote compliance with international norms against

[11] Jo & Simmons, 2016.

expulsion. Projects that aim to build social cohesion between core and non-core groups and reduce exclusionary elite rhetoric may be effective interventions to eliminate a critical precondition for expulsion (exclusionary ideologies).

To be sure, governments of high-risk countries may neither have nor seek to cultivate strong ties with IOs. Regardless, IOs should persist in engaging, rather than isolating, these regimes.

IOs also influence government decisions on expulsion through their actual or anticipated responses. IOs may unintentionally signal indirect support by ignoring expulsion decrees or small-scale expulsions that may test the waters for larger events. The lack of international reaction, or response, to small-scale expulsion episodes often emboldens governments to later enact much larger expulsion policies.

- Recommendation 6: All expulsions, regardless of their size, must be quickly identified and condemned. When prevention fails, IOs should ensure criminal accountability for mass expulsion policies.

Unlike other atrocities, prominent leaders and scholars, with the backing of IOs, have endorsed or supported the use of expulsion. This support includes facilitating or backing bilateral or multilateral "population transfer/exchange" treaties as well as assisting governments in physically extracting expellees from their territory. Hence, IOs have played an important role in both constraining *and* enabling mass expulsion.

- Recommendation 7: Internationally negotiated "population transfers" or "population exchanges" should be removed from diplomatic negotiations as well as support or assistance to governments in expelling targeted groups. Officials should abandon proposals of expulsion as an "orderly and humane" policy option.

Some may suggest that Recommendation 7 is "pushing at an open door," implying that "population transfers/exchanges" are no longer politically relevant. However, as recently as 2018, leaders of Serbia and Kosovo discussed a potential land swap, and subsequent "population transfers," between the majority-Serb northern Kosovo and the majority-Albanian Preševo Valley in southern Serbia[12]—a plan that was referred to as a "peaceful ethnic cleansing."[13] Advocates of expulsion as a conflict resolution policy often suggest that it is better than the alternative, with the unnamed alternative often assumed to be genocide or mass killing. That is a false binary. There are a series of alternative policy options for managing diverse populations without resorting to elimination. These include control, arbitration, territorial management (i.e., autonomy or federation), and power-sharing arrangements.[14] All of these policy options should be placed on the negotiating table and pursued in earnest instead of the eliminationist policy of mass expulsion.

8.2 Remaining Questions

Given the understudied nature of mass expulsion, many areas merit further scholarly investigation. Four broad research areas are ripe for additional exploration: variation in eliminationist strategies, internal mass expulsion, pre–twentieth-century expulsions, and the consequences of expulsion.

8.2.1 Variation in Eliminationist Strategies

This study exclusively examined the policy of mass expulsion. The logical corollary to the question of why governments expel is why governments expel rather than use alternative eliminationist policies. Another fruitful area of inquiry is to examine variation in eliminationist strategies,[15] from genocide and mass expulsion to coercive assimilation, partition, or the recognition of secession. While there are seeds of answers to this question in the work of some scholars,[16] choices among these grim strategies have yet to be comprehensively analyzed. Several important questions to investigate include: Are eliminationist policies substitutes or complements? Are they escalatory? Are they restrained by the same factors? Are they likely to target the same groups?[17] These questions could be addressed using a

[12] Dragojlo & Bami, 2020; Kupchan, 2018.
[13] Bajrami, 2018; Kupchan, 2018.
[14] McGarry & O'Leary, 1993; O'Leary, 2001, pp. 28–29, 38–53.
[15] McGarry & O'Leary, 1993; O'Leary, 2001.
[16] E.g., Mann, 2005; Stanton, 2016; Straus, 2015; Valentino, 2004.
[17] Garrity & Mylonas, 2025.

cross-regional comparative approach to examine the treatment of different ethnic groups within a single state. For example, one might compare variation in the Ottoman Empire's treatment of the Armenians, Greeks, and Kurds in the early twentieth century, or Burma's treatment of the Tamils, Rohingya, and Karen after independence.

8.2.2 Internal Mass Expulsion

The GSME dataset captures incidents of cross-border expulsion and excludes cases of internal expulsion. The questions why and how governments expel populations *within* the state are outside the scope of this project. One reason was empirical feasibility. The Internal Displacement Monitoring Centre (IDMC), "the world's definitive source of data and analysis on internal displacement,"[18] does not begin its data collection until 1998. However, research into internal expulsion starting in 1998, using the IDMC data, is a fertile area for future research. The motivations outlined in the expulsion typology could be tested in the domestic context to see whether they still hold or if different dynamics are at play when populations are forcibly moved within a state. Questions of how internal expulsion differs from more generalized internal displacement and whether policies of segregation, apartheid, gentrification, and development-induced displacement fit within the concept of internal expulsion are important to assess.

8.2.3 Pre–Twentieth-Century Expulsions

This work focused on modern mass expulsions from the beginning of the twentieth century to the present. Yet, as noted in the introduction, mass expulsion is far from a new or modern phenomenon; it dates as far back as the Assyrian Empire in the eighth century BCE.[19] One area of further research would be a systematic analysis of pre–twentieth-century expulsions, perhaps with a particular focus on colonial or settler expulsions. Documenting these cases would allow one to explore whether expulsion motivations are consistent over time or if different patterns explain trends in earlier periods. As the international system has evolved, research could

[18] Internal Displacement Monitoring Centre, 2024.
[19] Bell-Fialkoff, 1999.

compare the restraints/constraints on expulsion before the turn of the twentieth century, if any, to those in the contemporary era.

8.2.4 Consequences of Expulsion

The literature on mass expulsion largely focuses on its causes and constraints, which is both essential for understanding the phenomenon and preventing its use. The aftermath of mass expulsion, however, is an underexplored area of research. For example, how did the expulsion of the *Volksdeutsche* in 1945 affect Czechoslovakia's postwar society? Or how did the 1972 expulsion of the Ugandan Asians affect the country's economy, both in the immediate aftermath of the expulsion and following their return at President Yoweri Museveni's invitation fourteen years later? Another area of inquiry is how expellees affect the societies to which they are expelled—the Rohingya in Bangladesh or the *Volksdeutsche* in Germany? Are expellees' experiences of arrival or return similar or different and how does that impact their integration or exclusion in the host/home society? As expulsion continues around the world, these are germane questions to investigate.

*

Tragically, mass expulsion is an eliminationist policy that is still very much in global use today. In the decade between 2010 and 2020, thirteen new expulsion episodes were initiated, and in each of those ten years, there was at least one ongoing expulsion somewhere in the world. For those affected by mass expulsion, their experience is anything but "orderly and humane"—families are separated, assets and property are confiscated, livelihoods are ruined, homes are destroyed, and in the most severe cases, lives are lost. Though mass expulsion may be less deadly than other atrocities, its continued use by governments around the world, its significant security and economic consequences, and its profound negative effects on the lives of expellees make it a critical area for research and policy attention. In telling the story of this understudied atrocity, this work aims to draw attention to the widespread use of this eliminationist policy. These modest policy implications and recommendations seek to aid policymakers and practitioners in designing strategies to constrain mass expulsion as a matter of priority for atrocity prevention. Given the millions affected by this abhorrent policy, additional research and action is both urgent and essential.

Appendix A

Mass Expulsion in International Law

Charter of the International Military Tribunal at Nuremberg (1945)

- Section II – Jurisdiction and General Principles, Article 6(c): "Crimes against humanity – namely, murder, extermination, enslavement, deportation, and other inhumane acts committed against any civilian population, before or during the war, or persecutions on political, racial or religious grounds in execution of or in connection with any crime within the jurisdiction of the Tribunal, whether or not in violation of the domestic law of the country where perpetrated."

Universal Declaration of Human Rights (1948)

- Article 9: "No one shall be subjected to arbitrary arrest, detention or exile."
- Article 13: "Everyone has the right to leave any country, including his own, and to return to his country."

Fourth Geneva Convention (1949)

- Article 49: "Individual or mass forcible transfers, as well as deportations of protected persons from occupied territory to the territory of the Occupying Power or to that of any other country, occupied or not, are prohibited, regardless of their motive."

UN Refugee Convention (1951)

- Article 32(1): "The Contracting States shall not expel a refugee lawfully in their territory save on grounds of national security or public order."
- Article 33(1): "No Contracting State shall expel or return ('refouler') a refugee in any manner whatsoever to the frontiers of territories where his life or freedom would be threatened on account of his race, religion, nationality, membership of a particular social group or political opinion."

European Convention for the Protection of Human Rights and Fundamental Freedoms, Protocol 4 (1963)

- Article 3(1): "No one shall be expelled, by means either of an individual or a collective measure, from the territory of the State of which he is a national.
- Article 3(2): "No one shall be deprived of the right to enter the territory of the state of which he is a national."
- Article 4: "Collective expulsion of aliens is prohibited."

International Covenant on Civil & Political Rights (1966)

- Article 12(4): "No one shall be arbitrarily deprived of the right to enter his own country."
- Article 13: "An alien lawfully in the territory of a State Party to the present Covenant may be expelled therefrom only in pursuance of a decision reached in accordance with law and shall, except where compelling reasons of national security otherwise require, be allowed to submit the reasons against his expulsion and to have his case reviewed by, and be represented for the purpose before, the competent authority or a person or persons especially designated by the competent authority."

American Convention on Human Rights (1969)

- Article 22(5): "No one can be expelled from the territory of the state of which he is a national or be deprived of the right to enter it."
- Article 22(6): "An alien lawfully in the territory of a State Party to this Convention may be expelled from it only pursuant to a decision reached in accordance with law."
- Article 22(9): "The collective expulsion of aliens is prohibited."

African Charter on Human and Peoples' Rights (1981)

- Article 12(2): "Every individual shall have the right to leave any country including his own, and to return to his country."
- Article 12(4): "A non-national legally admitted in a territory of a State Party to the present Charter, may only be expelled from it by virtue of a decision taken in accordance with the law."
- Article 12(5): "The mass expulsion of non-nationals shall be prohibited. Mass expulsion shall be that which is aimed at national, racial, ethnic or religious groups."

International Convention on the Protection of the Rights of All Migrant Workers and Members of Their Families (1990)

- Article 22(1): "Migrant workers and members of their families shall not be subject to measures of collective expulsion. Each case of expulsion shall be examined and decided individually."
- Article 23: "Migrant workers and members of their families shall have the right to have recourse to the protection and assistance of the consular or diplomatic authorities of their State of origin or of a State representing the interests of that State whenever the rights recognized in the present Convention are impaired. In particular, in case of expulsion, the person concerned shall be informed of this right without delay and the authorities of the expelling State shall facilitate the exercise of such right."

Rome Statute of the International Criminal Court (1998)

- [Crimes against humanity] Article 7(1)(d): "Deportation or forcible transfer of population."
- Article 7(2)(d): "'Deportation or forcible transfer of population' means forced displacement of the persons concerned by expulsion or other coercive acts from the area in which they are lawfully present, without grounds permitted under international law."

Arab Charter on Human Rights (2004)

- Article 26(2): "No State party may expel a person who does not hold its nationality but is lawfully in its territory, other than in pursuance of a decision reached in accordance with law and after that person has been allowed to submit a petition to the competent authority, unless compelling reasons of national security preclude it. Collective expulsion is prohibited under all circumstances."
- Article 27(2): "No one may be exiled from his country or prohibited from returning thereto.

Appendix B

List of Mass Expulsion Episodes (1900–2020)[1]

#	Expelling Country	Year(s)	Number of Persons Expelled[a]	Target Group
1	Greece	1912	10,000	Muslims
2	Serbia	1912–1913	10,000–20,000	Albanians
3	Greece	1913	15,000	Bulgarians
4	Bulgaria	1913–1914	70,000	Greeks
5	Bulgaria	1913–1914	48,500–48,570	Muslims
6	Turkey	1913–1914	46,700–46,764	Bulgarians
7	Greece	1913–1914	100,000–125,000	Muslims
8	Turkey	1913–1914	150,000–279,000	Greeks
9	France	1919–1921	100,000–150,000	Germans
10	Bulgaria	1919–1928	30,000–50,000	Greeks
11	Greece	1919	53,000–100,000	Bulgarians
12	Turkey	1922	868,186–1,000,000	Greeks
13	Turkey	1922–1924	35,000	Armenians
14	Greece	1923–1926	355,635–356,000	Muslims
15	Turkey	1923–1926	189,916–190,000	Greek Orthodox Christians
16	United States	1929–1939	500,000–2,000,000	Mexicans, Mexican-Americans
17	Mexico	1931–1932	3,000	Chinese
18	Cuba	1933–1934	8,000	Haitians
19	Dominican Republic	1937–1938	10,000–30,000	Haitians, Dominico-Haitians
20	Cuba	1937–1939	29,900	Haitians
21	Germany	1938–1939	40,000–50,000	Jews (Austrian)
22	Germany	1939–1941	365,000–1,000,000	Jews (Polish), Poles
23	Bulgaria	1940	100,000	Romanians

continued

[1] Data comes from the Government-Sponsored Mass Expulsion (GSME) dataset (Garrity 2022).

continued

#	Expelling Country	Year(s)	Number of Persons Expelled	Target Group
24	Romania	1940	61,000	Bulgarians
25	Germany	1941	100,000–130,000	Jews (French), French
26	Bulgaria	1942–1943	210,000	Greeks, Serbs
27	Peru	1942–1943	1,771–1,800	Japanese
28	Greece	1944–1945	18,000	Albanians
29	Poland	1944–1946	482,000–518,000	Belorussians, Ukrainians, Lithuanians
30	Soviet Union	1944–1946	1,496,000–2,100,000	Poles, Jews (Polish)
31	Czechoslovakia	1945–1946	50,000–91,079	Ukrainians
32	Soviet Union	1945–1946	33,961–42,000	Czechs, Slovaks
33	Czechoslovakia	1945–1947	2,252,544–3,000,000	Germans
34	Poland	1945–1947	6,000,000–8,250,000	Germans
35	Hungary	1945–1947	176,843–500,000	Germans
36	Romania	1945–1947	50,000–300,000	Germans
37	Yugoslavia[b]	1945–1947	250,000–271,000	Germans
38	Czechoslovakia	1946	200,000	Magyars (Hungarians)
39	Hungary	1946	200,000	Slovaks
40	Hungary	1946	40,000	Serbs, Croats
41	Yugoslavia	1946	40,000	Magyars (Hungarians)
42	Netherlands	1946–1948	3,000–3691	Germans
43	Israel	1947–1949	600,000–800,000	Palestinians
44	Bulgaria	1950–1951	152,000–155,000	Turks
45	United States	1954–1955	1,000,000–1,300,000	Mexicans, Mexican-Americans
46	United Kingdom (British Imperial Sierra Leone)	1956–1957	30,000–50,000	Guineans
47	Egypt	1956–1957	20,200–25,000	Jews
48	Indonesia	1957–1958	50,000–60,000	Dutch
49	Cote d'Ivoire	1958	1,000–2,000	Togolese, Beninese
50	Burma (Myanmar)[c]	1962–1964	300,000	Indians (Tamils)

#	Expelling Country	Year(s)	Number of Persons Expelled	Target Group
51	Gabon	1962	2,700	Congolese (Brazzaville)
52	Republic of Congo	1962	3,000	Beninese
53	Niger	1963–1964	6,918–16,000	Beninese
54	Democratic Republic of Congo	1964	1,000–3,000	Congolese (Brazzaville), Burundians, Malians
55	Cote d'Ivoire	1964	16,000	Beninese
56	Turkey	1964–1965	36,000–47,000	Greeks
57	France (French Somaliland)	1967	2,000–10,000	Somalis
58	Israel	1967–1968	270,000–390,000	Palestinians
59	Sierra Leone	1968	2,000–8,000	Ghanaians
60	Honduras	1969	60,000–130,000	Salvadorans
61	Ghana	1969–1970	200,000–1,000,000	Nigerians, Togolese, Burkinabe, Nigeriens
62	Uganda	1970	30,000	Kenyans (Luo)
63	Libya	1970	20,000	Italians
64	Cambodia	1970	200,000–250,000	Vietnamese
65	Zambia	1971–1972	150,000	Rhodesians, Batswana, Zaireans, Tanzanians, Somalis
66	Iraq	1971	11,000–60,000	Iranians
67	Uganda	1972	50,000–80,000	South Asians
68	Iraq	1974	60,000	Iranians, Kurds
69	Turkey	1974–1975	168,000–200,000	Greek Cypriots
70	Cyprus	1974–1975	37,000–60,000	Turkish Cypriots
71	Algeria	1975–1976	30,000	Moroccans
72	Cambodia	1975–1978	150,000–200,000	Vietnamese
73	Libya	1976	13,700	Tunisians
74	Republic of Congo	1977	5,000–6,000	Malians
75	Vietnam	1977–1979	400,000–1,000,000	Chinese
76	Burma (Myanmar)	1978	200,000	Rohingya
77	Burundi	1978	40,000–50,000	Zaireans

continued

continued

#	Expelling Country	Year(s)	Number of Persons Expelled	Target Group
78	Gabon	1978	6,000–12,000	Beninese
79	Bangladesh	1978–1979	187,000–190,000	Rohingya
80	Chad	1979	1,000	Beninese
81	Kenya	1979	2,500–4,000	Ugandans
82	Zambia	1979	4,000	Zaireans, Tanzanians, Malawians, Somalis, Mozambicans
83	Thailand	1979–1980	49,000–54,000	Cambodians
84	Iraq	1980	20,000–25,000	Iranians
85	Kenya	1980–1981	3,000	Tanzanians, Ugandans
86	Gabon	1981	5,000–10,000	Cameroonians
87	Sierra Leone	1982	1,000	Guineans (Fulani)
88	Uganda	1982	44,000–75,000	Banyarwanda
89	Mongolia	1983	1,764–10,000	Chinese
90	Nigeria	1983	1,500,000–2,000,000	Ghanaians, Nigeriens, Cameroonians, Chadians, Togolese, Beninese
91	Nigeria	1985	200,000–700,000	Ghanaians, Nigeriens, Cameroonians, Chadians
92	Cote d'Ivoire	1985	10,000	Ghanaians
93	Libya	1985	42,000–80,000	Tunisians, Egyptians
94	Mauritania	1989	70,000–85,000	Senegalese, Mauritanians (Black Africans)
95	Senegal	1989	80,000–100,000	Mauritanians ("White Moors")
96	Bulgaria	1989	250,000–310,000	Turks
97	Kenya	1989–1990	5,000	Somalis
98	Kenya	1990	1,000	Ugandans, Rwandans
99	Saudi Arabia	1990	750,000–1,000,000	Yemenis
100	Bhutan	1990–1992	106,000–110,000	Nepalis
101	Kuwait	1991	200,000–400,000	Palestinians, Iraqis
102	Dominican Republic	1991	35,000–60,000	Haitians, Dominico-Haitians
103	Burma (Myanmar)	1991–1992	250,000–260,000	Rohingya
104	Yugoslavia	1991–1992	250,000	Croats

#	Expelling Country	Year(s)	Number of Persons Expelled	Target Group
105	Yugoslavia	1992–1995	2,000,000	Bosnians (Muslims & Croats)
106	Bangladesh	1992–1997	230,000	Rohingya
107	South Africa	1993–1994	136,279–152,205	Mozambicans
108	Greece	1993–1994	96,000–100,000	Albanians
109	Croatia	1995	180,000–200,000	Serbs
110	Democratic Republic of Congo (Zaire)[d]	1995	14,000–15,000	Rwandans, Burundians
111	Libya	1995	80,000	Sudanese, Mauritanians
112	Tanzania	1996	250,000–500,000	Rwandans
113	Dominican Republic	1996–1997	30,000	Haitians, Dominico-Haitians
114	Ethiopia	1998–1999	54,000–75,000	Eritreans
115	Yugoslavia	1998–1999	740,000–900,000	Kosovar Albanians
116	Eritrea	1998–2000	49,000–70,000	Ethiopians
117	Dominican Republic	1999–2000	10,000–20,000	Haitians, Dominico-Haitians
118	United Arab Emirates	2002	1,200	Afghans
119	Angola	2003–2005	80,000–300,000	Congolese (Kinshasa)
120	Tanzania	2006–2007	17,000–60,000	Rwandans, Burundians
121	Russia	2006–2007	2,300	Georgians
122	Iran	2007	160,000–390,000	Afghans
123	Angola	2008–2009	154,000–160,000	Congolese (Kinshasa)
124	Democratic Republic of Congo	2009	30,000–40,000	Angolans
125	Thailand	2009	4,689	Hmong
126	France	2009–2011	23,014–28,955	Roma
127	Uganda	2010	1,700	Rwandans
128	Angola	2011–2012	60,590–105,000	Congolese (Kinshasa)
129	Iran	2012–2013	349,500	Afghans
130	Burma (Myanmar)	2012–2013	19,000–20,000	Muslims (Rohingya & Kaman)

continued

continued

#	Expelling Country	Year(s)	Number of Persons Expelled	Target Group
131	Tanzania	2013	8,509–52,576	Rwandans, Burundians, Ugandans
132	Republic of Congo	2014	179,000–245,000	Congolese (Kinshasa)
133	Cameroon	2015–2019	100,000–109,000	Nigerians
134	Dominican Republic	2015–2019	250,000–310,000	Haitians, Dominico-Haitians
135	Pakistan	2016	500,000–565,000	Afghans
136	Burma (Myanmar)	2016–2018	812,000–831,500	Rohingya
137	Algeria	2016–2020	67,000	Sub-Saharan Africans
138	Angola	2018	330,000–400,000	Congolese (Kinshasa)
139	Turkey	2018	137,000–300,000	Syrian Kurds (Afrin)

[a] Numbers listed indicate the range of low- and high-end estimates.
[b] References to Yugoslavia refer to the Socialist Federal Republic of Yugoslavia from 1945–1992, and the Federal Republic of Yugoslavia from 1992–2003.
[c] For consistency, the country is referred to as "Burma (Myanmar)" throughout the dataset. The country's official name was changed from the Union of Burma to the Union of Myanmar in 1989.
[d] The Democratic Republic of the Congo was known as Zaire from October 1971 to May 1997.

Bibliography

Archives Consulted[1]

International Committee of the Red Cross, Geneva (*the ICRC Archive citation format uses its French name: Archives du Comité international de la Croix-Rouge, ACICR*)

League of Nations Archives (UN Archives at Geneva), Geneva

League of Nations Library, Geneva

- Lausanne Conference on Near Eastern Affairs 1922–1923: Records of Proceedings and Draft Terms of Peace. (1923). His Majesty's Stationery Office.
- Conférence de Lausanne sur les affaires du Proche-Orient, 1922–1923: Recueil des actes de la Conférence, première série. (1923). Protocoles des séances plénières et procès-verbaux et rapports de la Première Commission. Paris: Imprimerie nationale.

United Nations High Commissioner for Refugees (UNHCR), Geneva

Other Primary Sources

Conventions, Treaties, & Legal Documents

African Union. (1981). *African (Banjul) charter on human and peoples' rights.* https://au.int/en/treaties/african-charter-human-and-peoples-rights

Constitution of the Union of Burma. (1947). Government Printing and Stationery.

Immigration and Nationality Act. (2025a). § 349, 8 U.S.C. 1451. https://uscode.house.gov/view.xhtml?req=granuleid:USC-prelim-title8-section1451&num=0&edition=prelim

Immigration and Nationality Act. (2025b). § 349, 8 U.S.C. 1481. https://uscode.house.gov/view.xhtml?req=granuleid:USC-prelim-title8-section1481&num=0&edition=prelim

Immigration and Nationality Act. (2025c). § 212(a)(9)(A), 8 U.S.C. § 1182(a)(9)(A), https://uscode.house.gov/view.xhtml?req=granuleid%3AUSC-prelim-title8-section1182&num=0&edition=prelim

Treaty of Sèvres. (1920, August 10). https://www.dipublico.org/100760/the-treaty-of-sevres-1920-the-treaty-of-peace-between-the-allied-and-associated-powers-and-turkey-signed-at-sevres-august-10-1920/

[1] Dates in archival citations follow the European format (day.month.year).

United Nations. (1945). *Charter of the United Nations*. https://www.un.org/en/about-us/un-charter/full-text

United Nations. (1948). *Convention on the prevention and punishment of the crime of genocide*. http://un-documents.net/a3r260.htm

United Nations. (1954). *Convention relating to the status of stateless persons*. https://www.unhcr.org/ibelong/wp-content/uploads/1954-Convention-relating-to-the-Status-of-Stateless-Persons_ENG.pdf

United Nations General Assembly, 47th Sess., 17th mtg., U.N. Doc A/47/PV.17 (1992, October 8). http://undocs.org/en/A/47/PV.17

UNHCR. (1951). *Convention and protocol relating to the status of refugees*. https://www.unhcr.org/en-us/3b66c2aa10

U.S. Department of State – Office of the Historian. (1945). *Foreign relations of the United States: Diplomatic papers, the Conference of Berlin (The Potsdam Conference), 1945* (Vol. II). U.S. Government Printing Office. https://history.state.gov/historicaldocuments/frus1945Berlinv02/d1380

Data & Statistics

Butcher, C., Goldsmith, B. E., Nanlohy, S., Sowmya, A., & Muchlinski, D. (2024). *Targeted Mass Killing (TMK)* Dataset (Version 1.2) [Dataset]. Harvard Dataverse. https://doi.org/10.7910/DVN/79DSXR

Center for Systemic Peace. (n.d.). *Political Instability Task Force (PITF) State Failure Problem Set, 1955–2018: Genocide/Politicide* [Dataset]. https://www.systemicpeace.org/inscrdata.html

Coppedge, M., et al. (2020). V-Dem [Country–Year/Country–Date] Dataset v10. Varieties of Democracy (V-Dem) Project. https://doi.org/10.23696/vdemds20

Eck, K., & Hultman, L. (2007). One-sided violence against civilians in war: Insights from new fatality data. *Journal of Peace Research*, *44*(2), 233–246. https://ucdp.uu.se/downloads/

Gleditsch, N. P., Wallensteen, P., Eriksson, M., Sollenberg, M., & Strand, H. (2002). Armed conflict 1946–2001: A new dataset. *Journal of Peace Research*, *39*(5), 615–637. https://ucdp.uu.se/downloads/

Internal Displacement Monitoring Centre. (2024). *Global internal displacement database*. https://www.internal-displacement.org/database/displacement-data/

Marshall, M. G., & Gurr, T. R. (2020). *Polity5: Political regime characteristics and transitions, 1800–2018: Dataset users' manual*. Center for Systemic Peace. https://www.systemicpeace.org/inscr/p5manualv2018.pdf

Marshall, M. G. (2021). *Polity5 project: Political regime characteristics and transitions, 1800–2018*. Center for Systemic Peace. https://www.systemicpeace.org/inscrdata.html

Sarkees, M. R. (2021). *Intra-state war data* (Version 5.1) [Dataset]. Correlates of War Data, 1816–2007. https://correlatesofwar.org/data-sets/COW-war

Sarkees, M. R., & Wayman, F. W. (2010). *Resort to war: 1816–2007*. CQ Press. https://correlatesofwar.org/data-sets/COW-war

United Nations Peacekeeping. (2021, November 30). *Troop and police contributions*. https://peacekeeping.un.org/en/troop-and-police-contributors

World Bank (2025a). *World Bank country and lending groups.* https://datahelpdesk.worldbank.org/knowledgebase/articles/906519-world-bank-country-and-lending-groups

World Bank. (2025b). *GDP per capita (current US$) – Bangladesh.* The World Bank Data. https://data.worldbank.org/indicator/NY.GDP.PCAP.CD?locations=BD

World Bank. (2025c). *Emergency multi-sector Rohingya Crisis Response Project.* https://projects.worldbank.org/en/projects-operations/document-detail/P167762?type=projects

Government Documents, Speeches, & Memoirs of Key Officials

Morgenthau, H. (2017 [1918]). *Ambassador Morgenthau's story: A personal account of the Armenian genocide.* Doubleday, Page & Company.

Ne Win. (1982, October 8). *Meeting held in the central meeting hall, President House, Ahlone Road* (*Working People's Daily*, Trans.). Burma Library. http://www.burmalibrary.org/docs6/Ne_Win%27s_speech_Oct-1982-Citizenship_Law.pdf

Nigerian External Publicity Division, Department of Information, Executive Office of the President. (1983). *Illegal immigrants.* Sea Press & Publicity Ltd.

Republic of Kenya. (1965). *African socialism and its application to planning in Kenya.* CIA Library. https://www.cia.gov/readingroom/docs/CIA-RDP78-03061A000300030007-0.pdf

Republic of Uganda. (1970). *The common man's charter.* The Government Printer.

News Media

Anderson, P. (2008, September 11). Kemalism. *London Review of Books*, 3–12.

Austria in Extremis. (1860, May 10). *The New York Times.* https://timesmachine.nytimes.com/timesmachine/1860/05/12/78621790.html?pageNumber=4

Bajrami, A. (2018, October 17). A Kosovo-Serbia land swap is ethnic cleansing by another name. Don't do it. *The Guardian.* https://www.theguardian.com/commentisfree/2018/oct/17/kosovo-serbia-land-swap-ethnic-cleansing

BBC. (2006, October 6). *Georgians deported as row deepens.* http://news.bbc.co.uk/1/hi/world/europe/5412672.stm

Beech, Hannah. (2024, December 28). Tormentors change, but not the torment. *The New York Times.* https://www.nytimes.com/2024/12/28/world/asia/myanmar-rohingya-abuse.html?searchResultPosition=44

Bentsi-Enchill, N. K. (1983a, February 7). Exodus from Nigeria 1: The return to Ghana. *West Africa*, No. 3417, 305–306.

Bentsi-Enchill, N. K. (1983b, February 14). Exodus from Nigeria 1: Ghana absorbs its own. *West Africa*, No. 3418, 382–385.

Crossette, B. (1991, November 19). Burmese warning on arms buildup. *The New York Times.* https://www.nytimes.com/1991/11/19/world/burmese-warning-on-arms-buildup.html

de Waal, T. (2023, September 26). The end of Nagorno-Karabakh: How western inaction enabled Azerbaijan and Russia. *Foreign Affairs.* https://www.foreignaffairs.com/armenia/end-nagorno-karabakh

Dragojlo, S. & Bami, X. (2020, June 16). Land swap idea resurfaces to haunt Serbia–Kosovo talks. *Balkan Insight*. https://balkaninsight.com/2020/06/16/land-swap-idea-resurfaces-to-haunt-serbia-kosovo-talks/

Edwards, C. (2023, September 23). Azerbaijan has reclaimed Nagorno-Karabakh. What does that mean for the tens of thousands living there? *CNN*. https://www.cnn.com/2023/09/23/asia/nagorno-karabakh-armenia-azerbaijan-reintegrate-intl/index.html

Foreign Broadcast Information Service (FBIS) daily reports. Readex.

Florido, A. (2015, September 8). Mass deportation may sound unlikely, but it's happened before. *NPR*. http://www.npr.org/sections/codeswitch/2015/09/08/437579834/mass-deportation-may-sound-unlikely-but-its-happened-before

Gray, C. J. (1998). Cultivating citizenship through xenophobia in Gabon, 1960–1995. *Africa Today*, *45*(3/4), 389–409.

Hauer, N. (2021, April 24). Armenia is still grieving: Losing a war has reopened old wounds in a battered nation. *Foreign Policy*. https://foreignpolicy.com/2021/04/24/armenia-azerbaijan-war-nagorno-karabakh-aftermath/

Ibrahim, Y. (1991, March 14). After the war: Kuwait; Palestinians in Kuwait face suspicion and probable exile. *The New York Times*. https://www.nytimes.com/1991/03/14/world/after-the-war-kuwait-palestinians-in-kuwait-face-suspicion-and-probable-exile.html

Kugelman, M. (2023, November 1). Why is Pakistan expelling 1.7 million Afghans? *Foreign Policy: South Asia Brief*. https://foreignpolicy.com/2023/11/01/pakistan-deports-million-afghans-undocumented-migrants/

Kupchan, C. A. (2018, September 13). An offensive plan for the Balkans that the U.S. should get behind. *The New York Times*. https://www.nytimes.com/2018/09/13/opinion/kosovo-serbia-land-swap.html

Lalani, Z. (1997). *Ugandan Asian expulsion: 90 days and beyond through the eyes of the international press*. Expulsion Publications.

Lawal, S. (2019, August 11). Ghana must go: The ugly history of Africa's most famous bag. *Mail & Guardian*. http://atavist.mg.co.za/ghana-must-go-the-ugly-history-of-africas-most-famous-bag

Noack, R. & Khan, H. N. (2023, November 16). Deported Afghans return home by the thousands to unexpected welcome. *The Washington Post*. https://www.washingtonpost.com/world/2023/11/16/afghanistan-refugees-deported-pakistan-taliban/

Noble, K. (1989, July 22). An African exodus with racial overtones. The *New York Times*. https://www.nytimes.com/1989/07/22/world/an-african-exodus-with-racial-overtones.html

Paddock, R. C. (2022, December 9). Myanmar's coup and its aftermath, explained. *The New York Times*. https://www.nytimes.com/article/myanmar-news-protests-coup.html

Radio Free Europe. (2014, July 3). European Court condemns Russia for 2006 expulsion of Georgians. https://www.rferl.org/a/georgia-russia-expulsions-human-rights/25444207.html

Refworld. (2018, October 30). Bangladesh, Myanmar to begin repatriating Rohingya in November. *Radio Free Asia*. https://www.refworld.org/docid/5c2cc3a313.html

Sattar, A. (2023, November 13). Pakistan opens 3 new border crossings to deport Afghans in ongoing crackdown on migrants. *Associated Press*. https://apnews.com/article/pakistan-border-crossings-afghans-deportation-2d0f27fefa4dcd28e8659a942ae88925

Suddath, C. (2010, August 26). Who are Gypsies, and why is France deporting them? *Time*. http://content.time.com/time/world/article/0,8599,2013917,00.html

Tempest, R. (1989, June 3). In Senegal and Mauritania, ethnic conflict rages amid talk of war. *Los Angeles Times*. https://www.latimes.com/archives/la-xpm-1989-06-03-mn-831-story.html

The Times of India. (1972, September 13). *Uganda orders expulsion of U.K. military*. ProQuest Historical Newspapers.

Verdon, L. (1983, January 31). Nigeria expels illegal aliens. *The Washington Post*. https://www.washingtonpost.com/archive/politics/1983/01/31/nigeria-expels-illegal-aliens/2e5fe7ed-077c-4732-927b-d087d92ee57a/

Walz, Jay. (1964, August 9). Turks expelling Istanbul Greeks; Community's plight worsens during Cyprus crisis. *The New York Times*. https://www.nytimes.com/1964/08/09/archives/turks-expelling-istanbul-greeks-communitys-plight-worsens-during.html

Welles, B. (1972, September 15). U.S. delays Uganda loan over Amin note on Jews. *The New York Times*. https://timesmachine.nytimes.com/timesmachine/1972/09/15/81959038.pdf?pdf_redirect=true&ip=0

Winfield, N. (2009, June 10). Gadhafi welcomes 'new era' in relations with Italy. *Associated Press*. https://www.heraldnet.com/news/gadhafi-welcomes-new-era-in-relations-with-italy/

Secondary Sources

Abbink, J. (1998). Briefing: The Eritrean–Ethiopian border dispute. *African Affairs*, *97*(389), 551–565.

Adachi, N. (2007). Racial journeys: Justice, internment and Japanese-Peruvians in Peru, the United States, and Japan. *The Asia-Pacific Journal*, *5*(9), 1–11.

Addo, N. (1982). Government-induced transfers of foreign nationals. In J. Clarke, and L. Kosinski (Eds.), *Redistribution of population in Africa* (pp. 31–38). Heinemann.

Adepoju, A. (1984). Illegals and expulsion in Africa: The Nigerian experience. *International Migration Review*, *18*(3), 426–436.

Adida, C. (2014). *Immigrant exclusion and insecurity in Africa: Coethnic strangers*. Cambridge University Press.

Ahmad, F. (1966). Great Britain's relations with the Young Turks 1908–1914. *Middle Eastern Studies*, *2*(4), 302–329.

Ahmad, F. (1982). Unionist relations with the Greek, Armenian, and Jewish communities of the Ottoman Empire. In B. Braude & B. Lewis (Eds.), *Christians and Jews in the Ottoman Empire: The functioning of a plural society, Volume 1* (pp. 401–434). Holmes & Meier Publishers, Inc.

Ahram, A. I., Köllner, P., & Sil, R. (Eds.). (2018). *Comparative area studies: Methodological rationales & cross-regional applications*. Oxford University Press.

Aiyar, S. (2015). *Indians in Kenya: The politics of diaspora*. Harvard University Press.

Akçam, T. (2012). *The Young Turks' crime against humanity: The Armenian genocide and ethnic cleansing in the Ottoman Empire*. Princeton University Press.

Alexandris, A. (1982). The Constantinopolitan Greek factor during the Greco-Turkish confrontation of 1919–1922. *Byzantine and Modern Greek Studies*, *8*(1), 137–169.

Alexandris, A. (1983). *The Greek minority of Istanbul and Greek-Turkish relations 1918–1974*. Center for Asia Minor Studies.

Alexandris, A. (2003). Religion or ethnicity: The identity issue of the minorities in Greece and Turkey. In R. Hirschon (Ed.), *Crossing the Aegean: An appraisal of the 1923 compulsory population exchange between Greece and Turkey* (pp. 117–132). Sage.

Amnesty International. (1992, April 30). *Union of Myanmar (Burma): Human rights violations against Muslims in the Rakhine (Arakan) State.* https://www.amnesty.org/en/documents/asa16/006/1992/en/

Amnesty International. (1992, September 30). *Myanmar: "No law at all": Human rights violations under military rule.* https://www.amnesty.org/en/documents/asa16/011/1992/en/

Amnesty International. (1999, May 21). *Ethiopia and Eritrea: Human rights issues in a year of armed conflict.* https://www.amnesty.org/en/documents/AFR04/003/1999/en/

Amnesty International. (2017, September 28). *Between a rock and a hard place: Thailand's refugee policies and violations of the principle of non-refoulement.* https://www.amnesty.org/en/documents/asa39/7031/2017/en/

Amnesty International. (2018, June 27). *"We will destroy everything": Military responsibility for crimes against humanity in Rakhine State, Myanmar.* https://www.amnesty.org/en/documents/asa16/8630/2018/en/

Amor, M. (2003). Violent ethnocentrism: Revisiting the economic interpretation of the expulsion of the Ugandan Asians. *Identity*, *3*(1), 53–66.

Anderson, D. (2005). *Histories of the hanged: The dirty war in Kenya and the end of empire.* W. W. Norton & Company Ltd.

Asia Watch. (1992, May 7). *Burma: Rape, forced labor, and religious persecution in northern Arakan.* https://www.hrw.org/reports/pdfs/b/burma/burma925.pdf

Atieno-Odhiambo, E. S. (1987). Democracy and the ideology of order in Kenya. In M. Schatzberg (Ed.), *The political economy of Kenya* (pp. 177–202). Praeger.

Aung, Tun Tun. (2007). *An introduction to citizenship card under Myanmar citizenship law.* https://www.google.com/url?sa=t&rct=j&q=&esrc=s&source=web&cd=&ved=2ahUKEwjdp6KMyrn1AhWLkokEHc2jC0AQFnoECAUQAQ&url=https%3A%2F%2Fniigata-u.repo.nii.ac.jp%2Frecord%2F7673%2Ffile_preview%2F01_0053.pdf&usg=AOvVaw0L5z2Z8BULbx4I4zT99Hos

Avirgan, T., & Honey, M. (1982). *War in Uganda: The legacy of Idi Amin.* Lawrence Hill & Company.

Baldwin, D. A. (1997). The concept of security. *Review of International Studies*, *23*(1), 5–26.

Barnett, M., & Finnemore, M. (2004). *Rules for the world: International organizations in global politics.* Cornell University Press.

Bass, G. (2013). *The Blood telegram: Nixon, Kissinger, and a forgotten genocide.* Vintage Books.

Bellamy, A. J. (2011). *Mass atrocities and armed conflict: Links, distinctions, and implications for the responsibility to prevent.* https://stanleycenter.org/publications/mass-atrocities-and-armed-conflict-links-distinctions-and-implications-for-the-responsibility-to-prevent/

Bell-Fialkoff, A. (1999). *Ethnic cleansing.* St. Martin's Press.

Bishku, M. B. (2003). Turkish-Bulgarian relations: From conflict and distrust to cooperation over minority issues and international politics. *Mediterranean Quarterly*, *14*(2), 77–94.

Bishku, M. B. (2017). Israel's relations with the East African states of Kenya, Uganda, and Tanzania: From independence to the present. *Israel Studies, 22*(1), 76–100.

Blalock, H. M. (1967). *Toward a theory of minority group relations.* Wiley.

Bonacich, E. (1973). A theory of middleman minorities. *American Sociological Review, 38*(5), 583–594.

Boura, C. (1999). The Greek millet in Turkish politics: Greeks in the Ottoman parliament (1908–1918). In D. Gondicas & C. Issawi (Eds.), *Ottoman Greeks in the age of nationalism: Politics, economy, and society in the nineteenth century* (pp. 193–203). The Darwin Press Inc.

Branch, D., & Cheeseman, N. (2006). The politics of control in Kenya: Understanding the bureaucratic-executive state, 1952–78. *Review of African Political Economy, 33*(107), 11–31.

Brubaker, R. (1996). *Nationalism reframed: Nationhood and the national question in the new Europe.* Cambridge University Press.

Bulutgil, Z. (2016). *The roots of ethnic cleansing in Europe.* Cambridge University Press.

Bulutgil, Z. (2018). The state of the field and debates on ethnic cleansing. *Nationalities Papers, 46*(6), 1136–1145.

Butcher, C., Goldsmith, B. E., Nanlohy, S., Sowmya, A., & Muchlinski, D. (2020). Introducing the targeted mass killing data set for the study and forecasting of mass atrocities. *Journal of Conflict Resolution, 64*(7–8), 1524–1547.

Butt, A. I. (2017). *Secession and security: Explaining state strategy against separatists.* Cornell University Press.

Cable, V. (1969). The Asians of Kenya. *African Affairs, 68*(272), 218–231.

Callahan, M. P. (2003). *Making enemies: War and state building in Burma.* Cornell University Press.

Casey, M. (2017). *Empire's guest workers: Haitian migrants in Cuba in the Age of US Occupation.* Cambridge University Press.

Center for Diversity & National Harmony. (2018). *Myanmar's citizenship law: An analysis.* https://www.cdnh.org/publication/myanmars-citizenship-law-an-analysis/

Cervenka, A. (1972). The Organization of African Unity in the seventies. *Verfassung Und Recht in Übersee/Law and Politics in Africa, Asia and Latin America,* 5(1), 29–39.

Chakravarti, N. R. (1971). *The Indian minority in Burma: The rise and decline of an immigrant community.* Oxford University Press.

Chandra, K. (2006). What is ethnic identity and does it matter? *Annual Review of Political Science, 9*(1), 397–424.

Chang, P. M. (1982). The Sino–Vietnamese dispute over the ethnic Chinese. *China Quarterly, 90,* 195–230.

Charney, M. W. (2009). *A history of modern Burma.* Cambridge University Press.

Cheesman, N. (2017). How in Myanmar "national races" came to surpass citizenship and exclude Rohingya. *Journal of Contemporary Asia, 47*(3), 461–483.

Chirot, D., & McCauley, C. (2006). *Why not kill them all? The logic and prevention of mass political murder.* Princeton University Press.

Christie, C. J. (1996). *A modern history of Southeast Asia: Decolonization, nationalism and separatism.* Tauris Academic Studies.

Clark, B. (2006). *Twice a stranger: How mass expulsion forged modern Greece & Turkey.* Granta Books.

Clayton, A. (1986). Foreign intervention in Africa. In S. Baynham (Ed.), *Military power and politics in black Africa* (pp. 203–258): Routledge.

Clogg, R. (1982). The Greek millet in the Ottoman Empire. In B. Braude & B. Lewis (Eds.), *Christians and Jews in the Ottoman Empire: The functioning of a plural society, Volume 1* (pp. 185–207). Holmes & Meier Publishers, Inc.

Clogg, R. (2021). *A concise history of Greece* (Fourth ed.). Cambridge University Press.

Cockett, R. (2015). *Blood, dreams and gold: The changing face of Burma*. Yale University Press.

Coles, J. L. (1983, April 16–18). *The problem of mass expulsion*. [A background paper prepared for the Working Group of Experts on the Problem of Mass Expulsions convened by the International Institute of Humanitarian Law, San Remo, Italy].

Collier, D., & Levitsky, S. (1997). Democracy with adjectives: Conceptual innovation in comparative research. *World Politics*, *49*(3), 430–451.

Cosemans, S. (2018). The politics of dispersal: Turning Ugandan colonial subjects into postcolonial refugees (1967–76). *Migration Studies*, *6*(1), 99–119.

Cosemans, S. (2021). *The internationalization of the refugee problem: Resettlement from the Global South during the 1970s* [Doctoral dissertation, KU Leuven].

Croissant, A. (2007). Muslim insurgency, political violence, and democracy in Thailand. *Terrorism and Political Violence*, *19*(1), 1–18.

Cullen, P. (2017a). *Kenya and Britain after independence: Beyond neo-colonialism*. Palgrave Macmillan.

Cullen, P. (2017b). Operation Binnacle: British plans for military intervention against a 1965 coup in Kenya. *The International History Review*, *39*(5), 791–809.

Cullen, P. (2018). 'Playing Cold War politics': The Cold War in Anglo-Kenyan relations in the 1960s. *Cold War History*, *18*(1), 37–54.

Curtis, M. (2004). *Unpeople: Britain's secret human rights abuses*. Vintage.

Davison, R. H. (1965). Turkish diplomacy from Mudros to Lausanne. In G. A. Craig & F. Gilbert (Eds.), *The diplomats 1919–1939: Volume 1 - The Twenties* (pp. 172–209). Princeton University Press.

De Bernières, L. (2004). *Birds without wings*. Vintage Books.

de Zayas, A. (1977). *Nemesis at Potsdam: The Anglo-Americans and the expulsion of the Germans*. Routledge.

de Zayas, A. (1988). A historical survey of twentieth century expulsions. In A. C. Bramwell (Ed.), *Refugees in the age of total war* (pp. 15–37). Unwin Hyman Ltd.

Douglas, R. M. (2012). Orderly and humane: The expulsion of the Germans after the Second *World War*. Yale University Press.

Downes, A. B. (2011). *Targeting civilians in war*. Cornell University Press.

Elie, J. (2010). The historical roots of cooperation between the UN High Commissioner for Refugees and the International Organization for Migration. *Global Governance*, *16*, 345–360.

Elkins, C. (2005). *Imperial reckoning: The untold story of Britain's gulag in Kenya*. Henry Holt and Company.

Emin, A. (1930). *Turkey in the World War*. Yale University Press.

Evans, R. J. (2005). *The Third Reich in power*. Penguin Books.

Fearon, J. D., & Laitin, D. D. (2011). Sons of the soil, migrants, and civil war. *World Development*, *39*(2), 199–211.

Ferguson, J. M. (2015). Who's counting? Ethnicity, belonging, and the national census in Burma/Myanmar. *Bijdragen tot de taal-, land-en volkenkunde/Journal of the Humanities and Social Sciences of Southeast Asia*, *171*(1), 1–28.

Finnemore, M. (2003). *The purpose of intervention: Changing beliefs about the use of force.* Cornell University Press.

Fleischman, J. (1994). Ethnic cleansing. *Africa Report, 39*(1), 45–46.

Foltz, W. J. (1988). Libya's military power. In R. Lemarchand (Ed.), *The green and the black: Qadhafi's policies in Africa* (pp. 52–69). Indiana University Press.

Frank, M. (2017). *Making minorities history: Population transfer in twentieth-century Europe.* Oxford University Press.

Fulford, L. (2023). *The exiled: Empire, immigration and the Ugandan Asian exodus.* Coronet.

Gardiner, C. H. (1975). *The Japanese and Peru 1873–1973.* University of New Mexico Press.

Garrity, M. (2022). Introducing the government-sponsored mass expulsion dataset. *Journal of Peace Research, 59*(5), 767–776.

Garrity, M. M. (2023a). What enables or constrains mass expulsion? A new decision-making framework. *Security Studies, 32*(3), 537–567.

Garrity, M. M. (2023b). "Ethnic cleansing": An analysis of conceptual and empirical ambiguity. *Political Science Quarterly, 138*(4), 469–490.

Garrity, M. M. & Mylonas, H. (2025). The various facets of eliminationist politics: Conflict, nation-building, and forced migration. *International Political Science Review, 46*(3): 336–352.

Garrity M M, and Mylonas H. (2026). Eliminationist politics: An analytical framework. *Journal of Ethnic and Migration Studies, 52*(4), 891–909.

Gertzel, C., Goldschmidt, M., & Rothchild, D. (Eds.). (1969). *Government and politics in Kenya: A nation building text.* East African Publishing House.

Gertzel, C. (1970). *The politics of independent Kenya 1963–8.* Northwestern University Press.

Ghai, Y. P. (1967). The government and the constitution in Kenya politics. *East Africa Journal, 4*(8), 9–14.

Ghai, D. P. (1970). The Bugandan trade boycott: A study in tribal, political, and economic nationalism. In R. Rotberg & A. Mazrui (Eds.), *Protest and power in black Africa* (pp. 755–770). Oxford University Press.

Ghai, D., & Ghai, Y. (1965). Asians in East Africa: Problems and prospects. *The Journal of Modern African Studies, 3*(1), 35–51.

Ghai, D., & Ghai, Y. (1971). The Asian minorities of East and Central Africa. Minority Rights Group, *Report Number 4*, 1–39.

Gilbert, M. (1994). *The First World War: A complete history.* Henry Holt and Company, Inc.

Gilbert, M. (2009). *The Routledge atlas of the Second World War* (2nd ed.). Routledge.

Gitelson, S. A. (1977). Major shifts in recent Ugandan foreign policy. *African Affairs, 76*(304), 359–380.

Gleditsch, K. S., & Ward, M. D. (1997). Double take: A reexamination of democracy and autocracy in modern polities. *Journal of Conflict Resolution, 41*(3), 361–383.

Goertz, G. (2017). *Multimethod research, causal mechanisms, and case studies: An integrated approach.* Princeton University Press.

Gökatalay, G. E. (2021). A crisis of legitimacy or a source of political consolidation? The deportation of Bulgarian Turks in 1950–1951 and the Democratic Party. *Middle Eastern Studies, 57*(6), 920–934.

Goodman, A. (2020). *The deportation machine: America's long history of expelling immigrants*. Princeton University Press.

Goodwin-Gill, G. S. (1978). *International law and the movement of persons between states*. Oxford University Press.

Greenhill, K. M. (2010). *Weapons of mass migration: Forced displacement, coercion, and foreign policy*. Cornell University Press.

Gupta, A. (1974). Ugandan Asians, Britain, India and the Commonwealth. *African Affairs*, *73*(292), 312–324.

Güven, D. (2021). The events of 6–7 September 1955: Greeks, Armenians and Jews within the context of the strategies of the Turkish Republic. In S. H. Astourian & R. H. Kévorkian (Eds.), *Collective and state violence in Turkey: The construction of a national identity from empire to nation-state* (pp. 277–302). Berghahn.

Habiburahman, & Ansel, S. (2019). *First, they erased our name: A Rohingya speaks* (A. Reece, Trans.). Scribe.

Hansen, R. (1999). The Kenyan Asians, British politics, and the Commonwealth Immigrants Act, 1968. *The Historical Journal*, *42*(3), 809–834.

Harff, B. (2003). No lessons learned from the Holocaust? Assessing risks of genocide and political mass murder since 1955. *American Political Science Review*, *97*(1), 57–73.

Hein, P. (2018). The re-ethnicisation of politics in Myanmar and the making of the Rohingya ethnicity paradox. *India Quarterly*, *74*(4), 361–382.

Henckaerts, J.-M. (1995). *Mass expulsion in modern international law and practice*. Kluwer Law International.

Herzig, P. (2006). *South Asians in Kenya: Gender, generation and changing identities in diaspora*. Transaction Publishers.

Himbara, D. (1994). *Kenyan capitalists, the state and development*. Lynee Rienner Publishers.

Hirschon, R. (2003). 'Unmixing peoples' in the Aegean region. In R. Hirschon (Ed.), *Crossing the Aegean: An appraisal of the 1923 compulsory population exchange between Greece and Turkey* (pp. 3–12). Sage.

Holliday, I. (2005). Doing business with rights violating regimes: Corporate social responsibility and Myanmar's military junta. *Journal of Business Ethics*, *61*(4), 329–342.

Honig, L. (2016). Immigrant political economies and exclusionary policy in Africa. *Comparative* Politics, *48*(4), 517–537.

Horowitz, D. (1985). *Ethnic groups in conflict*. University of California Press.

Howell, J. (1968). An analysis of Kenyan foreign policy. *The Journal of Modern African Studies*, *6*(1), 29–48.

Huang, C., & Ginn, T. (2022). The World Bank window for host communities and refugees: Opportunities for learning and expansion in Africa and beyond. *Center for Global Development*. https://www.cgdev.org/blog/world-bank-window-host-communities-and-refugees-opportunities-learning-and-expansion-africa

Human Rights Watch. (1992, March). *Denying human rights and ethnic identity: The Greeks of Turkey*. https://www.hrw.org/sites/default/files/reports/TURKEY923.PDF

Human Rights Watch. (1994, February). *Albania: The Greek minority*. https://www.hrw.org/reports/1995/Albania.htm#P303_56040

Human Rights Watch. (1996, September). *The Rohingya Muslims: Ending a cycle of exodus?* https://www.hrw.org/legacy/summaries/s.burma969.html

Human Rights Watch. (2000, May). *Burma/Bangladesh, Burmese refugees in Bangladesh: Still no durable solution.* https://www.hrw.org/reports/2000/burma/index.htm

Human Rights Watch. (2003, January). *The Horn of Africa war: Mass expulsions and the nationality issue* (June 1998–April 2002). https://www.hrw.org/sites/default/files/reports/ethioerit0103.pdf

Human Rights Watch. (2007a, May 16). *Last hope: The need for durable solutions for Bhutanese refugees in Nepal and India.* https://www.hrw.org/report/2007/05/16/last-hope/need-durable-solutions-bhutanese-refugees-nepal-and-india

Human Rights Watch. (2007b, September 30). *Russia targets Georgians for expulsion: Government targeted ethnic group in response to political conflict.* http://pantheon.hrw.org/legacy/english/docs/2007/09/30/russia16977.htm

Human Rights Watch. (2008, February 1). *Bhutan's ethnic cleansing.* https://www.hrw.org/news/2008/02/01/bhutans-ethnic-cleansing

Human Rights Watch. (2011a, September 28). *France's compliance with the European Free Movement Directive and the removal of ethnic Roma EU citizens.* https://www.hrw.org/news/2011/09/28/frances-compliance-european-free-movement-directive-and-removal-ethnic-roma-eu

Human Rights Watch. (2011b, September 29). *France: One year on, new abuses against Roma.* https://www.hrw.org/news/2011/09/29/france-one-year-new-abuses-against-roma

Human Rights Watch. (2013, April 22). *"All you can do is pray": Crimes against humanity and ethnic cleansing of Rohingya Muslims in Burma's Arakan State.* https://www.hrw.org/report/2013/04/22/all-you-can-do-pray/crimes-against-humanity-and-ethnic-cleansing-rohingya-muslims

Human Rights Watch. (2017, February 13). *Pakistan coercion, UN complicity: The mass forced return of Afghan refugees.* https://www.hrw.org/sites/default/files/report_pdf/pakistan0217_web.pdf

Human Rights Watch (2024a, August 12). *Myanmar: Armies target ethnic Rohingya, Rakhine.* https://www.hrw.org/news/2024/08/12/myanmar-armies-target-ethnic-rohingya-rakhine

Human Rights Watch. (2024b). *World Report 2025: Myanmar—Events of 2024.* https://www.hrw.org/world-report/2025/country-chapters/myanmar

Hurewitz, J. C. (1956). *Diplomacy in the Near and Middle East: A documentary record, 1914–1956.* D. Van Nostrand Company, Inc.

Jo, H., & Simmons, B. A. (2016). Can the International Criminal Court deter atrocity? *International Organization, 70*(3), 443–475.

Ibrahim, A. (2018). *The Rohingya: Inside Myanmar's genocide.* Hurst & Company.

Içduygu, A., Sule, T., & Soner, A. B. (2008). The politics of population in a nation-building process: Emigration of non-Muslims from Turkey. *Ethnic and Racial Studies, 31*(2), 258–389.

International Crisis Group. (1999, November 30). *Burundian refugees in Tanzania: A key factor in the Burundi peace process.* https://www.crisisgroup.org/africa/central-africa/burundi/burundian-refugees-tanzania-key-factor-burundi-peace-process#:~:text=1999%203%20minutes-,Burundian%20Refugees%20in%20Tanzania%3A%20A%20Key%20Factor%20in%20the%20Burundi,are%20reported20to%20have%20fled

Jacob, A. (1971). Israel's military aid to Africa, 1960–66. *The Journal of Modern African Studies, 9*(2), 165–187.

Jamal, V. (1976). Asians in Uganda, 1880–1972: Inequality and expulsion. *The Economic History Review*, *29*(4), 602–616.

Jha, S. (2013). Trade, institutions, and ethnic tolerance: Evidence from South Asia. *American Political Science Review*, *107*(4), 806–832.

Jørgensen, J. J. (1981). *Uganda: A modern history*. St. Martin's Press.

Kaliber, A. (2019). Re-engaging the self/other problematic in post-positivist international relations: The 1964 expulsion of Greeks from Istanbul revisited. *Southeast European and Black Sea Studies*, *19*(3), 365–386.

Kasfir, N. (1976). *The shrinking political arena: Participation and ethnicity in African politics, with a case study of Uganda*. University of California Press.

Kasozi, A. B. K. (1994). *The social origins of violence in Uganda, 1964–1985*. McGill-Queen's University Press.

Karpat, K. H. (1982). Millets and nationality: The roots of the incongruity of nation and state in the post-Ottoman era. In B. Braude & B. Lewis (Eds.), *Christians and Jews in the Ottoman Empire: The functioning of a plural society, Volume 1* (pp. 141–169). Holmes & Meier Publishers, Inc.

Karpat, K. H. (1985). *Ottoman population 1830–1914: Demographic and social characteristics*. University of Wisconsin Press.

Keesing's Contemporary Archives. (1963–1964). Volume No. XIV. Keesings Publications Limited.

Keesing's Contemporary Archives (1965–1966). Volume No. XV. Keesings Publications Limited.

Keesing's Contemporary Archives (1967–1968). Volume No. XVI. Keesings Publications Limited.

Keesing's Contemporary Archives. (1971–1972). Volume No. XVIII. Keesings Publications Limited.

Keesing's Record of World Events. (1957). Volume 1. https://web.stanford.edu/group/tomzgroup/pmwiki/uploads/1024-1957-12-KS-a-AMS.pdf

Khalil, G. (1993). The catastrophic cyclone of April 1991: Its impact on the economy of Bangladesh. *Natural Hazards*, *8*(3), 263–281.

Kieser, H. L. (2018). *Talaat Pasha: Father of modern Turkey, architect of genocide*. Princeton University Press.

Kostanick, H. L. (1955). Turkish resettlement of refugees from Bulgaria, 1950–1953. *Middle East Journal*, *9*(1), 41–52.

Kulischer, E. M. (1948). *Europe on the move: War and population changes, 1917–47*. Columbia University Press.

Kyaw, N. N. (2015). Alienation, discrimination, and securitization: Legal personhood and cultural personhood of Muslims in Myanmar. *The Review of Faith & International Affairs*, *13*(4), 50–59.

Kyaw, N. N. (2017). Myanmar's other Muslims: The case of the Kaman. In A. South & M. Lall (Eds.), *Citizenship in Myanmar: Ways of being in and from Burma* (pp. 279–300). ISEAS – Yusof Ishak Institute.

Kyemba, H. (1977). *A state of blood: The inside story of Idi Amin*. Ace Books.

Ladas, S. (1932). *The exchange of minorities: Bulgaria, Greece and Turkey*. The MacMillan Company.

Lall, M. C. (2001). *India's missed opportunity: India's relationship with the non resident Indians*. Ashgate.

Lambrecht, C. (1995). The return of the Rohingya refugees to Burma: Voluntary repatriation or refoulement? U.S. Committee for Refugees.

Lee, E. (2019). *America for Americans: A history of xenophobia in the United States.* Hachette Book Group.

Legum, C. (1971). *Africa contemporary record: Annual survey and documents 1970–1971*, Volume 13. Rex Collings.

Legum, C. (1972). *Africa contemporary record: Annual survey and documents, 1971–1972*, Volume 4. Rex Collings.

Legum, C. (1980). *Africa contemporary record: Annual survey and documents, 1978–1979*, Volume 11. Africana Publishing Company.

Lemarchand, R. (Ed.) (1988). *The green and the black: Qadhafi's policies in Africa.* Indiana University Press.

Leopold, M. (2020). *Idi Amin: The story of Africa's icon of evil.* Yale University Press.

Lewis, B. (2002). *The emergence of modern Turkey.* Oxford University Press.

Lichtenheld, A. G. (2020). Explaining population displacement strategies in civil wars: A cross-national analysis. *International Organization, 74*(2), 253–294.

Lieberman, B. (2006). *Terrible fate: Ethnic cleansing in the making of modern Europe.* Ivan R. Dee.

Lingaas, C. (2020). *The concept of race in international criminal law.* Routledge.

Lipman, J. K. (2020). *In camps: Vietnamese refugees, asylum seekers, and repatriates.* University of California Press.

Llewellyn-Smith, M. (1998). *Ionian vision: Greece in Asia Minor, 1919–1922.* University of Michigan Press.

Loescher, G. (2001). *The UNHCR and world politics: A perilous path.* Oxford University Press.

Macartney, C. A. (1931). *Refugees: The work of the League.* League of Nations Union.

Macartney, C. A. (1934). *National states and national minorities.* Oxford University Press.

McDowall, D. (2000). *A modern history of the Kurds.* I. B. Tauris.

McGarry, J. (1998). 'Demographic engineering': The state-directed movement of ethnic groups as a technique of conflict regulation. *Ethnic and Racial Studies, 21*(4), 613–638.

McGarry, J., & O'Leary, B. (Eds.). (1993). *The politics of ethnic conflict regulation: Case studies of protracted ethnic conflicts.* Routledge.

MacLean, K. (2019). The Rohingya crisis and the practices of erasure. *Journal of Genocide Research, 21*(1), 83–95.

MacLeod, M. C. (1998). Undesirable aliens: Race, ethnicity, and nationalism in the comparison of Haitian and British West Indian immigrant workers in Cuba, 1912–1939. *Journal of Social History, 31*(3), 599–623.

Mahoney, J., & Goertz, G. (2004). The possibility principle: Choosing negative cases in comparative research. *American Political Science Review, 98*(4), 653–669.

Maloba, W. O. (2017). *The anatomy of neo-colonialism in Kenya: British imperialism and Kenyatta, 1963–1978.* Palgrave Macmillan.

Mamdani, M. (1975). Class struggles in Uganda. *Review of African Political Economy, 4*(Nov), 26–61.

Mamdani, M. (2022). *From citizen to refugee: Uganda Asians come to Britain* (Third ed.). Daraja Press.

Mann, M. (2005). *The dark side of democracy: Explaining ethnic cleansing.* Cambridge University Press.

Mansel, P. (1996). *Constantinople: City of the world's desire, 1453–1924.* St. Martin's Press.

Martin, D. (1974). *General Amin*. Faber and Faber.

Marx, A. (2002). The nation-state and its exclusions. *Political Science Quarterly, 117*(1), 103–126.

Mattausch, J. (1998). From subjects to citizens: British 'East African Asians.' *Journal of Ethnic and Migration Studies, 24*(1), 121–141.

Maurice, F., Sir. (1943). *The Armistices of 1918*. Oxford University Press.

Maxon, R. M. (1995). Social & cultural changes. In B. A. Ogat & W. R. Ochieng (Eds.), *Decolonization & independence in Kenya, 1940–93* (pp. 110–147). Ohio University Press.

Mazower, M. (2004). *Salonica, city of ghosts: Christians, Muslims and Jews 1430–1950*. HarperCollins.

Mazower, M. (2009). *No enchanted palace: The end of empire and the ideological origins of the United Nations*. Princeton University Press.

Mazrui, A. A. (1964). The United Nations and some African political attitudes. *International Organization, 18*(3), 499–520.

Mazrui, A. (1979). Casualties of an underdeveloped class structure: The expulsion of Luo workers and Asian bourgeoisie from Uganda. In W. A. Shack & E. P. Skinner (Eds.), *Strangers in African societies* (pp. 261–278). University of California Press.

Melady, T. P., & Melady, M. B. (1976). *Uganda: The Asian exiles*. Orbis Books.

Midlarsky, M. I. (2005). *The killing trap: Genocide in the twentieth century*. Cambridge University Press.

Mirković, D. (1996). Ethnic conflict and genocide: Reflections on ethnic cleansing in the former Yugoslavia. *The Annals of the American Academy of Political and Social Science, 548*(1), 191–199.

Mohiddin, A. (1969). Socialism or capitalism? Sessional paper No. 10 revisited. East Africa Journal, 6(3), 7–16.

Morris, B. (1999). Righteous victims: A history of the Zionist-Arab conflict, 1881–2001. Vintage Books.

Morris, B., & Ze'evi, D. (2019). *The thirty-year genocide: Turkey's destruction of its Christian minorities, 1894–1924*. Harvard University Press.

Mourelos, Y. G. (1985). The 1914 persecutions and the first attempt at an exchange of minorities between Greece and Turkey. *Balkan Studies, 26*(2), 389–413.

Mueller, S. D. (1984). Government and opposition in Kenya, 1966–9. *The Journal of Modern African Studies, 22*(3), 399–427.

Müller-Crepon, C., Schvitz, G., & Cederman, L.-E. (2024). "Right-peopling" the state: Nationalism, historical legacies, and ethnic cleansing in Europe, 1886–2020. *Journal of Conflict Resolution, 69*(2–3), 211–241.

Mutibwa, P. (1992). *Uganda since independence: A story of unfulfilled hopes*. Africa World Press, Inc.

Myint-U, T. (2021). *The hidden history of Burma: Race, capitalism, and the crisis of democracy in the 21st century*. W. W. Norton & Company.

Mylonas, H. (2012). *The politics of nation-building: Making co-nationals, refugees, and minorities*. Cambridge University Press.

Mylonas, H. (2015). Methodological problems in the study of nation-building: Behaviorism and historicist solutions in political science. *Social Science Quarterly, 96*(3), 740–758.

Mylonas, H., & Radnitz, S. (Eds.). (2022). *Enemies within: The global politics of fifth columns*. Oxford University Press.

Naim, A. (2005). Perspectives—Jomo Kenyatta and Israel. *Jewish Political Studies Review*, *17*(3/4), 75–80.

Naimark, N. (2001). *Fires of hatred: Ethnic cleansing in twentieth-century Europe*. Harvard University Press.

Nanlohy, S. (2024). Geopolitics and genocide: Patron interests, client crises, and *realpolitik*. *Journal of Global Security Studies*, *9*(1), ogad023.

Norwich, J. J. (2013). *A short history of Byzantium*. Penguin Books.

Nowik, L. (2015). East African Indians: How many are they? In M. Adam (Ed.), *Indian Africa: Minorities of Indian-Pakistani origin in Eastern Africa* (pp. 99–176). Mkuki na Nyota Publishers Ltd.

O'Brien, J. (1972). *Brown Britons: The crisis of the Ugandan Asians*. Runnymede Trust Publication.

O'Brien, J. (1973). General Amin and the Uganda Asians: Doing the unthinkable. *The Round Table*, *63*(249), 91–104.

OCHA. (2024, July 1). *Myanmar Humanitarian Update No. 39*. https://www.unocha.org/publications/report/myanmar/myanmar-humanitarian-update-no-39-1-july-2024

Ochieng, W. R. (1995). Structural & political changes. In B. A. Ogat & W. R. Ochieng (Eds.), *Decolonization & independence in Kenya, 1940–93* (pp. 83–109). Ohio University Press.

Oded, A. (2006). Israeli-Ugandan relations in the time of Idi Amin. *Jewish Political Studies* Review, *18*(3/4), 65–79.

Office of the High Commissioner for Human Rights (OHCHR). (2017, September 13–24). *Mission report of OHCHR rapid response mission to Cox's Bazar, Bangladesh*. https://www.ohchr.org/Documents/Countries/MM/CXBMissionSummaryFindings October2017.pdf

Ojo, O., & Sesay, A. (1986). The O.A.U. and human rights: Prospects for the 1980s and beyond. *Human Rights Quarterly*, *8*(1), 89–103.

O'Leary, B. (2001). The elements of right-sizing and right-peopling the state. In B. O'Leary, I. Lustick, & T. Callaghy (Eds.), *Right-sizing the state: The politics of moving borders* (pp. 15–73). Oxford University Press.

Oran, B. (2003). The story of those who stayed: Lessons from articles 1 and 2 of the 1923 convention. In R. Hirschon (Ed.), *Crossing the Aegean: An appraisal of the 1923 compulsory population exchange between Greece and Turkey* (pp. 97–115). Sage.

Orchard, P. (2010). The perils of humanitarianism: Refugee and IDP protection in situations of regime-induced displacement. *Refugee Survey Quarterly*, *29*(1), 38–60.

Pallis, A. A. (1925). Racial migrations in the Balkans during the years 1912–1924. *The Geographical Journal*, *66*(4), 315–331.

Palmier, L. H. (1961). Indonesian-Dutch relations. *Journal of Southeast Asian History*, *2*(2), 24–34.

Parnini, S. N. (2013). The crisis of the Rohingya as a Muslim minority in Myanmar and bilateral relations with Bangladesh. *Journal of Muslim Minority Affairs*, *33*(2), 281–297.

Parson, J. D. (1973). Africanizing trade in Uganda: The final solution. *Africa Today*, *20*(1), 59–72.

Parsons, T. (2007). The Lanet incident, 2–25 January 1964: Military unrest and national amnesia in Kenya. *The International Journal of African Historical Studies*, *40*(1), 51–70.

Patel, H. H. (1972). General Amin and the Indian exodus from Uganda. *A Journal of Opinion*, *2*(4), 12–22.

Pedersen, S. (2015). *The guardians: The League of Nations and the crisis of empire*: Oxford University Press.

Pentzopoulos, D. (1962). *The Balkan exchange of minorities and its impact upon Greece.* Mouton & Co.

Permanent Committee on Geographical Names. (2007). An introduction to the toponymy of Burma. *The National Archives—UK Government Web Archive.* https://webarchive.nationalarchives.gov.uk/ukgwa/20140402150947/http://www.pcgn.org.uk/burma%200907.pdf

Petersen, R. D. (2002). *Understanding ethnic violence: Fear, hatred, and resentment in twentieth-century Eastern Europe.* Cambridge University Press.

Piper, T. (1994). Myanmar: Exodus and return of Muslims from Rakhine state. *Refugee Survey Quarterly, 13*(1), 11–29.

Pohl, J. O. (1999). *Ethnic cleansing in the USSR, 1937–1949.* Praeger.

Polybius (1918). *Greece before the conference.* Methuen & Co. Ltd.

Pondi, J.-E. (1988). Qadhafi and the Organization of African Unity. In R. Lemarchand (Ed.), *The green and the black: Qadhafi's policies in Africa* (pp. 139–149). Indiana University Press.

Posner, M. (1974). *Violations of human rights and the rule of law in Uganda: A study by the International Commission of Jurists.* https://www.icj.org/wp-content/uploads/2013/06/Uganda-violations-of-human-rights-thematic-report-1974-eng.pdf

Power, S. (2002). *"A problem from hell": America and the age of genocide.* Basic Books.

Psomiades, H. J. (1968). *The eastern question: The last phase.* Institute for Balkan Studies.

Psomiades, H. J. (2011). Fridtjof Nansen and the Greek refugee crisis, 1922–1924. *The Journal of Modern Hellenism, 29*, 213–230.

Ragin, C. C. (2000). *Fuzzy-set social science.* University of Chicago Press.

Rau, B. N. (1948). The constitution of the Union of Burma. *India Quarterly, 4*(2), 109–120.

Robinson, G. (2010). *"If you leave us here, we will die": How genocide was stopped in East Timor.* Princeton University Press.

Robson, L. (2017). *States of separation: Transfer, partition and the making of the modern Middle East.* University of California Press.

Rosen, S. J. (2012). Kuwait expels thousands of Palestinians. *Middle East Quarterly, 19*(4), 75–83.

Rosenberg, S. P. (2012). Genocide is a process, not an event. *Genocide Studies and Prevention, 7*(1), 16–23.

Rothchild, D. (1970a). Citizenship and national integration: The non-African crisis in Kenya. *Studies in Race and Nations, 1*(3), 1–32.

Rothchild, D. (1970b). Kenya's Africanization program: Priorities of development and equity. *American Political Science Review, 64*(3), 737–753.

Rothchild, D. (1973). *Racial bargaining in independent Kenya: A study of minorities and decolonization.* Oxford University Press.

Salehyan, I., Siroky, D., & Wood, R. M. (2014). External rebel sponsorship and civilian abuse: A principal-agent analysis of wartime atrocities. *International Organization, 68*(3), 633–661.

Sartori, G. (Ed.) (1984). *Social science concepts: A systematic analysis.* Sage Publications.

Schabas, W. A. (2000). *Genocide in international law: The crime of crimes.* Cambridge University Press.

Seidenberg, D. A. (1996). *Mercantile adventurers: The world of East African Asians, 1750–1985*. New Age International.

Semelin, J. (2007). *Purify and destroy: The political uses of massacre and genocide*. Columbia University Press.

Sharma, V. D., & Wooldridge, F. (1974). Some legal questions arising from the expulsion of the Ugandan Asians. *International and Comparative Law Quarterly, 23*(2), 397–425.

Skocpol, T. (1979). *States and social revolutions: A comparative analysis of France, Russia and China*. Cambridge University Press.

Smith, M. (1991). *Burma: Insurgency and the politics of ethnicity*. Zed Books.

Smith, M. (1994). *Ethnic groups in Burma: Development, democracy and human rights*. Anti-Slavery International.

Smith, M. (1999). *Burma: Insurgency and the politics of ethnicity* (Updated ed.). University Press.

Soifer, H. (2020). Shadow cases in comparative research. *Qualitative and Multi-Method Research, 18*(2), 9–18.

Stanton, G. H. (1996). The ten stages of genocide. *Genocide Watch*. https://www.genocidewatch.com/tenstages

Stanton, J. A. (2016). *Violence and restraint in civil war: Civilian targeting in the shadow of international law*. Cambridge University Press.

Steinberg, D. I. (1980). Burma: Ne Win after two decades. *Current History, 79*(461), 180–184.

Steinberg, D. I., & Fan, H. (2012). *Modern China-Myanmar relations: Dilemmas of mutual dependence*. Nordic Institute of Asian Studies Press.

Straus, S. (2001). Contested meanings and conflicting imperatives: A conceptual analysis of genocide. *Journal of Genocide Research, 3*(3), 349–375.

Straus, S. (2012). Retreating from the brink: Theorizing mass violence and the dynamics of restraint. *Perspectives on Politics, 10*(2), 343–362.

Straus, S. (2015). *Making and unmaking nations: War, leadership, and genocide in modern Africa*. Cornell University Press.

Straus, S. (2016). *Fundamentals of genocide and mass atrocity prevention*. United States Holocaust Memorial Museum.

Tägil, S. (1990). From Nebuchadnezzar to Hitler: The question of mass expulsion in history up to World War II. In R. Göran (Ed.), *The uprooted: Forced migration as an international problem in the post-war era* (pp. 59–85). Lund University Press.

Tandon, Y. (1972). The expulsions from Uganda: Asians' role in East Africa. *Patterns of Prejudice, 6*(6), 1–8.

Tandon, Y., & Raphael, A. (1978). *The new position of East Africa's Asians: Problems of a displaced minority* (Report No. 16). Minority Rights Group Ltd.

Tangri, R. K. (1966). Asians in Kenya: A political history. *Africa Quarterly, 6*(2), 107–127.

Ther, P., & Siljak, A. (Eds.). (2001). *Redrawing nations: Ethnic cleansing in East-Central Europe, 1944–1948*. Rowman & Littlefield Publishers, Inc.

Ther, P. (2014). *The dark side of nation-states: Ethnic cleansing in modern Europe*. Berghahn Books.

Tignor, R. L. (1998). *Capitalism and nationalism at the end of empire: State and business in decolonizing Egypt, Nigeria, and Kenya, 1945–1963*. Princeton University Press.

Tinker, H. (1990). Indians in Southeast Asia: Imperial auxiliaries. In C. Clarke, C. Peach, & S. Vertovec (Eds.), *South Asians overseas: Migration and ethnicity* (pp. 39–56). Cambridge University Press.

Treier, S., & Jackman, S. (2008). Democracy as a latent variable. *American Journal of Political Science*, *52*(1), 201–217.

Turits, R. L. (2002). A world destroyed, a nation imposed: The 1937 Haitian massacre in the Dominican Republic. *Hispanic American Historical Review*, *82*(3), 589–635.

Uche, C. (2017). The British government, Idi Amin and the expulsion of British Asians from Uganda. *Interventions*, *19*(6), 818–836.

Ulfelder, J., & Valentino, B. (2008). *Assessing the risks of state-sponsored mass killing*. Paper presented at the Political Instability Task Force, Washington, D.C. https://papers.ssrn.com/sol3/papers.cfm?abstract_id=1703426

Umozurike, U. O. (1979). The domestic jurisdiction clause in the OAU charter. *African Affairs*, *78*(311), 197–209.

UN Commission on Human Rights. (1993, February 17). *Report on the situation of human rights in Myanmar. E/CN.4/1993/37*. https://digitallibrary.un.org/record/159740?ln=en

UN Human Rights Council. (2018, September 12). *Report of the independent international fact-finding mission on Myanmar*. https://www.ohchr.org/sites/default/files/Documents/HRBodies/HRCouncil/FFM-Myanmar/A_HRC_39_64.pdf

Üngör, U. Ü. (2008). Seeing like a nation-state: Young Turk social engineering in Eastern Turkey, 1913–50. *Journal of Genocide Research*, *10*(1), 15–39.

U.S. Committee for Refugees. (1980). *World refugee survey*. American Council for Nationalities Service.

Valentino, B. (2004). *Final solutions: Mass killing and genocide in the 20th century*. Cornell University Press.

Van Hear, N. (1998). *New diasporas: The mass exodus, dispersal and regrouping of migrant communities*. UCL Press.

Vinnai, V. (1974). The creation of an African civil service in Kenya. *Law and Politics in Africa, Asia and Latin America*, *7*(2), 175–188.

Walton, C. (2013). *Empire of secrets: British intelligence, the Cold War and the twilight of empire*. The Overlook Press.

Walton, M. J. (2013). The "wages of Burman-ness": Ethnicity and Burman privilege in contemporary Myanmar. *Journal of Contemporary Asia*, *43*(1), 1–27.

Waterbury, M. A. (2020). Kin-state politics: Causes and consequences. *Nationalities Papers*, *48*(5), 799–808.

Weiner, M. (1978). *Sons of the soil: Migration and ethnic conflict in India*. Princeton University Press.

Weiner, M. (1992). Security, stability, and international migration. *International Security*, *17*(3), 91–126.

Weiner, M. (1993). Rejected peoples and unwanted migrants in South Asia. In M. Weiner (Ed.), *International migration and security* (pp. 149–178). Westview.

Whitaker, B. E. (2002). Changing priorities in refugee protection: The Rwandan repatriation from Tanzania. *Refugee Survey Quarterly*, *21*(1/2), 328–344.

Winter, R. P. (1983). *Refugees in Uganda and Rwanda: The Banyarwanda tragedy*. U.S. Committee for Refugees.

Wood, E. J. (2006). Variation in sexual violence during war. *Politics and Society*, *34*(3), 307–341.

Woodward, P. (1978). Ambiguous Amin. *African Affairs, 77*(307), 153–164.

Yegar, M. (1972). *The Muslims of Burma: A study of a minority group.* Otto Harrassowitz.

Yegar, M. (2002). *Between integration and secession: The Muslim communities of the Southern Philippines, Southern Thailand, and Western Burma/Myanmar.* Lexington Books.

Yegen, M. (2009). "Prospective Turks" or "pseudo-citizens": Kurds in Turkey. *Middle East Journal, 63*(4), 597–615.

Zolberg, A. (1983). The formation of new states as a refugee-generating process. *Annals of American Academy of Political and Social Science, 467*(1), 24–38.

Zolberg, A. R., Suhrke, A., & Aguayo, S. (1986). International factors in the formation of refugee movements. *International Migration Review, 20*(2), 151–169.

Zürcher, E. (1998). The Ottoman Empire and the armistice of Mudros. In H. Cecil & P. H. Liddle (Eds.), *At the eleventh hour: Reflections, hopes and anxieties at the closing of the Great War, 1918* (pp. 266–275). Leo Cooper.

Index

For the benefit of digital users, indexed terms that span two pages (e.g., 52–53) may, on occasion, appear on only one of those pages.

Tables and figures are indicated by an italic *t* and *f* following the page number.